Where Few Have Been

Sir Hubert Wilkins and the Antarctic

Trish Burgess and Annette Carter

Connor Court Publishing Pty Ltd

Published in 2025 by Connor Court Publishing Pty Ltd.

Copyright © Trish Burgess & Annette Carter

ALL RIGHTS RESERVED. This book contains material protected under International and Federal Copyright Laws and Treaties. Any unauthorised reprint or use of this material is prohibited. No part of this book may be reproduced or transmitted in any form or by any means, electronic or mechanical, including photocopying, recording, or by any information storage and retrieval system without express written permission from the publisher.

Connor Court Publishing Pty Ltd.
PO Box 7257
Redland Bay QLD 4165
sales@connorcourt.com
www.connorcourt.com

ISBN: 9781923224827

Cover illustration: With special thanks to Matilda Michell.

Printed in Australia.

Alone and apart, defiant and inexorable, Antarctica beckons to the mystic. For the man who cannot dream, for the explorer with no soul, it is a white hell. But for the visionary it is a white heaven, and it is no fortuitous accident that makes the same men return time and again to its pitiless wastes, some of them to master a few of its secrets, many of them to die.

The White Desert, Noel Barber, 1958, p. 9.

This book is dedicated to Elizabeth Chipman

with our thanks for her encouragement and support and for giving us access to all her papers in the National Library of Australia. We recognise the extensive efforts Elizabeth made to collect material for a biography of George Hubert Wilkins.

Contents

	Acknowledgements	vii
	Introduction – George Hubert Wilkins.	1
1	Wilkins – learning to "live rough".	7
2	1920-22: British Expedition to Graham Land – The John Cope disaster!	17
3	1921-22: Shackleton-Rowett Expedition – Wilkins joins *Quest* as Naturalist on Shackleton's final voyage.	43
4	1928-1929: The Wilkins-Hearst Antarctic Expedition. Wilkins and Eielson: the first people to fly in the Antarctic.	77
5	1929-1930: The Second Wilkins-Hearst Expedition. Support from the "Discovery Committee" and the use of their ship, RRS *William Scoresby*.	105
6	1933-1934: The First Ellsworth Trans-Antarctic Expedition. *Wyatt Earp* enters the scene. Ellsworth engages Wilkins. After one trial flight the plane was damaged, the expedition was over.	127
7	1934-1935: The Second Ellsworth Expedition. And the weather defeats them again, and again.	145
8	1935-1936: The Third Ellsworth Expedition – Success! And Rescue!	157
9	1938-1939: The Fourth Ellsworth Antarctic Expedition – Claiming Land.	167
10	1957-1958: Operation Deep Freeze III. Wilkins Final Antarctic Trip with US Navy for International Geophysical Year.	191
	Epilogue: Death and Legacy. What did George Hubert Wilkins achieve during his Antarctic expeditions and what is his legacy?	233

Photo by Paul Dalrymple. "Mug shot" of Wilkins at Little America V or McMurdo Station in December 1957.[1]

---

[1] Personal correspondence, Paul Dalrymple to a Wilkins' family member, 18 January 2014. See Chapter 10: During the IGY (International Geophysical Year) Paul served two consecutive years, 1957-1959, at Little America V and at Amundsen-Scott South Pole Station.

Acknowledgements

We, the authors Annette and Trish, must start this acknowledgement with our thanks to Elizabeth Chipman, to whom this book is dedicated, for allowing us full and complete access to all her papers at the National Library of Australia. The material she collected and the research she did for her proposed biography of this fascinating man has been a guiding light for us through our own research for and the writing of *Where Few Have Been*: *Sir Hubert Wilkins and the Antarctic*.

To the Byrd Polar and Climate Research Center, custodians of the Sir George Hubert Wilkins Papers, at Ohio State University, AND to their Polar Curator, Laura Kissel, go our immense thanks for the incredible support and help given to us over several years. And thanks also to that Center for the Award of the 2024-2025 Polar Archives Research Award, which enabled Annette to spend three weeks in their Archives in September 2024. And thanks to Radford College, the Department of Defence and Annette's helpful family for allowing her to go! Laura, you are something very special to this book!

While many people have supported us in all sorts of ways, two of the most appreciated as well as the most useful and unwavering were Dr Bruce Moore and Dr Mike Ryan, who proof read – and made valuable suggestions – on the whole manuscript. Thanks Bruce and Mike. And for his long-term and on-going transcribing of Wilkins' diaries and other very useful information, we thank Philip van Dueren. Others who have supplied information or done some manuscript reading, often both, have been Alan Capp, Commander Peter Cooke-Russell, RAN RTD, Dr David Harrowfield of Christchurch NZ, Dr Joe Johnston, 2022 Phil Law Medal recipient and former President of ANARE, Jeff Maynard, author and Wilkins "encyclopedia on legs", the late Dr Ian Norman, Malcolm Robertson, Convenor of Canberra ANARE Club, and Wilkins family member Kaye Ridge in South Australia.

Illustrations are an expensive part of any book. Thanks to all those people who have donated to us the free use of their own work or work to which they own the copyright. They include Matilda Michell for the portrait of Wilkins on the cover; world renowned and specialist Antarctic-photographer Colin Monteath of Christchurch NZ; Margaret Mortimer, Antarctic tourism pioneer, who cooked for the yacht crew, the first people (1988) to climb Mount Minto in the Transantarctic Mountains; Richard Gillam of Jersey, fellow passenger on a 2013 voyage through the South Atlantic and his photographic skills with Wilkins's finch (*Nesospiza wilkinsi*), and Professor Simon Harley of Edinburgh University, a modern-day Antarctic researcher/explorer in one of the same areas as Hubert Wilkins' on the 1938-1939 Expedition. The Romsdal Museum in Molde, Norway now holds several photo albums from crew members of the *Wyatt Earp* on her 1930s voyages, which have been accessed by us through their always helpful Curator, Kenneth Staurset Fåne.

We are extremely thankful for the amazing resources of the following institutions in Canberra, interstate and overseas: the Australian War Memorial, the National Archives of Australia, the National Library of Australia (especially Trove and the always helpful Special Collections staff), the National Museum of Australia, the State Libraries of New South Wales and Victoria, and all their kind, professional and helpful staff. Other places which hold Wilkins-related material which we have used include The National Archives in London, the National Library of New Zealand, the Scott Polar Research Institute in Cambridge, England, and the University of Wisconsin-Milwaukee, Yale University and Johns Hopkins University, in the United States of America.

On-going thanks to Professors Tom Frame and David Lovell, both former Directors of the John Howard Prime Ministerial Library, who have been strong and enthusiastic supporters from the start of this project in 2021. Thanks also to Professor Emma Sparks, Rector of UNSW Canberra, for encouraging Trish, as an Adjunct Fellow, to keep working on this project. Thanks too to the Library at the Australian Defence Force Academy that has enabled us to have most of their Antarctic collection close at hand, that is, at home, for several years now!

Trish's husband, Jim, as with all things Antarctic, had supportive comments to make, until his sudden death in early 2023. Thanks Jimbo.

To our publisher Anthony Cappello and the support people at Connor Court Publishing in Brisbane, a big thank you for the work they have done to bring our manuscript to a published book! Very much appreciated.

Trish Burgess and Annette Carter
28 April 2025

Introduction

George Hubert Wilkins

Dr Brendan Nelson, in his Foreword to *The Unseen Anzac*,[1] sums Wilkins up very well: "By any standard the life of George Hubert Wilkins was an extraordinary one. From humble beginnings in rural South Australia, Wilkins became a renowned photographer and cinematographer, aviator, war correspondent, scientist, author, and, above all else, polar explorer."

For a man born in 1888, George Hubert Wilkins achieved many things worth noting before we focus on the Antarctic aspects of his life. Wilkins was the first person to film fighting on a battlefield, during the First Balkan War in 1912 and, also later, in World War I. During the Balkan War he filmed and photographed from the air and the ground for newsreels and newspapers. During World War I he served as an Australian Official War Photographer. He was awarded the Military Cross and Bar, the only Australian official war photographer to have been decorated.

He was the first person to navigate a plane that traversed the Arctic Circle, crossed the Arctic and flew over the Arctic ice cap (with pilot Carl Ben Eielson). Eielson later accompanied him in the Antarctic where they became the first people to fly, explore and map areas from the air. On the Second Hearst Expedition he was the first person to take a car to the Antarctic! Between the Arctic and Antarctic flights Wilkins was invited as naturalist, but also became photographer, on Shackleton's final voyage on the *Quest*. After Shackleton's death, on the journey home through the South Atlantic, Wilkins was the first person to identify an unknown bird, now called the *Wilkins's Bunting* on Nightingale Island near Tristan da Cunha. And he was the first person to command a submarine to the Arctic ice cap.[2]

---

[1] Jeff Maynard, *The Unseen Anzac*, Scribe Publications, Melbourne, 2015, p. ix.
[2] Simon Nasht, *The Last Explorer: Hubert Wilkins – Australia's Unknown Hero*, Hachette Australia, Sydney, 2005, 2nd ed reprint 2014, p. 250.

As early as 14 November 1928, the *Sydney Morning Herald* reported that Wilkins "feeds on perilous adventures as a child does on milk"![3]

There is something similar about all of his polar travels. They were not easy – given the dates – 1912-1931. There was a constant and never-ending battle with the elements, the cold in particular, and the need to plan meticulously for the unknown ahead. And, presumably, to have Plan B ready and waiting should things go awry. No doubt growing up on an outback Australian farming property gave him plenty of opportunities to learn about survival. There was a severe four-year drought from 1901. No snow, but temperatures ranging from minus 5°C to 44.9°C. By the time he left the area as a teenager he would have had a fair idea of how extremes of temperature needed to be dealt with.

It is generally agreed by historians and biographers that, as stated by him, George Hubert Wilkins was the youngest and last child of Henry (Harry) Wilkins and Louisa (Smith). Whether he was the youngest of eleven, twelve or thirteen is debatable. Jeff Maynard says "youngest of eleven, possibly twelve children".[4] While his mother, interviewed by Associated Press in Adelaide on 23 April 1928, for a news article which appeared in the *New York Times* on 24 April 1928, had this to say about her youngest child:

> "We mothers don't say much, but we feel a lot," said Mrs. Wilkins, 86-year-old mother of Captain George H, Wilkins, as she talked with vivacity today, despite her years, of her son's great Polar feat.
>
> "I am very glad George has done what he set out to do," she continued with beaming face. "It is twenty years since he first went away, and he has never lived at home since. Like all his brothers, he was a good son, kind both in words and action. He has always been a great reader, and made more of what he learned in a little country school than many men have been able to on college educations."

---

[3] All newspaper references in this book are sourced through Trove, courtesy of the National Library of Australia, unless otherwise stated.
[4] Jeff Maynard, *The Illustrated Sir Hubert Wilkins*, Netfield Publishing, Melbourne, 2022, p. 9.

The article ended with "Mrs. Wilkins is the mother of twelve children."

George Hubert Wilkins was born on 31 October 1888, at the family property "Netfield", at Mount Bryan East in country South Australia, about 200 kms from Adelaide. He died at Framingham, Massachusetts in the United States, on 30 November 1958. Called George throughout his childhood and until he was knighted in 1928, he then chose to be known as Sir Hubert. However, he was more like an only child. Five or six of his siblings died in infancy and his brother Tom, the only one living at home when he was born, left when George was four or five.[5] He loved books and read whenever he could lay his hands on one. His knowledge and love of nature, the outdoors, wildlife and, in particular, a fascination with the weather, were deep-seated in him from his earliest days. His interest in the weather stayed with him all his life and he had great ambitions to set up a series of weather stations across the Arctic and the Antarctic to provide better weather forecasting generally and, in particular, to help farmers. This goal added impetus to many of his travels over the years.

Drought and advancing age forced his parents to leave the country and move to Adelaide in 1905, where George studied electrical engineering at the South Australian School of Mines and Industries. He was an apprentice at Bullock & Fulton, Electrical Engineers and Contractors, from November 1905 to September 1908.[6] During these years he also studied mechanical engineering and took music and singing lessons, learning to play several instruments. He had an excellent voice, but aware that his strict Protestant parents would not allow him to sing in public, he sometimes used the name "Bert Wilkie" to enter singing contests.

About May 1908, he became involved with Bruce's Carnival, a tent-show, which used an electric engine to light their activities in places without access to electricity. In Adelaide Wilkins was working nearby when the Carnival engine refused to start and he was asked

---

[5] John Grierson, *Sir Hubert Wilkins: Enigma of Exploration*, Robert Hale Limited, London, 1960, p.13.
[6] Jeff Maynard, *The Illustrated Sir Hubert Wilkins*, p.14.

to "make it go". He did, and it was here he saw his first cinema machine, and so began his career as a cinematographer.

In April 1909 he stowed away on a ship to Sydney – and did not, as related in Lowell Thomas's *Sir Hubert Wilkins*, take the wrong ship to London via Algiers, become kidnapped by Arabs and eventually escape with the help of a young lady! In Sydney, however, he did begin a life of adventure and exploration which covered every continent and ocean and both the North and South Poles. He documented this in diaries, letters, reports, newspaper articles and books as well as in photographs and film. A surprisingly large amount of this material is still available today in archives and museums around the world and, in particular, in the Byrd Polar and Climate Research Center Archival Program at Ohio State University in America and the National Library of Australia in Canberra.

During nearly three years in Sydney, he worked as an electrician at first fixing engines that provided light for (Frank) Waddington's Pictures, another moving picture tent type theatre. From that he operated projectors and acquired his own equipment to make films. "In January 1912 Waddington opened the first purpose-built movie theatre in Australia and showed films continuously throughout the day and evening. Wilkins assisted Waddington design and fit out the theatre".[7] Moving pictures were the rage in Sydney with many new venues opening up. Wilkins, once he had his own camera, taught himself to film, process and produce newsreels and worked on early Australian feature films.

On 21 February 1912 he left Sydney for London, arriving there nearly seven weeks later on 8 April.

With a lively imagination, some of his journeys were written up as factual diaries, some as possible future film and radio scripts, and some with a solid base of fact and a little fiction occasionally added! Wilkins had a wonderful ability to paint a picture with his words and as such was in demand by various newspapers to provide "on the spot" dispatches. A great example of this is his book

---

[7] Jeff Maynard, *The Illustrated Sir Hubert Wilkins*, p.19.

Undiscovered Australia,[8] the account of his expedition in 1923-1925. for the British Museum, to tropical Australia. As author, he is named as Capt. Sir G.H. Wilkins, M.C. and it clearly shows a great talent – to make a report of a scientific expedition into a very readable document.

Many of the biographies about Wilkins have all but ignored the incredible exploration and documentation of his nine Antarctic journeys. This book aims to fill these gaps.

---

[8] Capt. Sir G.H. Wilkins, M.C., *Undiscovered Australia: Being an Account of an Expedition to Tropical Australia to Collect Specimens of the Rarer Native Fauna for the British Museum, 1923-25*, Ernest Benn Limited, London, 1928.

Informal photograph of Captain George Hubert Wilkins taken in Australia in 1922. From the Australian War Memorial and courtesy of George Hubert Wilkins Papers Box 35_9_1, BPRC, OSU.

1

WILKINS – LEARNING TO "LIVE ROUGH"

A brief history and what prepared him for the Antarctic: living rough in the First Balkan War, the Vilhjalmur Stefansson-led Canadian Arctic trip (very rough and very cold), and the World War I battlefields.

Before Wilkins left Australia the Gaumont Film Company offered him a job in London.[1] Arriving in England on 8 April 1912, he was employed as a cinematographer making newsreels. He learned to fly a plane soon after his arrival, probably at Hendon, the country's first aerodrome and flying school. At least two people have been mentioned as having taught him and it is likely that he learned from more than one pilot. Claude Grahame-White, the first in England to have an aviator's certificate, built the centre at Hendon and Wilkins had his first flight with him when on assignment for Gaumont. He was soon frequently filming from the air.

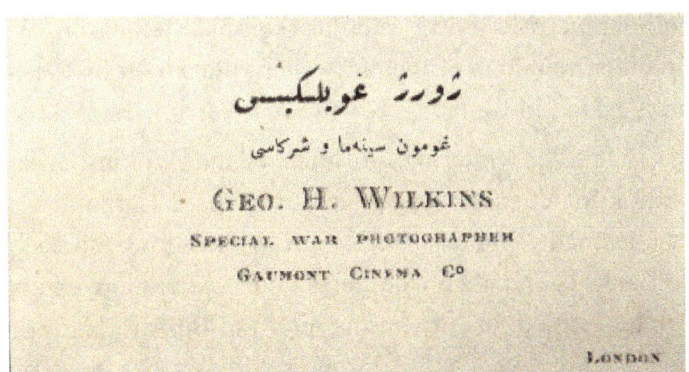

OSU Box PA.2017.003.0001, Folder 1, Sir George Hubert Wilkins Papers, SPEC.PA.56.0006, Byrd Polar and Climate Research Centre, Ohio State University.[2]

---

[1] Ian Macfarlane, *Ten Remarkable Australians,* Connor Court, Brisbane, 2019, p. 99.
[2] Future references to the Sir George Hubert Wilkins Papers will appear as Sir George Hubert Wilkins Papers, BPCRC, OSU.

At the start of the First Balkan War in 1912, Gaumont and the *Daily Chronicle* in London sent Wilkins to Turkey to report on it. He carried a business card which read *Geo. H. Wilkins, Special War Photographer, Gaumont Cinema Co. London*, in both English and Turkish.[3] Arriving in Constantinople (now Istanbul) he and other newspaper people had to wait two weeks before they were taken by train to the battle front. For several weeks Wilkins filmed and sent reports to London. He continued filming newsreels and by this time films made in colour were the latest thing. In 1913 Gaumont sent Wilkins to the West Indies to film a colour advertising documentary for the Cadbury chocolate company. During Wilkins' absence from London, Gaumont received a request for his services as the photographer for the Canadian Arctic Expedition led by Vilhjalmur Stefansson. Gaumont and Wilkins agreed and in June 1913 he joined the Expedition in Victoria, British Columbia. They travelled north with several ships. Wilkins was to spend nearly three years in the Arctic. His diaries, letters and stories document this time, including living with the Inuits from whom he gained his extensive knowledge about dealing with snow, ice, cold and the other hinderances to living in polar regions. Stefansson, Wilkins and the other members of the party spent the winter of 1914-1915 on Banks Island in Canada's North West Territories.

In 1915, "After wintering on Banks Island, Wilkins led a small party 800 kilometres across the ice to Bernard Harbour, Canada. There he learned of the war in Europe. Wilkins took more supplies back to Banks Island, then wintered again".[4] After more exploration in 1916, he learned, in July on his return to Bernard Harbour, that the war in Europe was still in progress. In October he started the long journey back to Australia, via London. In a letter dated 27 November 1916, Frank Hurley invited Wilkins to dine with Lady Kathleen Scott, the widow of "Scott of the Antarctic". She "made

---

[3] Jeff Maynard, *The Illustrated Sir Hubert Wilkins*, p. 21.
[4] Jeff Maynard, p. 37.

a point of meeting the interesting polar explorers".[5] Hurley and Wilkins first met on 30 November, at a soirée at Lady Scott's home. Hurley was already a renowned photographer who had just returned from the Antarctic with Shackleton's British Imperial Trans-Antarctic Expedition of 1914-1916. Their paths would cross again about six months later.[6]

Wilkins' father died while he was overseas and he had not seen his mother since he left Adelaide in 1909. He visited her in Adelaide before going on to Melbourne where he enlisted in the Australian Flying Corps, planning to be a pilot.

Records in the Australian Archives (NAA: B2455. WILKINS GEORGE HUBERT, on following page) show that on his "Attestation Paper of Persons Enlisted for Service Abroad" dated 4 May 1917, he listed his "Trade or Calling" as Explorer. Then aged 28-6/12 he had already made his mark in the world and begun what would be a long list of "first" achievements.

---

[5] Simon Nasht, *The Last Explorer*, p. 52.
[6] "Sir Hubert Wilkins – The Man and His Work – Captain Hurley on a Friend", *Telegraph* (Brisbane), 8 October 1931, p. 6.

AUSTRALIAN MILITARY FORCES.
AUSTRALIAN IMPERIAL FORCE.

Attestation Paper of Persons Enlisted for Service Abroad.

No. 26.

Name in full — Surname: WILKINS
Christian Name: George Robert Hubert

Unit: 9th Reinf. Aus Flying Corps

Joined on: 1st May 1917

Questions to be put to the Person Enlisting before Attestation.

1. What is your Name? — George Hubert Wilkins
2. In or near what Parish or Town were you born? — In the Parish of Burra, in or near the Town of Burra, in the County of South Australia
3. Are you a natural born British Subject or a Naturalized British Subject? — British Subject
4. What is your Age? — 28 yr
5. What is your Trade or Calling? — Explorer
6. Are you, or have you been, an Apprentice? —
7. Are you married? — No.
8. Who is your next of kin? — (Brother) Thomas Walter Wilkins, Dulwich, South Australia
9. What is your permanent address in Australia? — Dulwich, South Australia
10. Do you now belong to, or have you ever served in, His Majesty's Army, the Marines, the Militia, the Militia Reserve, the Territorial Force, Royal Navy, or Colonial Forces? — Canadian Naval Service 3½ yrs
11. Have you stated the whole, if any, of your previous service? — Yes
12. Have you ever been rejected as unfit for His Majesty's Service? — No
13. (For married men, widowers with children, and soldiers who are the sole support of widowed mother)—
14. Are you prepared to undergo inoculation against small pox and enteric fever? — Yes

I, George Hubert Wilkins, do solemnly declare that the above answers made by me to the above questions are true, and I am willing and hereby voluntarily agree to serve in the Military Forces of the Commonwealth of Australia within or beyond the limits of the Commonwealth.

And I further agree to allot not less than two-fifths of the pay payable to me from time to time during my service for the support of my wife and children.

Date 4/5/17

Signature of person enlisted: Geo H Wilkins

Having enlisted in Melbourne on 4 May 1917, Wilkins was back in London by July with other reinforcements for the Australian Flying Corps. He only met the medical requirements after a specialist tested his eyes, because the military tests said he was colour blind (which he was not!). Nevertheless, Wilkins was told he would not be flying but would be joining Captain Frank Hurley, who had been appointed official photographer for the Australian Imperial Force (AIF). Wilkins was assigned to this new position by Captain Charles E.W. Bean, official Australian war historian of the newly created Australian War Records Section (AWRS), who had personally chosen Wilkins to be Hurley's assistant and official photographer of historical events. On 17 August 1917 Wilkins and Hurley travelled by ferry to France and while they were in Calais:

> We met Bean and he explained our various duties. Hurley was to photograph scenes suitable for propaganda and press releases, while I was expected to photograph actual frontline scenes and incidents, showing everything the camera could represent. This meant that I would often have to photograph before sunrise amid the smoke and dust of battle. From a photographic point of view the film would be bad, but from an historical point of view very valuable.[7]

Wilkins and Hurley worked and lived together throughout the following three months. It is not hard to imagine the devastation and appalling sights they saw and recorded both in photographs and moving film. Frequently they were on the front line and, although they did not take part in the fighting, Wilkins often helped retrieve wounded men. No doubt through this difficult time they shared stories of their Arctic and Antarctic experiences. In November 1917 Hurley was sent to Palestine and in December Wilkins and Bean were in London for the first photographic exhibition arranged by the newly formed Imperial War Museum. Many photographs taken by Wilkins during this time appeared in Bean's Volume XII of the *Official History of Australia in the War of 1914-1918*. Jeff Maynard's book *The Unseen Anzac* gives a detailed and fascinating

---

[7] Wilkins' manuscript quoted in *The Unseen Anzac*, p. 71.

account of this period and the time immediately following the end of the War on 11 November 1918.

Wilkins, the only Australian Official War Photographer to have received a military Medal, was Mentioned in Dispatches (MiD)[8] for providing information about German troop movements, gained as he followed Australian soldiers to photograph them in action. In June 1918 he was awarded the Military Cross (MC) for entering No Man's Land to rescue wounded soldiers under fire. And in September he received a Bar to the Military Cross for leading a group of inexperienced American soldiers, whose officers had been killed, through a dangerous action during the Battle of the Hindenburg Line. During World War I, 37,104 Military Crosses were awarded and 2,984 of those recipients received a Bar.

Following the end of the War, Bean wanted to return to Gallipoli and photograph the whole area, calling his plan the "Gallipoli Mission":

> Displaying the zeal with which he now approached anything to do with the history of Australians in the war, Bean named the planned trip the 'Gallipoli Mission'. He and Wilkins would be accompanied by artists George Lambert, two assistants, two map makers, and Lieutenant Hedley Howe, who had landed at Gallipoli on Anzac Day, and who could retrace the movements of the first men ashore. The eight members of the mission left London on 18 January 1919 and travelled to Turkey. While the rest of the team waited at Chanak, Bean and Wilkins went to Constantinople to buy maps.[9]

Wilkins "had brought 200 glass plate negatives with him. On those negatives he made a record that has since become a national treasure – the deathly quiet beach and hills of Gallipoli, captured while many of the dead still lay where they had fallen".[10] Today these, with other material collected by the AWRS from 1917 to

---

[8] World War II Australian War Correspondent and Photographer Damien Parer was Mentioned in Despatches on 15 March 1945.
[9] Jeff Maynard, *The Unseen Anzac*, p.181.
[10] Jeff Maynard, pp.182-183.

1919, form the basis of the Australian War Memorial collection in Canberra.

National Archives of Australia. NAA: A14518, H5173. Notation by J.K. Davis on front of photo says: "Captain G.H. Wilkins M.C. and Bar, J.K. Davis, Lieut R.A.N.R., Major Eric Webb, D.S.O., M.C., Magnetic Observer, Australian Antarctic Expedition, London 1918".[11]

In 1957, Wilkins responded to a request for information from Mr. R.A. Swan, for a book that he was writing. The letter includes a chronological list of his visits to Antarctica. It is reproduced below and details of each visit are in the following chapters of this book. Swan's book, *Australia in the Antarctic: Interest, Activity and Endeavour*, was published in 1961 by Melbourne University Press, after Wilkins death.

---

[11] Taken in London 1918, almost certainly by Frank Hurley. Hurley met Davis and Webb on the AAE voyage in 1911-1914. He met Wilkins in London in 1916. Hurley and Wilkins worked together as Official War Photographers in France in 1917. Davis and Wilkins corresponded over many years, until Wilkins' death in 1958.

> 37 West 53rd Street
> New York. 19. N.Y
> 15 August 1957.
>
> Dear Mr Swan:
>
> The photograph I mentioned in my previous letter is not in the New York apartment and because of the rush of duty with the Army I do not know when I will be able to get to the farm- which is about 200 miles from New York.
>
> In the meantime I am sending a photograph of myself, a photograph of the plane I used to fly from Point Barrow, Alaska around the North Pole to Spitsbergen, a distance of about 2500 miles in 20 hours 20 minutes. Many accounts state 2200 miles for this flight. That is the distance we would have travelled if we had gone over the Pole, but we went around the Pole.
>
> The airplane in the photograph taken at Deception Island, 1928, is the same plane; used to fly for the first time over the Antarctic continent. From the plane I dropped proclamations authorized by and under the direction of King George Vth, claiming the Graham Land area for the British Empire. Other proclamations were hand planted on the Graham Land area and the British flag flown.
>
> The picture of the two penguins standing at attention beside the Australian flag was taken in the Vestfold Hills area, Antarctica. It was in that area I planted (1938-39) proclamations similar to the ones left on Graham Land, except that the Vestfold Hills proclamations stated " As far as this act will allow, claim is laid to this area for the Australian Commonwealth. "
>
> Chronological record of my visits to Antarctic.
>
> 1919-20. 2nd in command British Antarctic Expedition. To Graham Land.
> 1922-23. Naturalist, Shackleton-Rowett Antarctic Expedition, traversing from Wedell Sea westward to Bouvet Island, Tristan da Cunha, Capetown.
> 1928-29. Wilkins-Hearst Antarctic Expedition. First flight over Antarctic.
> 1929-30. Wilkins Antarctic Expedition. (Hearst gave some funds to the first expedition, but not to the second.) Further flights and discovery of islands in Wedell Sea and Pacific Ocean sectors.
> 1933-34. Ellsworth Antarctic Expedition. (Ellsworth provided the funds but did not join the expedition until it was leaving South Africa, and left at the first port of call on the return journey. I organized and managed all of the "Ellsworth" Antarctic Expeditic
> 1934-35. From Ross Sea area to Deception Island, Snowhill Island, Graham Land .
> 1935-36. To Deception Island, Dundee Island and Ross Sea area.
> During this expedition Herbert Hollick-Kenyon flew and navigated the airplane from Dundee Island to within sight of Little America, making several stops on the way. Kenyon was under oath to me not to fly above or under cloud; to land and await clear weather before continuing. I had promised to pick up Ellsworth and Kenyon at Little America on Jan 19th, 36. While on the way , in agreement with the Australian Government, the Wyatt Earp was delayed so that the Discovery could go in ahead and " rescue " Ellsworth and Kenyon. The Wyatt Earp picked up Ellsworth and Kenyon from the Discovery, near Little America on the 19th.
> 1938-39. " Ellsworth " expedition to the Vestfold Hills area. This expedition was prematurely ended as a result of one man crushing his knee in a crevasse. *Hubert Wilkins*

Letter from Hubert Wilkins to R.A. Swan from the Papers of Elizabeth Chipman, National Library of Australia, MS9635, MS Acc11.071. Written in August 1957 just before Wilkins' final trip to the Antarctic (see Chapter 10). Unable to ascertain copyright.[12]

---

[12] All further references to the Papers of Elizabeth Chipman are from National Library of Australia, MS9635, MS Acc11.071. This collection comprises research notes pertaining to the life of Sir George Hubert Wilkins, compiled for a biography that was not completed.

The photo below, taken by Wilkins, is referred to in his letter to Swan:

> The picture of the two penguins standing at attention beside the Australian flag was taken in the Vestfold Hills area, Antarctica. It was in that area that I planted (1938-39) proclamations similar to ones left on Graham Land, except that the Vestfold Hills proclamations stated "As far as this act will allow, claim is laid to this area for the Australian Government."

See further details in Chapter 9.

OSU Box 36_1_4, Sir George Hubert Wilkins Papers, BPCRC, OSU.

2

1920-22 British Expedition to Graham Land – The John Cope disaster!

Misled by the lure of planes, Wilkins joined this expedition to discover it had only four members, the funds raised had been spent, there were no planes and no ship and the leader had little idea about leading!

Wilkins returned to London from Gallipoli on 21 April 1919, the same month that John Lachlan Cope released details of a very large, ambitious and costly expedition to the Antarctic. Cope and Wilkins met and Wilkins agreed to join what was originally proposed as the British Imperial Antarctic Expedition 1920-1922. It was to be the largest, grandest and best equipped expedition yet to head south. It gradually diminished in size and goals and eventually became known as the British Expedition to Graham Land 1920-1921. Cope worked extremely hard to obtain funds and sponsorships. He would be leader of the expedition and he promised "flying opportunities" as part of it. Planes built for World War I were easily available now the War was over. Cope's plans were to take 12 planes to Graham Land on whaling ships and stage them, with fuel, along the coast towards the Antarctic mainland where they would establish a base well inside the Antarctic Circle. By leap frogging planes, men and fuel they would have two planes at the base from where they would fly to the South Pole and back. Also included in his plans was the establishment of permanent bases for weather forecasting from the frozen continent. Both, the opportunity for flying and weather bases, were at the top of Wilkins' wish list.

John Lachlan Cope was born in 1893. He studied medicine at Cambridge but gave up before he graduated in order to join Shackleton's Imperial Trans-Antarctic Expedition (Ross Sea Party) 1914-1917. Despite not having graduated in medicine (he eventually did in 1933) Shackleton took him as surgeon and biologist on board *Aurora*. This Expedition, one of the greatest of the 'Heroic Age' of polar exploration has been covered by many writers. The Ross Sea Party from the *Aurora* was to meet the party from the *Endurance* who planned to sledge across the Antarctic from the Weddell Sea. Both groups suffered extraordinary hardships with the Ross Sea Party referred to in books titled *The Lost Men*, *Polar Castaways*, *The Forgotten Men* or *Marooned in the Antarctic*.

> When Sir Ernest Shackleton's dreams of crossing Antarctica foundered with his expedition ship *Endurance* in the ice of the Weddell Sea in October 1915, he could only wonder what had become of his support party on the other side of the continent.[1]

The Ross Sea Party was to lay supply depots to support the traverse party from *Endurance* led by Shackleton. Their ship *Aurora* broke from her winter moorings at Cape Evans in a blizzard in May 1915. *Aurora* was trapped in the ice drifting about 1600 miles until February 1916. Ten men were left stranded and without proper equipment and supplies. Cope, with nine others, had no choice but to winter there and, under extremely difficult conditions, they laid the planned depots across the Ross Ice Shelf as far as Mount Hope. *Aurora* made it to New Zealand where she was refitted and, under the command of Captain J.K. Davis,[2] reached the seven survivors of the Ross Sea Party on 10 January 1917, after more than 18 months of tremendous adversity. And Cope wanted to return!

World War I had started before *Endurance* sailed from Plymouth on 26 October 1914 and before *Aurora* had left Hobart on 24 December 1914. The Ross Sea Party had no news from the rest of the world until the rescue voyage of *Aurora* arrived in January 1917. Her return brought the information that World War I was still going and, once back in England, many of the returning men immediately signed up to serve in the armed forces. Cope joined the Royal Navy and met Wilkins in London, possibly through Frank Hurley. Hurley

---

[1] Richard McElrea and David L. Harrowfield, *Polar Castaways: The Ross Sea Party (1914-17) of Sir Ernest Shackleton*, Canterbury University Press, Christchurch, New Zealand, 2004. Inside front cover.

[2] Later to become lifelong friend and correspondent of Wilkins.

was, of course, a member of Shackleton's *Endurance* Party but it is unlikely Cope and Hurley met in the Antarctic.

Wilkins agreed to join the expedition but first he needed to go to Australia, as soon as possible and for several reasons. He wanted to visit his mother and family in Adelaide and to go Melbourne to finish his work on the Gallipoli photographs. He also needed to apply for his discharge from the AIF. Wilkins jumped at the chance to participate in the England-Australia Air Race in 1919. Australian Prime Minister Billy Hughes put up a £10,000 prize for the first flight from England to Australia. The race was restricted to Australian entrants. Wilkins became navigator for the *Blackburn Kangaroo*. Their flight departed on 21 November and all went reasonably well across Europe, with only minor hiccups due to weather, mechanical problems and getting bogged. Their good fortune ran out on 8 December 1919 when, 80 miles after leaving Crete, oil began leaking from the port engine. They turned and made a crash-landing close to the takeoff site. All were unharmed although the plane was damaged. It was abandoned there and Wilkins returned to London where he and Cope discussed plans for Cope's British Imperial Antarctic Expedition 1920-22, soon to become known as the British Expedition to Graham Land 1921, and planned to leave the following year.

On 23 January 1920, Cope released more details of the Expedition, which included a planned attempt to reach the South Pole by air:

> The Plane ... is being specially constructed and will be so designed that it can land on ice by means of skids. Three men will make the dash for the pole from the top of the great ice barrier at the Bay of Whales. From the starting point it will be a continuous climb since the plane will have to cross a mountain range with peaks 11 000 ft high. The pilot will be Capt G.H. Wilkins. With a full load and crew the airplane will weigh 12 000 pounds. Its speed will average 98 miles an hour.[3]

---
[3] Neville Parnell and Trevor Boughton, *Flypast: A Record of Aviation in Australia*, AGPS Press, Canberra, 1988, p. 33.

Through 1919 and into 1920 Cope worked hard seeking finance, participants and supporters for his Expedition. He met with the Royal Geographical Society seeking their support, which was not forthcoming. Frank Debenham, of Scott's 1910-1913 expedition, reported after Cope had visited him in Cambridge: "There was a long talk during which we jointly and severally told him we thought he was not the person to lead such an expedition and also that his plans were poor and in some respects ridiculous."[4]

THE ANTARCTIC.

DR. COPE'S EXPEDITION.

LONDON, Dec. 2.

The Blackburn Company is constructing a Blackburn single-engined biplane, entirely different from the "Kangaroo," to accompany Dr. Cope's expedition to the Antarctic, to make the final dash of 400 miles to the pole.

Its construction presents enormous difficulties owing to it being necessary for the machine to have great lifting capacity. It will carry four men, including Dr. Cope and Captain Wilkins, a considerable quantity of equipment such as sledge and camping outfit, shovels, spades, tent, cooking stove, and provisions to last 10 weeks, to meet an emergency in the event of the machine crashing, necessitating a return on foot. It will carry sufficient petrol to cover 12,000 miles, owing to the fact that it is not likely to be able to follow a direct course.

The journey to the Pole from the Great Barrier will be flown at 5000 feet, but the machine must be capable of flying at 11,000 feet, which, owing to the rarefied atmosphere, is equal to 21,000 feet in lower altitudes. The machine must be warmed throughout, and the whole fuselage airtight. It is impossible to use wheels for the undercarriage. Skids will replace them. A machine fitted with the latter will be sent to Scandinavia in January to test their suitability.

A water-cooled engine is out of the question, owing to the certainty of freezing. An air-cooled engine is impracticable, owing to the fragility of the cylinder under intense cold, therefore they are adopting an oil-cooled engine. The machine will be shipped complete, but will be partly dismantled, the wings being folded back.

[5]

---

[4] Debenham 1919 in David L. Harrowfield, "The British Imperial Antarctic Expedition 1920-1922: Paradise Harbour, Antarctic Peninsula", *Polar Record* 9 (1958) pp. 97-134.

[5] *Sydney Morning Herald*, 6 December 1919, p.13.

Despite this and other similar reactions Cope pressed ahead. Wilkins dined with him at least twice in March 1920 and met him again in May[6] that year. Cope invited and named men who, he said, would take part including Major (later Sir) Raymond Priestley, a veteran of Shackleton's 1907-1909 and Scott's 1910-1913 expeditions. From the same Scott expedition, two other members were named by Cope as being offered places. Hurley sent an application from Australia to be photographer and others with polar experience were invited.

> The Chief Scientist initially appointed early in 1919 was Robert C. Mossman a meteorologist [of Bruce's Scottish National Antarctic Expedition 1902-1904]. Although 'his medical examination was satisfactory' (Cope 1919b) he was for reasons unknown replaced with an Australian George Hubert Wilkins.[7]

On 28 May 1920, Wilkins finally left London for Australia. His AIF records[8] show the following note: "Failed to complete flight from Gt Britain to Aust & returned to England & will remain on leave w/o pay or allowances until arrival in Australia. The cost of passage viz. £50 to be charged against deferred pay on allotment to the 'Bremen'". He travelled on the *Breman* to Fremantle and overland to Adelaide, arriving on 17 July. Here he visited his family, rejoined the ship on 19 July to Melbourne and Sydney arriving on 24 July. Under the heading "A Distinguished South Australian. Return of Capt. Wilkins, M.C." it was reported:[9]

> Few South Australians have had so many romantic experiences as has Capt. G. H. Wilkins, M.C. and Bar, who returned to Adelaide on Saturday after an absence of three years from the Commonwealth. ... He is under orders to report to Victoria Barracks, Melbourne, for special duty before he receives his discharge from the A.I.F.

The newspaper article briefly outlines his presence as

---

[6] Wilkins' Diary 1920, Sir George Hubert Wilkins Papers, BPCRC, OSU.
[7] Harrowfield, *Polar Record* 49 (2013) pp.118-139.
[8] National Archives of Australia File NAA: B2455, p. 58.
[9] *Register* (Adelaide), 19 July 1920, p. 7.

photographer at the Balkan war, time with Stefansson in the Arctic and joining the Australian Flying Corps. It refers to meeting Capt. Frank Hurley and serving in France with him and to his tour of Gallipoli and Palestine with Mr. C.E.W. Bean after the war. It also mentions Wilkins return to London following the crash-landing of the *Blackburn Kangaroo* with a sub-heading "Antarctic Expedition in View":

> Capt. Wilkins returned to London to organize the scientific staff of the British Imperial Antarctic Expedition. Owing to a difficulty in securing a suitable boat for operations in polar areas, and because of various misunderstandings between Dr. J.L. Cope, the leader and certain scientific societies in England, it was decided that the expedition could not leave this year, but it was agreed that a small party of men with sledges and dogs should go south at an early date in one of the whaling boats, to complete an important geographical survey of a section of the original plan. This party will proceed to Ross Sea, and follow as nearly as possible the configuration of the Antarctic coastline, depending almost entirely for food on seals and penguin. They will be picked up early in 1922 or 1923. This coast is 1,000 miles from point to point, and the knowledge of its geography and geology is of the utmost importance to those interested in polar matters. Capt. Wilkins will accompany this expedition as second in command, if his military duties in connection with the pictorial history of the war will enable him to do so.

In Sydney on 24 July, he signed the official form to be discharged from the AIF and his appointment was terminated from the 2nd Military District (Sydney) on 7 September 1920. Following this Wilkins returned to Melbourne to finish some of the photographic work for Bean and the Australian War Museum (later Australian War Memorial) including selecting photographs for enlargement. While in Australia he received a cable from Cope, the content of which came as a big surprise, advising that the size, equipment and number of participants for the Expedition had shrunk to almost nothing! The use of planes had been discarded, they would travel on a Norwegian whaling ship (rather than their own) and most of the funds raised had been spent. Cope wanted Wilkins to go to

Canada and purchase dogs. Having been offered a job in Australia, Wilkins commented:

> The whole thing was a hard blow. I really had no desire at all to go along with the expedition if we could not use planes. The Australia offer was an important one, and in the circumstances it was a sacrifice to give it up. However, I agreed that I would meet Cope and his party in Montevideo, stipulating that he would have to arrange for the dogs himself. This was the inauspicious start of perhaps the most mismanaged Antarctic expedition in history, one from which I was to learn, by horrible example, all about how *not* to direct an expedition into the unknown.[10]

Wilkins made a quick visit to his mother in Adelaide and left there on 4 October 1920, to make his way to Montevideo. It was an amazing journey – just to get to the starting point of the Antarctic Expedition. Wilkins went by train to Melbourne, bus to Sydney, ship to Auckland, train to Wellington, ship (SS *Marama*) to San Francisco (calling at Rarotonga and Tahiti) arriving on 5 November. He then travelled by train to New Orleans where, on 9 November, he spent a day "getting passports etc." On 10 November he boarded a ferry, with a Mississippi River Pilot, which followed the River to the Bar.

On 15 November, at 3 pm he arrived in Panama and transferred his baggage to *Huasco*, a Chilean passenger/cargo ship. He "looked about Colon and Christobal" the Panamanian port on the Caribbean Sea, near the Atlantic entrance to the Panama Canal. From here he posted "a concertina-folded postcard of colour views of the Panama Canal to Captain Davis without comment, except to say that he would be leaving the next day for Valparaiso (Chile) where he expected to arrive on 30th".[11] *Huasco* sailed the following day for the Canal taking a day to travel its length and into the Pacific Ocean. Land hadn't been sighted for two days before they went up

---

[10] Lowell Thomas, *Sir Hubert Wilkins: His World of Adventure*, Readers Book Club, London, 1962, p.108.
[11] Papers of Elizabeth Chapman: Timeline 1920. Letter Wilkins to Davis 15 November 1920.

a river about 40 miles to Guayaquil, Ecuador, and loaded bananas, mangoes, limes and pineapples. Going down river on 20 November they "had a good view of the mountains of Peru above the clouds. 1800 ft but no snow". The ship followed the coast and they went ashore at Pimentel, Callao and Mollendo in Peru, before arriving in Arica, Chile on 28 November, sailing the same day for Santiago and arriving on 29, and at Antofagasta on 30 November.

Wilkins' Diary for the first few days of December is illegible but he stayed in Los Andes overnight on 4 December, leaving by train the next morning, travelling over the mountains to Mendoza in Argentina. Leaving there on 6 December, on 7 December he boarded a "boat" to Montevideo, the capital of Uruguay. He enquired at the Harbour Master's office and several other places for news of Cope. He caught up with a number of people and enjoyed some social life: "Drive with Cloughs round beach. Dinner at Royal Hotel", "Dinner at Bucks", "Dinner at Cloughs. Stayed up until 2 am". "Went out walking in afternoon. Tea at Hotel. Dinner at Pocitos. Met the Italian Prince. Dance afterwards. Drove home with Cloughs at 3 am." On 12 December Wilkins boarded the Norwegian whaling factory ship *Solstreif* after lunch but as they were not sailing until 3 am, he went ashore with several others for dinner, taking Cope "home". However, because of a gale the ship was unable to sail until 7.30 pm on 13 December. Wilkins noted that *Solstreif* was a "decent boat. Officers all speak English. Good meals."

Someone somewhere, probably in London, was obviously releasing fanciful news to the press! Where or how the *Launceston Examiner* acquired the information they printed on 29 September 1920 (p.5), is not known but they reported under the heading "ANTARCTIC EXPLORATION: COPE'S EXPEDITION":

> The British Imperial Antarctic expedition consisting of Lieut Cape [sic], Messrs. G.H. Wilkins, C.M. Lester and T.W. Bagshawe have left London for Christiania, whence they start on a preliminary trip to the Antarctic, via the Falklands and Deception Island to Hope Bay, Graham Land, where they will establish a base and spend a year exploring the Weddell Sea and Deception Island. Then they return to London to arrange

a big expedition, occupying five years during which specially-prepared aeroplane will make a dash for the Pole.

At that time Cope was on his way from London to Norway to join the Norwegian whaling factory ship *Thor I*.[12] Bagshawe (on *Svend-Foyn I*) and Lester (on *Ørn II*) both departed on two further factory ships with most of the expedition's stores, from Cardiff, about the second week of October. Bagshawe and Lester arrived in Montevideo on 7 November.

Brian Roberts who prepared the first *Chronological List of Antarctic Expeditions*, summed it up:

> Four men were taken to South Shetland Islands by whaling vessels; the leader and H.G. [sic] Wilkins returned to England, but T.W. Bagshawe and M.C. Lester wintered at Waterboat Point on west coast of Graham Land recording meteorological, tidal and zoological observations.[13]

Wilkins' diaries tell that the *Solstreif* arrived in Port Stanley in the Falkland Islands about 9.30 pm on Saturday 18 December 1920, and it was "too dark to see much after passing the lighthouse". The following day he managed to buy eight dogs "after lots of trouble. Nobody there taking much interest" and they left the Falklands late that day. "Pilot did not come out with us as promised so I didn't get a chance to post my letters".

Financially things had gone badly wrong. Cope had spent too much of the expedition funds and the Norwegian whaling firms, owned by Lars Christensen, were aware of this and were very reluctant to allow Cope or his men or their supplies to travel on the whaling vessels. Christensen tried to delay Cope's departure. He did this by telling the captain of his ship "not to support Cope and by ordering the hold up of stores unless payments were forthcoming".[14]

Bagshawe and Lester made their way to Deception Island,

---

[12] Harrowfield, *Polar Record* 49 (2013) p. 122.
[13] Brian Roberts, "Chronological List of Antarctic Expeditions", *Polar Record* 9 (1958) pp. 97-134, 191-239.
[14] Lester 1920, in Harrowfield, *Polar Record* 49 (2013) p. 122.

arriving on 20 November. They spent their time, until Wilkins and Cope arrived on 24 December on the *Solstreif*, learning about whaling on several of the Norwegian ships as well as investigating some of the local penguin colonies and the geology of the island. At this time they "had heard nothing of Wilkins and the sledge dogs, nor had they received orders or advice from Cope".[15]

From Wilkins 1921 Diary it seems that having arrived at Deception Island, where the new Norwegian factory ship *Ronald* was tied up,[16] Cope and his small group had meals aboard the *Ronald* but slept ashore. "We had an excellent lunch with red wine, beer & liqueur to help it down. The meals are good on board the Ronald but not quite so good as on the Solstreif." On 1 January 1921 Wilkins noted he had spent all morning "going over" the Debrio Cinema camera. He said that "the machine works rather stiffly, needs the oil washing out of it although the temperature today is well above freezing. The 3" lens will not fit without a good deal of work so I shall have to the best I can with the 2" that is fitted to the camera."

It seems from several accounts that Wilkins came to an arrangement with Lars Christensen. He agreed that he would provide film of the complete whaling operations suitable for the Norwegians to use as publicity. He would hand over the film and his camera in exchange for the whalers transporting the party and their supplies to a suitable place to set up their winter base.

More from his Diary on the same day:

> After lunch Hamilton & I went up to the cliffs on the south of the entrance in the neighbourhood of Needle Rock. We took four of the dogs with us & they proved an inconvenience when climbing, some times going ahead & dropping rocks on us or pushing us to one side. They could scramble up first as steep places as we could. We photographed a Cape pigeon on the nest.

---

[15] Harrowfield, p. 123.
[16] Bjorn L. Basberg, "The Floating Factory Ship: Dominant Designs and Technological Development of Twentieth-Century Whaling Factory Ships", *Northern Mariner* 8:1 (1998) pp. 21-27.

Needle Rock at entrance to Deception Island, 2010. ©Margaret Mortimer.

And on Sunday 2 January 1921, Wilkins' Diary records:

> The whalers were working this morning so I got out the cinema camera to try & get some pictures but the light was not good & by the time I had the platform rigged from which to photograph the flensing platform it had started to snow. I eventually took a few feet of the men working in the snow & perhaps the snowflakes will show on the picture anyway. I must take that subject again in good light for I am afraid the platform was not solid enough … The barometer is going down & it looks as if we are in for some bad weather, If it would only clear up for a couple of days I daresay I could get all the pictures done & we could get away south.

Wilkins comments that he has not seen Cope since breakfast or the other two all day. Cope wanted to search for a suitable landing site to set up their base.

On 3 January Wilkins records another side of his personality which played a persistent and interesting part in his life: "Had a discussion about spiritualism this morning after breakfast. The Capt & Hamilton interested but the Dr very skeptical."

Hearing from the whalers that there was heavy sea ice in Antarctic Sound, which made the planned Snow Hill Island inaccessible for their winter base, Cope decided to use Hope Bay but was again thwarted by ice. Again, we have Wilkins' Diary, still on 3 January:

> Cope on board when we finished lunch. Says he has been on board "Orn" which would take him down but not send him back when he wants to come so he can't go with her. He says the Capt of Thor I will take us down & land us now as soon as the cinema pictures are taken & handed over but will not allow us to have the Norwegian gear until we are landing. This is rather foolish & we will find ourselves on the beach with nothing ready for a journey. We particularly want to get at the finnesko [boots of tanned reindeer skin with the hair on the outside] to repair them for the rats have been at them. I also want to fix up fur suits & make hoods for the parkas if they are not already on them.

Wilkins continued:

> Cope showed me a letter he wrote to Mr. Lars Christensen in which he complains of his treatment & Hansens behaviour & although there is room for a little complaint he is not quite fair to Hansen. It is another case of not stating all the facts, a thing impossible in a letter. Cope says he has asked Hamilton to arrange for a relief expedition for us next year, or for a government vessel to come & pick us up, which I think is utterly unjustified under the circumstances.

With the camera and processed film handed to the Norwegians and the site for the winter base agreed, transport of men and stores was organised and on 12 January 1921, all were landed at what was named by Lester and Bagshawe as Waterboat Point. It is between Paradise Harbour and Andvord Bay on the west coast of Graham Land. Now a designated historic site, only the base of the water boat, foundations of doorposts and an outline of the hut and extension still exist. Nearby are the remains of the disused Chilean González Videla Antarctic Base.

Waterboat Point, 3 March 2003. ©Trish Burgess.

And adjacent Paradise Harbour, 3 March 2003. ©Trish Burgess.

Wilkins wrote a letter dated 11 January 1921, while on board the whale catcher *Odd II*, en route from Deception Island to their drop off point at the selected site for their base. It was obviously not a pleasant trip with Wilkins referring to the vessel as "WHALE PITCHER"! The letter was sent to J.K. Davis, with a copy enclosed for Frank Debenham. It should be noted that Debenham in a letter dated 16 August 1921, thanked Wilkins for "the long letter, just received, via John K. Davis". It seems the letter took seven months to reach Debenham – probably not unusual for Antarctic mail and especially a letter sent care of Davis, who could have been anywhere in the world when it arrived! If it had been received more quickly in England many of the later "problems" might have been avoided!

Having arrived at their new home, the next week was spent in turning the upturned waterboat into a livable structure. Again, from Wilkins' Diary – starting on 13 January and over several days:

> (13th) Decided to live in the waterboat & build an outhouse over the opening & outside.
>
> (14th) Started to build frame work of house today & got it mostly up. Very few big nails so am not sure it will hold up in a gale but if cases are packed around I daresay it will be O.K.
>
> (16th) Busy finishing roof & front of house today. Also fixing 3 drum stove in outhouse. It will probably smoke very badly for the front opening is so large. Went out to get a seal on the ice, shot it 3 times with Bagshawe's revolver but still it got away.
>
> (17th) Putting windows & attic in hut today. Made windows of food bags. Took the whole boat around to the cache of supplies & brought back instruments etc including gramophone.
>
> (18th) Saw a Cape pigeon tonight at midnight. About finished house building last night & got to be at midnight after having a few tunes on the gramophone. Not any very good records to light so far, a couple of Besses of Barn Band[17] not too bad. Overslept again this morning got up 9.30. Soon as fed dogs Lester saw a seal on the ice so we got out sled boat & went after it. My revolver misfired 4 times then went off, the bullet going right through the seal's head. It only shook him for a moment, he then got up to struggle away & I had to finish him with the tomahawk. It was a very big male with loose front teeth. Many fish in stomach (Rock cod?) too far digested to keep. Lester &

---

[17] Besses o' th' Barn Band is one of the oldest and most famous brass bands in the world, formed in 1818. www.besses.co.uk.

I fixed up boat & went for a short sail. Cope cooked seal meat on drum stove. Foggy in morning clear at 4.30 today high tide. Made a door for drum stove from biscuit tins ok.

Wilkins' Diary has no information until 3 February. However, from Harrowfield[18] we learn a good deal from the journal (diary) articles of Bagshawe and Lester. Bagshawe states that "There was little prospect in moving far from base and on 25 January, Cope announced that he proposed to return on the first whaler to Montevideo. Later he would obtain a schooner and return next season and the expedition would then move to Hope Bay."

Wilkins' Diary resumed on 3 February:

(3rd) Wind sprang up last night from S.E. a new direction for this place. It was very gusty & averaged about 27 mph. It was still blowing this morning & we did not get up until 9.45 am. Killed a seal (female) with fetus about 4" long. It was a large one. A sea elephant came up into shallow water near the hut at 7.15 we are waiting to see if it will come right back.

(6th) Went to Andvord Bay & stayed the night. 4 glaciers at its bottom, one running to SE looks as if it could be climbed. A low slope on south side of Bay would afford a landing. Bay must be much bigger than marked on chart judging from the time it took for me to row to the bottom. Only saw two places where it might be easy to get on the land past ice. Slept in boat from 12am until 4am.

(7th) Climbed the cliff at foot of Bay & got some grass. Many sea gulls and few skuas. Rowed around Nth side of Bay & landed on a sandy beach above which is a penguin rookery. South Glacier slope looked more promising than ever on the way home but we could not see what is beyond it. It too may end at a steep cliff. Got home at 8 pm. A sea elephant on the rocks at entrance. I should pack up a week's provisions & off to the bay tomorrow to wait for fine day to try the slope but …

(12th) Took sights from Lemaire Island, sth side of Andvord Bay & w side. I got a good view of plateau & saw that it might be fairly easy to reach it via the SE glacier. Could not see signs

---

[18] Harrowfield, *Polar Record* 49 (2013) p. 123.

of high land there & plateau to the eastwards. Shot 2 sheathbills & 2 young shags on Andvord Bay.

(13th) Clear & sunshine but the boat was high & dry owing to low tide before we finished breakfast (12 noon). We went up on ice slope & got sight of mountains on Anvers & Brabant Islands.

Wilkins' Diary entries from 15 to 23 February, show only one word each day – "Hut" – except for 18 February "Boat Journey Andvord Bay. Choked with ice. Saw catcher pass." On 24 February "Discarded botany point[??]. Going home this year." On the following days his only comments are "25th Made ready to board whaler", "26th Left Waterboat Point 4 am for Sven Foyn Harbour", "27th Wilhelmina Bay", "28th Arrived Thor I 2.40 Left 6.20 Sailing 8.30", and "1st March Arrived Solstreif 7.20". Entries on 2 and 3 March simply said "Solstreif", and his final entry on 4th March "Visited Waterboat Point. Came back & settled on the Solstreif …? to reach Monte Video at last."

There is a melancholy feeling to Wilkins' last entries and together with his lack of information, given previous insightful comments, it is probable that he was undergoing some sadness and concern about leaving Lester and Bagshawe behind, despite their voiced keenness and willingness to remain at Waterboat Point, unsupported for nearly 12 months, through the winter, and alone.

Strangely, however, Wilkins' Diary does not describe in any detail the voyage that Lester reports in his journal. Wilkins records they left Waterboat Point on 26 February, for Sven Foyn Harbour and Wilhelmina Bay and, in fact, Wilkins' brief entries have him on board *Solstreif* on 1 March. Whereas Lester, quoted in Harrowfield, has Cope, Wilkins and Lester departing on 1 March on an extraordinary four-day voyage in their lifeboat to arrange transport: "The four-day voyage covered 90 nautical miles (166 km), accomplished little, and was not without incident." Further Lester states that the three returned to Waterboat Point on 5 March in the catcher *Graham* and that the Norwegian Captains Andersen and Hansen gave Lester and Bagshawe the opportunity to leave on *Svend Foyn I* and assured them, that if Cope was unable to return for them, he, Hansen personally, would collect them the following season. It would not be surprising, particularly with the long daylight hours, if any of them confused the actual date!

Lester and Bagshawe committed to staying through the winter, and on 4 March, Cope and Wilkins left Waterboat Point. In a letter to J.K. Davis dated 11 September, from London, Wilkins says "Anyway they decided to stay and Cope and I went off to live on the Whaler [*Solstreif?*] until they should start for home. It was a fortnight after we left the boys before the Whaler left". This would have been at the end of the whaling season with the whole Norwegian whaling fleet leaving together. After about five days sailing the ship called at the Falklands (Port Stanley). Wilkins, in Lowell Thomas's biography[19] states:

> When we reached the Falklands, the affair became most unpleasant. I was taken before the Governor, virtually under arrest, and charged with abandoning these two. A fuss was made about their being "boys", when actually they were young men. The father of one of them had consented to his coming with Cope only with the understanding that I assumed full responsibility and would take his son in hand. Although I had never heard of this until we were in the Falklands, the father held me responsible, and so did the British Governor and the Royal Geographical Society. Although Cope was nominally the expedition leader, the officials knew I had more experience than Cope and was of a different temperament, so I should bear the blame. I tried to convince them that the two lads were safe enough, because they were within thirty miles of one whaling station and 110 miles of another, where any of the whalers could pick them up next year. Nevertheless, the whole affair was most disagreeable for me.

While it is likely that Wilkins came under some criticism, it has not been possible to find corroboration of the event above as told by Wilkins. It may be a little exaggerated as has happened in other events he has related.

---

[19] Lowell Thomas, *Sir Hubert Wilkins: His World of Adventure*, p. 117.

From Port Stanley Wilkins sailed to Montevideo ("wire" from Wilkins to Frank Debenham from here on 19 May) and then New York (where he was writing letters on 11 June) and he sailed for London on 10 July 1921. Meanwhile in England letters were flying around between Frank Debenham (co-founder and unpaid Director of the new Scott Polar Research Institute in Cambridge), Arthur Hinks (Secretary of the Royal Geographical Society), and Bagshawe Senior (father of T.W. Bagshawe left at Waterboat Point). Both Debenham and Hicks had interacted with Cope when he was setting up the expedition and both were very unimpressed to the point that neither they nor the bodies they represented were prepared to support Cope.

Wilkins' wire from Montevideo to Frank Debenham in Cambridge, was communicated to Arthur Hicks in London in a letter dated 19 May 1921, and reads:

COPE, LESTER, IRRESPONSIBLE, IGNORANT DANGEROUSLY INCOMPETENT EXPEDITIONARY MATTERS. BAGSHAWE CONTENTEDLY INACCURATE PLANS UNSERIOUSLY ATTEMPTED BAGSHAWE LESTER WINTERING IDLY UNCOMFORTABLE. COPE DISHOURABLE ATTEMPTING FURTHER COMPLICATIONS. WILKINS

In the same letter Debenham says "The rich adjectives are almost sufficient comment but in the same mail comes a cutting from a M.V. (Montevideo) Sunday paper with a satirical cutting about 'Friend Cope' accepting an invitation to do a turn for a Variety Show there." He continues "The only thing quite clear is that there has been a most effective 'bust up' and we may hear later the sordid details. Wilkins promises to write me from New York".

Elizabeth Chipman comments[20] "Presumably Debenham was ready to believe that Wilkins was prone to exaggeration, but held back his criticism in the light of his own knowledge of Cope and the ridicule implied in the press clipping."

It seems likely that news of Wilkins' return to London became known, or information on Cope's return, for on 21 July, Bagshawe

---

[20] Papers of Elizabeth Chipman.

Senior writes to the Secretary (Arthur Hicks) of the Royal Geographical Society. Chipman quotes:

> Bagshawe's letter makes no mention of Wilkins. It states that his son "is now isolated", "away from all communication until early next year" and "the only apparent chance of their being picked up in the early part of next year is by Norwegian Whalers". His anxiety for his son is obvious: "I do not know what is likely to happen to these two young men who are alone at the base". He asks if the Society is "moving in any way in the matter?".

Hicks responds the following day (22 July) saying that he has heard from Frank Debenham "of the position your son was left by Messrs. Cope and Wilkins in the Antarctic Continent for the winter..." Chipman comments:

> He is quick to include Wilkins in the blame, which is hardly fair. It was Cope's expedition; it was his responsibility. This is the beginning of the Royal Geographical Society, through Hicks, animosity to Wilkins. The remainder of the letter is a statement freeing the Royal Geographical Society for any blame, and denying any responsibility for providing any assistance.

Bagshawe immediately replies to Hicks asking for any advice and saying he did not know the Royal Geographical Society had "formally repudiated the Expedition". He also advises that during the week he had "been also to lobby Sir Ernest Shackleton, who advises him that Wilkins is in London and will go South with him."

Hicks' reply to Bagshawe on 25 July has a further comment on Wilkins as he "passes Bagshawe off to Frank Debenham, on the grounds that Debenham "knows far more of the circumstances of the expedition than I do, and has had letters from your son, as well as from Wilkins". And "I did not know that Wilkins was in London – he has not been here. I should like to have an opportunity of cross questioning him on the extraordinary action in leaving your son and his companion alone".

Frank Debenham wrote to Hicks on 27 July, "I didn't know

Wilkins was in London: he promised to write me from New York but did not. As soon as I do see him I shall get the whole story and will let you know his end of the story." Debenham is not at all worried about the fate of the young men: "There can be no real difficulty in picking them up next year as they are at one of the whalers' regular haunts. What is more important is that when picked up they should come clear back to England and not be waylaid by Cope with fresh schemes".

In a handwritten letter dated 16 August 1921,[21] Debenham replied to Wilkins' letter of 11 January 1921, and quoting Chipman again, "asking for the truth of the details of the Cope expedition, and asking for his help in getting Bagshawe and Lester safely back to England from Andvord Bay. He is very supportive of Wilkins' actions, and it is obvious he has not been swayed in any way by Hicks of the Royal Geographical Society." Debenham included such comments as "By this time you must have heard many opinions of Cope from this end and I can only say I have never had to do with such a specious rascal". And "nothing but the fact that you were to be there would have persuaded me that there was a chance of success". "We would willingly have blocked the expedition at Monte Video if we had been able, but could neither do that nor warn you & the other two." And, supportively, "I for one fully endorse your action on leaving the expedition but am very sorry it didn't take place earlier".

Wilkins agreed to join the Shackleton-Rowett Expedition as Naturalist and Photographer. On 15 August 1921 he writes to the British Museum offering, on behalf of Shackleton, specimens to be collected on the Expedition. The Expedition sailed from St Katharine Docks in London on 17 September 1921.

On 11 September, Wilkins writes to Captain Davis, bringing him up to date on the Cope expedition, and telling him of his plans as part of the Shackleton-Rowett Expedition. But he obviously still had concerns about Lester and Bagshawe, the young men left to winter on their own, as he wrote to them from the *Quest* in Montevideo in

---

[21] SPRI, MS720: ER Correspondence received by Debenham, circa 1920-1922 [Regarding the British Expedition to Graham Land 1920-1922 (leader John Lachlan Cope) relating to its formation and conduct].

a letter dated 28 November 1921. They received it on 13 January 1922, when they were picked up by Norwegian whalers from their Waterboat Point base. The whalers, in fact, arrived to collect them on 18 December 1921, but Lester and Bagshawe insisted on staying the full 12 months, to complete their scientific work. After leaving the stubborn and dedicated winterers well provisioned and in no danger, the whalers returned on 13 January 1922. Wilkins' letter to Lester and Bagshawe is in the archives of the Scott Polar Institute in Cambridge (SPRI), with an annotation noting the day it was received.[22]

The following chapter tells of Wilkins and his time on the Shackleton-Rowett Expedition but one last, and important, event in relation to the Cope Expedition, when Wilkins had returned to London, needs mentioning. On the day before he left again, this time on a journey "to take official film of the work of the committee" of the (Society of) Friends (Quakers) travelling through Austria, Poland, Russia, Czechoslovakia, Latvia and Lithuania, Wilkins visited the Royal Geographical Society offices and wrote an eleven-page document, on the Society's letterhead, to the Secretary, Arthur Hinks. Dated 6 November 1922, it is quoted below and the under-linings are Wilkins:

> During the last few days I have heard from various sources that many people including yourself have had opinions as to my actions in connection with Cope's Expedition to the Antarctic that have been based on an incomplete knowledge of circumstances.
>
> - I have also been ill informed as to some of the circumstances and feel now that it is necessary to acquaint you with my understanding of the position. In order to do this clearly I will go over the happenings in chronological order.
> - After a certain party had withdrawn a promise to advance the money for a boat being built for Cope the plans resolved into a small expedition to the West side of Grahams Land & on to Charcot land. I had given my promise to Mr. Cope to go through with the Expedition & because of this people had advanced him

---

[22] SPRI, MS931/1/7; D Letter to Bagshaw and Lester 28 November 1921.

considerable sums in cash and as a good deal of this had been spent on purchasing stores & supplies I was bound to keep faith with those people.

- Military duties necessitated my return to Australia & upon receiving a guarantee from Cope that he had further backing I was to meet him in America. I received cable guarantees & was forced to give up a Government appointment in order to keep my word which was more binding than any legal agreement that might have been drawn up.

- I met Cope in South America & found that the guarantees were not substantial & that he had made arrangements to carry out plans entirely different to those we had discussed in London. It was then too late to retract & I agreed to go on and do what was possible for <u>that Summer</u> in the Antarctic, but if conditions at the end of the season would allow work of a satisfactory nature to be done during the winter then I might decide to stay on.

- After meeting the two other members of the Expedition I realized that only under extremely favourable conditions could we do more than the Summer's work. I informed Mr. Cope of this & the Whaling Captains at my suggestion landed us on Grahams Land <u>promising to call for us at the end of the season</u>.

- Towards the end of the Season Mr. Cope informed Messrs Lester, Bagshawe & myself that he had come to the conclusions that we could not do satisfactory work during the winter or even next summer without a boat at our disposal & proposed that we three should remain while he returned to civilization & secured a boat.

- Lester & Bagshawe agreed in the first place to remain if I would do so. I pointed out the futility of this, said I had no confidence in Cope getting a boat and advised them to return with the whalers at the end of the Season. This they agreed to do but overnight Cope persuaded them to stay and they stated that even though Cope could not return the next year with a boat of his own they were particularly anxious to spend a winter in the Antarctic, at Deception Island even, if no-where else was suitable.

- I gave as my opinion that it was perfectly safe for them to stay at Andvord Bay. They had an abundance of food (for two years[without?] other supplies but meat). Together with any number of sea elephants & seals & <u>provided always that they did not go out on the sea ice or on the glaciers</u>, they could come to no harm.

- In my opinion they were temperamentally suited as companions under such conditions but pointed out that it was an utter waste of time & I personally could not afford to indulge in the gratification of an idle boast of wintering in the Antarctic. I would however do my best to give them an opportunity of changing their minds after they had been together for a few days & before I finally left the neighbourhood. Together with Cope & Lester I made a boat journey of five days & completed arrangements whereby Cope & myself <u>and the others if they cared to</u> could return to Monte Video on the "Solstreif". Bagshawe who had been alone during that time expressed himself as being quite happy & determined to stay on. Lester also was keen to stay. There was still a fortnight to the end of the Season & Captain Hansen of the "Solstreif" promised me definitely that he would send one of his boats to give those two an opportunity of changing their minds & returning to Monte Video.

- The day before our departure I made arrangements with Capt Hansen to call at Andvord Bay for the boys hoping that by that time they would be tired of playing "Robinson Crusoe" & would return with us.

- Mr. Cope knowing this went to Capt Anderson Manager of the "Solstreif" Company who was superior in position to Capt Hansen but who could not speak English & demanded that he should in no way interfere with his (Copes) Expedition by sending a catcher to his base & threatened if he did so to report him to the Colonial Office & Royal Colonial Institute, of which Cope was a member, & so stop Capt Andersons cruise for hunting whales. In front of Capt Hansen & Dr Neilson I asked Capt Anderson to reconsider his decision if only from a humanitarian point of view & call on the boys & at any rate give them a chance to decide for themselves.

- Even then Cope demanded he should not do this & Capt Anderson acceded. I asked Capt Hansen & Dr Neilson to bear witness to this & they agreed. Confirmation of this may be had from them at the end of this whaling season if necessary. My statement then was that as I did not consider it a matter of life & death I would go no further in the matter.

- The Boys would be exposed to no grave danger & I had Captain Anderson's (of the Sven Foyn) promise to call for Bagshawe & Lester as soon as possible next year & received also both Captain Hansen's & Captain Anderson's (of the Solstreif) promises to call & see that the boys were brought back the next year.
- I told Cope I would expose his action to the people to whom he was more or less responsible (Messrs Debenham & Priestly) which I did.
- About two {?} nights before we left for Monte Video a catcher passed the hut at Andvord Bay & saw the two Boys & waved to them so I knew they were alright so far.
- At that time there was no question of whalers not visiting South Shetlands in 1921 & in my mind was a plan to return myself with an aeroplane that year. (This plan was completed but forgone at the urgent request of Sir Ernest Shackleton to join him & make use of his aeroplane).
- When there was any doubt about whalers visiting South Shetlands this year I drafted a report of the means to use for getting the boys back, copies of this report I posted to the Governor of Falklands Island through Major Hamilton the Resident magistrate to Mr. Bagshawe & Mr. Debenham. It was not necessary to go ahead with these plans for the whalers did proceed to South Shetlands and everything happened as expected in 1920.
- With regard to whisky that was left at Cope's base. I knew from personal experience that neither of the boys cared for strong drink & also that under the conditions in which they lived there is no desire for it by normal human being and although it was landed without my knowledge & I was as a matter of fact under the impression that arrangements we had made for it to be left at Deception Island had been carried out, I did not worry.
- Less than ¼ bottle had been consumed during more than the 2 months when the four of us lived at Andvord Bay so the whisky was not in any way a consideration.
- The point that I had no knowledge of until recently was that Mr. Bagshawe Sen had placed his boy under my charge. I had no communication with Mr. Bagshawe Sen whatever until September last year, when I reported to him the best means of bringing his boy home in case the whalers did not go South.

- I am very sorry to have to take up your time with this but have gone blindly on assuming that people understood my moral character sufficiently well to discredit any rumour of base action no matter how wrong my judgement in other matters may be or how much I should be blamed for going through, as far as possible with a proposition on which I had given my word of honour. Although Cope was not found to live up to his promises that was no real excuse for me to behave in the same manner.
- Please pardon this scribbled account but as I am leaving tomorrow for an extensive trip through middle Europe on official & Secret duties I have not time to get it typed.

This is private & confidential to you but I hope you will consider yourself at liberty to use anything I have stated to help me with reference to statements that are being circulated and are to the effect that I abandoned two boys on an Antarctic island, they being in a starving condition without food but 25 cases of whisky to drink.

3

1921-22 SHACKLETON-ROWETT EXPEDITION – WILKINS JOINS *QUEST* AS NATURALIST ON SHACKLETON'S FINAL VOYAGE

With the seasick photographer sent home from Lisbon, Wilkins takes on the cinematography and photography. Wilkins is not on the ship the night Shackleton dies as he and the Expedition's geologist, George Douglas are sent ahead of the Expedition to work on South Georgia.

Following the British Expedition to Graham Land led by Dr John Cope, Wilkins was recruited as Naturalist by Sir Ernest Shackleton for an expedition on board the *Quest*. Shackleton had already led two British expeditions to the Antarctic. Using the ship *Endurance* on his previous expedition, the Imperial Trans-Antarctic Expedition (1914-1917), had planned to cross the Antarctic from the Weddell Sea to the South Pole and then to the Ross Sea. *Endurance* was trapped in pack ice from December 1914 to November 1915, when the ship was crushed and sank. The story of the epic journey of the men after losing their ship is one of the greatest and most amazing tales of the Antarctic.[1]

John Quiller Rowett, a school friend of Shackleton and a British businessman, was the only financial backer for this new expedition and it was consequently named the "Shackleton-Rowett Expedition". The romantic-sounding voyage was sailing off to find "lost islands". Shackleton told the press that "the whole expedition, in fact, will touch the places of which just the barest fringe of knowledge exists, and not always as much as that, but

---

[1] They 'camped' on the ice until April 1916, before taking to *Endurance's* boats and rowed and sailed for seven days to Elephant Island. Days later, Shackleton and five crew members made the 800-mile journey to South Georgia in the *James Caird*. All were finally rescued in September 1916.

just enough to make us want to know much more".[2] Wilkins had arranged for a metal airplane, similar to the type used by explorer Roald Amundsen, to be delivered to Cape Town and picked up by the *Quest*. Wilkins expected to survey "two hundred miles of the coastline of King Edward VII Land, giving the pilots and mechanics an opportunity to test the all-metal machine under Antarctic conditions".[3]

Quest was a converted 111-ft Norwegian sealing ship. Rowett paid for her to be refitted for this expedition which included re-rigging and the addition of a deckhouse. Wilkins reflects on his recruitment by Shackleton when writing for the American Geographical Society in 1929:

> He [Shackleton] opened negotiations and finally persuaded me to postpone my plan [to accompany the Norwegian whalers in 1921-22 with two Junker monoplanes to Port Lockroy, near Antwerp Island, and from there make flights in seaplanes as far as possible] and join him on his expedition, during which we might fly not only at Graham Land but at other points along the Antarctic coast line.

Prior to departure Wilkins talked to the press about the detailed itinerary for the Shackleton-Rowett Expedition. The plan was to call in at a port in France before going to the Savage Islands, off the west coast of Africa, then to St Paul's Island, on the Equator. Wilkins observed that the islands were not often visited and "are said to be very interesting, and we may find on them some new forms of bird and plant life". After that, the Expedition would make its way to Trinidad:

> In the petrified forests of Trinidad the land crabs, ramble and rattle over the mineralized relics of an earlier age, fighting to the death over a morsel of refuse washed up by the tide, or raiding the nests of the gulls and terns. A moving picture and study of nature under these conditions – for it is on these

---

[2] "30,000-miles voyage: Shackleton's 'Quest'", *Daily Standard* (Brisbane), 13 October 1921, p. 2.

[3] "Captain Wilkins: Preparations for Antarctica", *Saturday Journal* (Adelaide), 8 August 1925, p. 1.

islands that the struggle for existence is greater than elsewhere – will prove of tremendous interest.[4]

From there the Expedition would visit the islands of Tristan da Cunha and Gough Island "a place that has only been visited twice before so far as we know, and there we shall probably find some new and interesting things".[5] After a planned restock in Cape Town, the Expedition would head south towards the Antarctic calling at Marion Island:

> We hope to reach the Antarctic barrier at a point known as Enderby Land, that was discovered over a hundred years ago, and has not been visited since, and from here we will try and follow the coastline for about 1,200 miles, covering an entirely new area ... We will leave the Antarctic coastline a few hundred miles from where I spent last summer, and go to the South Georgia Islands, where we will be again, sometime in April, in touch with civilization.[6]

> From South Georgia we go to Bouvet Island, a place little known and then back to South America, probably to Punta Arenas, where we will get mail and supplies about the end of May next year. We then go across the Pacific Ocean looking for two groups of islands that have been reported several times but not definitely located and so far as we know nobody has ever landed on them. We hope to find them on our way to New Zealand, where we expect to arrive sometime in July. We shall restock again here and then set out for South Africa and back to England, thus going round both the length and breadth of the earth. It is an exceptionally fine opportunity to visit most of the little-known parts of the globe and to do some extremely useful work in collecting natural history information and mapping these known and little-known islands.

---

[4] Hubert Wilkins, "The Wilkins-Hearst Antarctic Expedition, 1928-1929", *Geographical Review* 19:3 (1929) p. 357, American Geographical Society Library, University of Wisconsin-Milwaukee Libraries. Further references to this source will be shown as "The Wilkins-Hearst Antarctic Expedition, 1928-1929", *Geographical Review*.

[5] "Seeking Lost Islands: Shackleton Expedition Itinerary", *The Mail* (Adelaide), 15 October 1921, p. 3.

[6] "To Antarctica: Much Travelled Young Australian Goes as Naturalist with Shackleton", *Daily Telegraph* (Launceston), 20 October 1921, p. 7.

It is also important from the point of view of establishing meteorological stations in a ring around the Antarctic, from where we may obtain information that would lead to the possibility of predicting the weather conditions in Australia, Africa, and South America for many months ahead. There is no doubt in the minds of scientific people that we will soon be able to forecast the weather conditions with comparative certainty. There will be seventeen of us, including a doctor, and we expect to have a very pleasant and profitable trip.

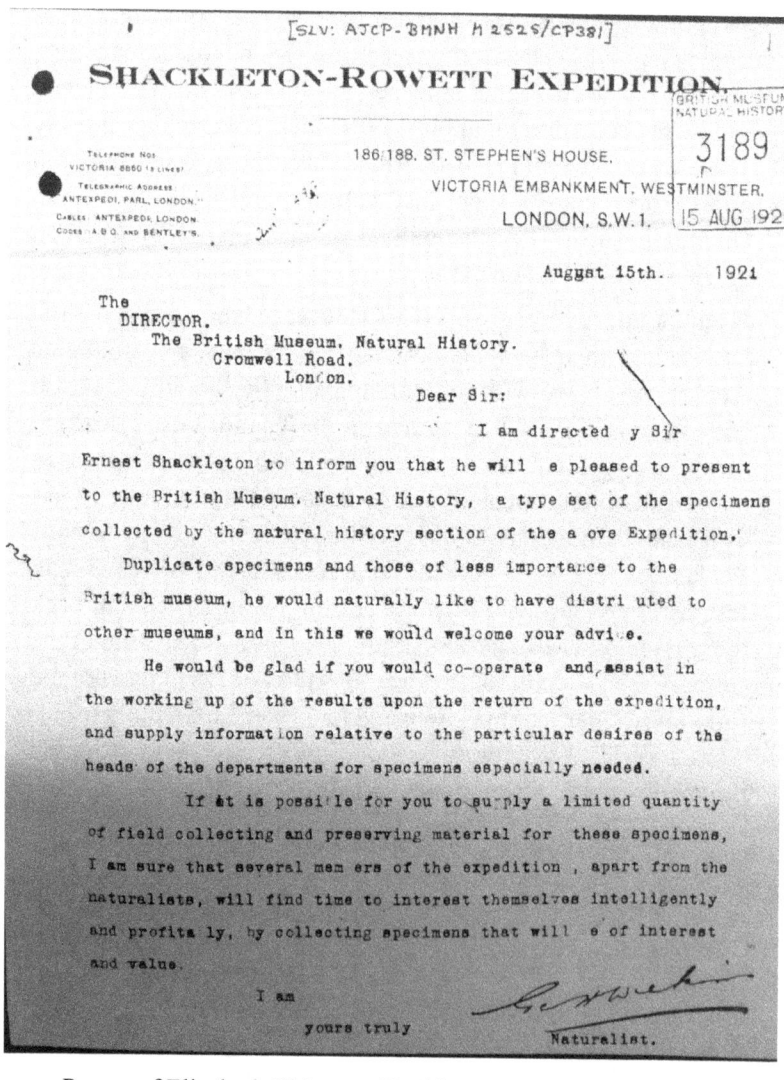

Papers of Elizabeth Chipman. Unable to ascertain copyright.

Also on board the *Quest* were James Marr,[7] an 18-year-old who was studying classics and biology at the University of Aberdeen, and Norman Mooney a 17-year-old. Both boys had been selected from thousands of Boy Scouts, by Lord Baden-Powell, founder of the Boy Scouts, to accompany Shackleton on the expedition. Originally, only one was to go but when Shackleton interviewed the finalists, he thought they were all "grand"[8] and made room for two.

Officers and expedition members on board *Quest* with the Boy Scouts sitting in the foreground.[9]

---

[7] Earning the nickname 'Boy Scout Marr', this voyage was the start of a life of Antarctic expeditions and research. Later Marr sailed with Sir Douglas Mawson on the British Australian and New Zealand Antarctic Research Expedition (BANZARE) and, as a marine biologist, took part in the Discovery Investigations of 1928-29, 1931-1933 and 1935-1937. During that latter voyage, Marr was on board *Discovery II* when she successfully located Lincoln Ellsworth and Herbert Hollick-Kenyon at "Little America" (see Chapter 8). During World War II he was expedition leader of Operation Tabarin, a secret British Antarctic Expedition to set up permanent bases on the Antarctic Peninsula. He established the base at Port Lockroy in 1944. In 1949 he became a Senior Scientific Officer at the National Institute of Oceanography, working there until his death in 1965.

[8] "Scout Pie", *Advocate* (Burnie), 22 June 1944, p. 4.

[9] Probably taken by Wilkins. Mitchell Library, State Library of New South Wales. Shackleton-Rowett Expedition 1921-1922. Slides 27. Item FL3444131.

The Shackleton-Rowett Expedition left London on 17 September 1921 and anchored at Gravesend, still on the River Thames, for the night. At 4 am, the anchor dragged, and the *Quest* rammed a collection of tugs which sprung the fulbrow and carried away the rigging from the other boat.[10] In the morning they docked in Sheerness to replace the fulbrow. Wilkins spent much of the next three days fitting out the darkroom and laboratory. Frank Wild, second in command, later wrote that:

> Wilkins and Bee Mason[11] [the photographer and cinematographer] had bunks in the converted forecastle, which contained the photographic dark room, a work bench for the naturalist, and numerous cupboards for storing of specimens. Wilkins, an old campaigner, had used much foresight and ingenuity in fitting it up, and had utilized the limited space to the utmost advantage.[12]

On 20 September 1921 Wilkins caught a train to London to order books, records and do several other jobs and was back on board the *Quest* by 25 September, when they set off again. During the days that followed Wilkins became part of the *Quest's* routine. He was on watch while also writing observations about the fauna, in this location mostly seagulls, petrels, herons, porpoises but also a butterfly! There was a robin that came on board, but Wilkins chose not to "take it". The robin returned a few times but then is not observed for a while and Wilkins thinks the cat probably got it!

Wilkins' frustrations with the crew and the ship itself are evident early in the voyage. On 30 September 1921, just 13 days into the trip, Wilkins wrote that:

> the saloon is the dirtiest place I have ever eaten in & that is saying something... There is no place to put dirty dishes & the sea slops in whenever there is the least roll. The table & stools

---

[10] In this chapter, if there is no reference provided, it has come from Wilkins' Diary. 1921. Sir George Hubert Wilkins Papers, BPCRC, OSU.
[11] John Charles Mason, filmmaker, explorer and naturalist, was noted for his early films about bee-keeping. Such was his association with bees that at some point in his life he changed his surname officially to Bee Mason.
[12] Frank Wild and A.H. Macklin, *Shackleton's Last Voyage. The Story of the Quest*, Frederick A. Stokes Co., New York, 1923.

are not fastened down & the floor is hardly ever washed & with people sleeping & casting off their dirty clothes down there it is in a proper mess. It shows distinct lack of organisation & economic thoroughness. Everybody is fed up.

The next day Wilkins made observations about the poor overall state of the *Quest*: "They had taken another reef in the mainsail & taken in the fore & stay sail. They also tried to reef the mizzen but it is rotten & started to rip. All tackle & gear is in a disgraceful shape – just as it was left from the last trip apparently". It was clear that the *Quest* was not suitable for the Expedition. The engines were already in difficulty and "getting worse and worse" requiring the ship to travel at half speed. On 1 October, a decision was made to call at Lisbon to "fix the engines". Lisbon was sighted on 3 October. Here, while the *Quest* was being repaired, Wilkins took the opportunity to get film developed and also to enjoy the hospitality at the British Club. "Met 3 Miss Harkers all very nice girls who can dance ... 2 of them had just returned from a visit to London. Danced until 1 am then went on to Maxims. Got home 3 am". Wilkins was able to pick up his developed photographs from the Army photographer on 8 October, but he was disappointed that they were not dark enough as "they had printed for the detail on the deck & not the skyline". This is a continuing theme throughout Wilkins' diaries: he is critical of his own photography work and often skeptical that it will turn out well.

Observing how the *Quest* reacted in the stormy weather, Wilkins commented on 12 October that he was "afraid by the way the ship rolls that there will be little opportunity for scrims & efficient work in the lab. It will be very difficult skinning birds in the forecastle. Took some cine of the cat & dog asleep together & some of The Boss leaning against the wind & roll of the ship". "The Boss" was the nickname given to Ernest Shackleton.

Wilkins wrote observations on the fauna almost every day in his Diary but his frustrations with the daily routines of the ship are never far away. The ship's watches continued four hourly and Wilkins was part of the relentless roster. He observed that "it thoroughly messes things up, we don't know one day from another & the dogwatch (two of two hours for dinner) every day assures that we only get at the most 6 hours sleep, in short intervals". By 15 October the Expedition was getting near to the Desertas Islands. Shackleton came to Wilkins to discuss the plans for the Expedition given that the engines were still not working at full capacity. Wilkins favoured the original plan of going to the Antarctic but raised the possibility of staying for a month or two at Gough Island.

On board the *Quest*. Query, the dog, and Wilkins in the centre. Mitchell Library, State Library of New South Wales. Shackleton-Rowett Expedition 1921-1922. Slides 27. Item FL3444123.

Several crew members had been seasick but Mason was still terribly ill and Shackleton made the decision to send him home from Lisbon. Wilkins had previously teased Mason as he was not fond of spiders. He had joked to the press prior to leaving that "there are spiders in the Antarctic, but as they are almost microscopic – about the size of a pin's head – Mason need have no fear of them". As a consequence of Mason going home, Shackleton approached Wilkins about also doing the cinematography and photography work on the Expedition but Wilkins had reservations. "I told him it was impossible to do justice to all three or even two [jobs] but if he could not get anyone else to do it I should do what I could. He has not made up his mind yet as to which plan he will endeavour to carry out. I daresay it will depend on how the engines run between here & St Vincent".

On 16 October the *Quest* arrived at Madeira. Wilkins was on watch until 4 am and "in spite of the fact that I was to do all cine & still work & had to get the camera ready I was called to help to scrub down decks at 6 am. When that was finished everyone else could sit around but I had to hurry on with the photographic work". While at Madeira, Wilkins went out in a car and collected butterflies, bugs and beetles. The next day, Wilkins hired horses and observed the birds and flora, specifically the prickly pear and "the finest grove of Eucalyptus trees" reminding him of his Australian homeland. On 18 October, he hired a car and did some more scientific collecting around Madeira. While in port the *Quest* had the engines repaired again as well as some carpentry work.

After Madeira the ship sailed for St Vincent. Wilkins disagreed with the plans for going to South Georgia and working there while looking for Aurora Islands: "Aurora Islands yes but not Sth Georgia, it has been done so often". The engines were still causing problems and Wilkins' frustration with Shackleton continued. On 21 October, Shackleton went to see Wilkins and said:

> that he had considered giving me full time for my work but would not do it for each of the others would want it too. He went on with a lot of rot about doing scientific work. He didn't care a damn about all the scientific work that ever was done or could be done & doesn't mind if we do any or not but every effort must be made to get a popular lecture for the public. He is interested solely in the adventure & geographical discoveries, all else can go to hell for all he cares. This shows now more his incompetence & inability… Sheer madness. He doesn't know anything about engines etc. but a kid could have made a better showing than this selection.

While at sea Wilkins made the most of the time on board and prepared the specimens that he had collected so they could be packaged and sent back to England. On 22 October he was busy labelling the moths caught at Madeira. "Must get them packed ready to send back. The Boss wants me to send specimens of some things to all the museums I know". But some mistakes were made in the processing: "Next day started preserving the plankton but forgot to put anaesthetizing solution in the jars so the plankton had died and were practically useless for specimens".

Wilkins, on board *Quest*, washing Query, the dog![13]

Quest arrived at St Vincent on 26 October. Wilkins set off with donkeys and his entomological gear. By 29 October he had amassed a collection of specimens and spent all day skinning an owl and sorting and pickling. The *Quest* left St Vincent for St Paul's, and from there the ship expected to call at Trinidad for a week and then to Rio de Janeiro to have the engines looked at, again. Wilkins wrote in his Diary that they should consider scrapping them and

---

[13] OSU Box 36_5_1. Sir George Hubert Wilkins Papers, BPCRC, OSU.

putting in oil engines, having internal combustion. A view he presumably shared with other people on board. His birthday came and went on the 31 October but he "did not think of it until dinner time".

On 3 November came the first recorded suggestion from Shackleton that George Vibert Douglas, the geologist on board, and Wilkins should be sent ahead of the expedition party. "The Boss talks about sending Doug & I on by whaler for ... [Buenos Aires] after we reach there by passenger steamer from Rio earlier to Sth Georgia ... Both rot". It is unclear why Wilkins is so reluctant to go ahead of the failing engines on the *Quest*. On the same day a small bird flew on board. Wilkins took its measurements and recorded its colours but let it go mentioning that if it comes back on board tomorrow, he will keep it. The next day a porpoise is hauled on board. Wilkins recorded its measurements and found 114 squid beaks in its stomach. The meat was sent to the larder and was "fair eating something like seal".

They arrived at St Paul's on 8 November and went ashore. The cine camera repeatedly broke but Wilkins still managed to get 400ft of movies. For the next few days Wilkins was occupied with skinning birds, pickling specimens, and blowing eggs.

By 21 November they were sailing along the coast near Rio de Janeiro. Shackleton informed Wilkins and Douglas that the steamer *Woodville* was leaving Montevideo on 25 November and he had asked that she wait for them and for them to try and get to South Georgia that way. He gave them £100. The *Quest* reached Montevideo on 26 November and *Woodville* came into the harbour just afterwards. Wilkins observed that "She is a steamer of about 2000 tons, very heavily loaded. Has not been waiting for us but will go out tomorrow. She is coaling today". Wilkins and Douglas are told that they can travel on the whaler by paying for food. The only conditions are that they are not to come on board until the last minute and not stay on board longer than necessary. After two days of enjoying themselves in Montevideo, with dancing and staying at Hotel Alhambra, on 28 November, Wilkins and Douglas took a tugboat to *Woodville*. "At 5.30 we heaved anchor & started for South Georgia. We have a spare cabin just off the Saloon which is rather cramped but not too uncomfortable".

Woodville is a stark contrast from the chores and duties on board the *Quest*. Wilkins spent the next few days reading and "loafing". On 8 December 1921, land was sighted. *Woodville* sailed into Prince Olav Harbour at 4 pm. The Norwegian whaling station's Catch Manager Lars Anderson came "on board and took the Woodville right in and tied up to an old hulk in a very seamanlike manner. It was quite noticeable after my recent experiences on the Quest where there is so much shouting and hollering when there is anything to be done with the ship". As *Woodville* came into the harbour, she disturbed thousands of birds feeding on the refuse from the whaling factory.

On shore Douglas and Wilkins met a Customs Officer named Simons who had been there for three years and:

> Was with Hurley when the latter was taking pictures for the last Shackleton Expedition. He says that Gold Harbour is best for birds, penguins particularly. He was down there this year with the South American Sealing Schooners. ... Whales are plentiful, they have 316 to date from October 1st & just the last day or two many have been caught. There are 23 lying at the buoys now.

Woodville unloaded her cargo and headed back to Montevideo to get more coal as there was none to spare at Prince Olav Station. The next day Wilkins and Douglas were informed that an old catcher, *Southern Breeze* was at their disposal. They prepared things for a scientific expedition to Ice Bay. Wilkins decided to take a half plate hand camera, his gun, as well as bird preserving material "to be used at Rosetta Harbour if there is anything there & we have any time". On 10 December they landed at Coal Harbour. Wilkins was encumbered by too much equipment and decided to only take his still camera as he couldn't carry the cine camera as well. In his Diary, he provided lots of details about the birds and also the flora:

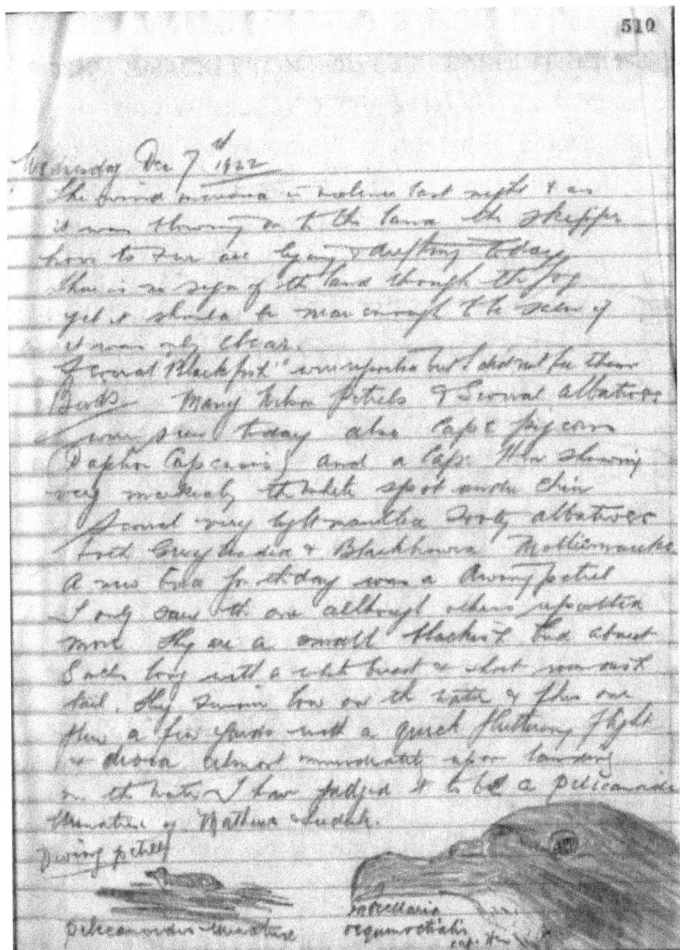

Page from Wilkins' Diary, showing Wednesday 7 December 1922 with sketches of birds. As Wilkins was not in the Antarctic in December 1922, it is assumed he has used the incorrect year here and it should be 1921.[14]

Very few flowering plants were noticed but some fine healthy grasses were seen. The commonest variety was the wiry tufted grass ... noticed in most virgin territories the world over the (Festuca erecta) mostly short & stiff or inclined to spread over the ground but in sheltered places growing to a height of 15 inches or more.

Wilkins and Douglas were ashore for only about 45 minutes and

---

[14] Wilkins' Diary 1921, Sir George Hubert Wilkins Papers, BPCRC, OSU.

then "went on to Ice Bay & decided to land on East side of the bay on what they call Matilda Bay, at the edge of a glacier which I photographed in colour & mono". After Wilkins and Douglas landed, it became apparent to Wilkins that he had brought too much gear for collecting and that he could "scarcely manage to get along even without any collected material". They decided to camp on the sandy beach, killed an elephant seal and cooked some of it for supper. They had a difficult time cooking it "due mainly to our inexperience or rather my forgetfulness for I had temporarily forgotten many of the tricks learned from the Eskimo". It rained during the night but Wilkins "slept very comfortably and warm but I think Douglas was cold". The wet weather hampered their efforts to get a fire going.

When the fog lifted on 11 December, Wilkins realised how perilously close they had walked to the edge of some steep slopes the previous day, places "we never would have ventured in good daylight". They set off with their packs to investigate the area but both "soon had severe spasms of cramps due to the wetting we had had and the unaccustomed exercise of lifting our feet so high". By nightfall, it was raining hard and they couldn't find shelter so they "spent the night huddled against a cliff. I kept awake & the blubber fire going all the time". As the next day dawned, Wilkins reflected that:

> Unfortunately we had made the mistake that I had so often made until I thought I would never have done it again & that was to have made a definite rendezvous at a definite time allowing only just sufficient time to reach a place. Had we not made arrangements for the whaler to pick us up at Rosetta Harbour early on Monday the next morning we would have camped again on the beach as soon as we reached it, but we could not afford to miss our appointment with the whaler for it was our first trip out & one they thought was foolhardy & dangerous & had we not been there to meet them they would have imagined all sorts of things & perhaps gone to a lot of trouble looking for us.

Wilkins and Douglas spent an hour crossing the peninsular and attempted to start a fire on the beach to warm themselves and dry their wet socks. They investigated a Gentoo penguin rookery before *Southern Breeze* arrived at 10 am. "We went aboard had a wash & good meal & finally arrived home in time for dinner at the Station". The next day Wilkins developed photos and blew specimen eggs. They then proposed a trip, leaving on 15 December, "to all the [whaling] stations finishing up at Grytviken where we hope to obtain the use of a small boat they have there & a man to accompany Douglas [to Green Bay]. If we cannot get anyone to go with him, I shall necessarily have to go with him & make the best of it". They left at 6 am on 15 December for Leith, Stromness, Husvik and Grytviken. Having welcome hospitality along the way, they then called on Mr. Binney, the magistrate, at Grytviken:

> Binney was not at all anxious to help & he told us frankly that he would not go out of his way to help anyone associated with Shackleton who he did not like ... Curiously enough, the people who were least willing, I might say conspicuously unwilling to help, were our own countrymen. This is not the first time, or the first place that this has been brought to my notice.

They spent the night on *Southern Breeze* and left at 4 am on 16 December. Wilkins then got "camping gear together for I have decided to try & camp on Bird Island, for a fortnight alone & do what collecting & photography I can". Without the spare time to wait for good weather, Wilkins set off for Bird Island at 6 am on 17 December, in strong winds and sleet. Unfortunately, the steering gear on *Southern Breeze* broke down as they arrived at Bird Island, which meant it was dangerous for the ship to wait amongst hidden rocks. In addition, "there was not room between the water's edge & the cliff to put up a tent & the cliffs were too steep to climb with any load". Reluctantly, Wilkins turned the rowing boat back towards *Southern Breeze* and crossed to Else Harbour instead. Here the sandy beach was sheltered from the heavy breaking seas "but the only place where a tent might be put was wind swept from both sides". The wind was strong and although the tent was erected, a heavy gust came and blew the whole side of the tent in. Again, Wilkins worried about being able to get around while carrying all his equipment. Walking was "frightfully difficult even without a load & I wondered how I should get on carrying the two cameras, the stand, a gun & collecting gear." One wonders whether Wilkins regretted his decision to camp alone when the rain was coming down, a thick mist had settled and he noted "one could not have had a much more miserable aspect & felt in a more miserable condition than I did as the *Breeze* steamed out of the harbour not to return until New Year's Eve". The same day he reflected that he "was quite disappointed with the site & wished I had risked all & stayed on Bird Island".

On 18 December Wilkins observed many skuas squabbling over the bones of the elephant seal he had killed the night before for supper. "They had picked them clean during the night. It really is surprising to find out how much the birds can eat in a short time." The weather was not suitable for photography. On a walk he found mating albatrosses and observed "It was as pretty a love scene as one could imagine & these birds seemed to show all the knowledge & delights of the human species in like conditions". The albatrosses "would walk straight up to their mates & a succession of greetings consisting of neck stretch & hissing, wing stretching & bill rubbing would go on & in practically every case this would end in less than five minutes with sexual connection. I had never heard of birds being so amorous." The next day he blew an albatross egg that he had brought back to the camp the previous day and had the contents as an omelette for breakfast. "It was excellent eating, the shell I kept for a specimen". The coal stove he had brought with him provided some warmth and comfort in the tent. His watch had stopped so he did not know the time but developed a daily routine. "I go out soon after breakfast, stay out as long as the light is good enough for photography, then come home, skin my specimens, have supper & go to bed".

After a bird stood next to its dead mate Wilkins remarked:

> I felt like a murderer & had a mind to give up the whole business of bird collecting but then decided it must be done so I shot the remaining bird almost with my eyes shut praying to some unknown power to forgive me & hoping that if there is such a thing as a Valhalla for birds that these two would go to

it. They are beautiful birds & in fine plumage. Have skinned them tonight.

Despite these feelings, he continued to collect bird specimens and found the entrance to a petrel burrow but got a nasty peck when he put "in a mittened hand". He persisted and retrieved two white chinned petrels. Good weather came on 21 December although Wilkins spent the day inside skinning birds! He observed "the scenery is really very beautiful ... It was one of those days that compensates for all the modern pleasures of civilization, one thrilled with the intoxicating air & marvelled at the beauty of nature in the virgin state". Realism hit again the next day as Wilkins wrote "The spell has passed, the world is ordinary again today". The weather proved, once again, to be not suitable for photography so on 23 December, Wilkins went out with his gun and hoped to shoot a Sooty albatross:

> After a while I had almost given up hope & was walking back along the cliff when a whirling of wings went over my head. I drew the gun to my shoulder cocking it on the way but before I had time to aim the gun went off & the beautiful Sooty albatross dropped not 20ft ahead of me. Had I stopped to aim I daresay I should have missed.

On his way back to camp he came across a Ringed Antarctic (Chinstrap) penguin that he added to his bag and two King penguins. Wilkins managed to render the first King penguin unconscious "with the aid of the pithing needle that I always carry on my mittens. Fortunately, the other one, had not quite reached the water & I managed to head him off & secure him after a lengthy chase. These penguins can move at an amazing rate for a bird that looks so clumsy".

There was a storm overnight on 24 December, and Wilkins was unable to sleep. After breakfast he started to skin the birds and then prepared his Christmas dinner:

> I roasted a duck, some onions & potatoes & had some peas from a tin. We were given Christmas pudding from the Quest but I had insisted on Douglas taking that & I had some tinned

cake that Bostock had given me, also some nuts, dry ginger, bottle of wine & one of good old brandy. I had a jolly fine meal which was quite acceptable in the cold conditions for the storm is still blowing.

On Christmas Day the weather improved and Wilkins was able to take some photographs. He had identified five distinct species of albatross. He had stored some blubber by the door but came home to find that skuas had stolen it. With the view to teach them a lesson, he shot three of them and skinned them and then a shag sitting nearby. The next day, after a clean-up, he collected an albatross and then "went along the beach to look for shells & picked up a few limpets & gastropods from the rocks. Also some small bivalves similar to those found on Grahamland".

Courting Albatross, taken by Wilkins on South Georgia on the Shackleton-Rowett Expedition.[15]

With the sun shining on 27 December, Wilkins hurried off without breakfast to take photographs. Although in waterproof

---
[15] Sir George Hubert Wilkins Papers, BPCRC, OSU.

bags, the difference in temperature had caused condensation and made the equipment damp. He managed to fix the camera and took a movie of a waterfall and some stills of the landscape as well as some of the fauna. "I wanted to get a general panorama in movies colour ... It meant three trips up the steep hillside with my gear & I was getting pretty tired. I had taken the movie & was setting up the still camera". While setting up the equipment he observed two men walking toward his camp. "I thought that they must be the men from Prince Olav come to fetch me before time, so I went on with my work. When I had exposed all my plates I saw these two walking round & round in widening circles as if they had lost something". The men had been collecting eggs and had lost the bucket of eggs they put down. Wilkins went back to his camp with the camera and made a hurried trip for the rest of my gear and then went down to the beach to catch the boat going back to the whaler. Wilkins was not feeling well. The "pain was so great I was doubled up" but he wanted to avoid letting the crew know he was ill otherwise they would take him home. The whaler made a stop to collect more eggs and Wilkins estimated they had collected 3,000. The whaler returned to "Else Harbour & anchored & then I went ashore as soon as I conveniently could & went to bed".

The whaler left the next morning and Wilkins remained on the island, still feeling ill. He found some relief by walking. By 29 December he had "severe stomach pain & headache all night, violently sick each time I tried to eat anything". Despite this, he still managed to collect some bird, moss and lichen specimens. "I do not know much about the mosses & grasses but hope that these may be of interest to the Museum people". He still felt weak and had occasional cramps the next day. *Southern Breeze* was due to arrive on New Year's Eve but turned up early in the afternoon of 30 December 1921. "They agreed to spend the night for I wanted to finish skinning the birds I had on hand & get in some albatross for skinning at Prince Olav ... We finished up & came on board the *Breeze* late tonight & will say goodbye to Else Harbour at daybreak in the morning". While sailing back, Wilkins asked to call at the

Bay of Isles for some bird specimens, which they did. Arriving back at Prince Olav Station:

> We got home just in time for dinner as then I was glad to get a bath & into civilized clothes & conditions once more & away from the blood & filth of birds carcasses for a day or so.
>
> We saw the old year out & saw the new year in with loud explosions from old dumps of burnt scrapings, guns firing, whistles screeching & hooters going. From the managers house we sent up unnumerable rockets & burnt Roman candles & what not & then as most of us were tired & I particularly had had a long & busy day we went to bed each no doubt forming resolutions for the New Year that had just dawned.

There was no news of *Quest* but she was expected in the next day or two. Wilkins was resigned that he would be hard at work as he had things to finish off before the ship arrived. "Bird skinning is a beastly business & after each collection I declare that I will not skin another." He continued with the specimens and some photographs of the whaling station for the next few days. By 5 January 1922 Wilkins had finished packing away all the skins, eggs and photographs:

> Bostock has promised that if we do not return this year that he will see that everything goes to the museum ... The old dog has kindly placed an attic over the hospital at my disposal for keeping the skins and it will do excellently. I could not have a better place. It is possibly a little warm but I do not think that there will be any trouble about rotting for it is absolutely dry.

Wilkins then added, "I must get The Boss to come up here and thank them personally or at least write a personal letter" for their hospitality. Sadly, this was something that he would now never get to do.

The *Quest* appeared the next day and Wilkins noticed that "the flag was at half mast as she came into the harbour" but had just casually thought "well I wonder who is dead now". Captain Mansen and Binney, the magistrate, were standing on the bridge "they greeted me with well I suppose you know that Shackleton is dead. I nearly dropped. Why Shackleton dead – he was the last chap

I would have thought of". Shocked, Wilkins boarded the *Quest*. He learned that the *Quest* had a good, fast trip from Rio but had met some bad weather. They had gone straight to Grytviken and Shackleton had gone ashore. Shackleton wrote: "At last, after 16 days of turmoil and anxiety, on a peaceful sunshiny day we came to anchor in Grytviken (South Georgia). How familiar the coast seemed!". He had been pointing out to everybody the places he knew. The last thing he wrote in his Diary was "In the darkening twilight I saw a lone star hover gem-like above the bay".[16] The crew went back on board:

> The Boss had a game of cards but went to bed early as did the others. At about 3 oclock in the morning The Boss called out for Macklin [the surgeon] who happened to be on watch & was passing his cabin door & asked him if he could give him a draught that might relieve a pain in the shoulders that he felt. Mac went off to his cabin to prepare the draught thinking that it was nothing serious & came back with a mixture. The Boss took it from him drank half of it & letting the glass drop out of his hand fell back on his pillow dead.

Nothing could be done to revive Shackleton and the doctor determined that he died from heart failure. Wilkins had been planning to write his biography "as I had hoped to do of other explorers" and was disappointed that he had only just begun to get the information from him. Having been frustrated with Shackleton on this expedition, Wilkins reflected that "he was a man with an undoubted personability & a doggedness of purpose that was irresistible but he was not a clever leader & his organisation of this expedition at least was shameful". Scathingly, he again commented that Shackleton was "so absolutely inefficient & cumbrous that I had often said before then that anyone with the least degree of moral courage & an inkling of desire to do solid work scientific or otherwise would have left the ship at Plymouth after the first three days experience".

With the death of Shackleton Wilkins wondered whether he should

---

[16] Frank Wild and A.H. Macklin, *Shackleton's Last Voyage. The Story of the Quest.*

return to England. Command of the Expedition fell to Frank Wild, who had been second in command and had previously accompanied Shackleton, Scott and Mawson on Antarctic expeditions. "I felt sure that without The Boss or the aeroplane we would never do anything worthwhile, my wasting a 12 month. However, there was John Quiller Rowett to consider & although it was going to be a hard task it was really 'up to us' to work harder now for his sake."

Wilkins used the next few days to get his cameras in order and developed plates and films. Shackleton's body was transported to Montevideo but, at the request of Lady Shackleton, he was returned to South Georgia and was buried in the small cemetery at Grytviken. His final resting place was "in high precipitous mountains, with hardly any level ground, and practically uninhabited"[17] in Grytviken cemetery.

Final farewell from the crew of *Quest* at Shackleton's grave before leaving Grytviken, South Georgia. Mitchell Library, State Library of New South Wales. Shackleton-Rowett Expedition 1921-1922. Slides 27. Item FL3444129.

Writing several years later, in an article in the *Sydney Morning Herald* on 4 January 1929, in a tribute from Deception Island, Wilkins fondly remembered Shackleton:

---

[17] "Shackleton's Death", *Newcastle Morning Herald and Miners' Advocate*, 29 April 1922, p.6.

> To-day holds a tinge of sadness for some of us. It is the anniversary of the day 'The Boss' Shackelton [sic], as we invariably called him in the Quest, anchored at South Georgia, not far from here, at the very gate of the Antarctic. I am proud to have served under him, and trust some day I may discover some worthy feature by which I can still further commemorate him. We who carry on Scott's and Shackleton's work in comparative ease and comfort realise that we cannot share the pedestal of fame with them, but there is still much to be done in the south. Whether we continue the work immediately depends upon the whims of the weather.

Douglas was at Cape George and Wilkins had to break the news of Shackleton's death when they picked him up on 9 January 1922. His reaction was like Wilkins and he "declared at once his intention of leaving the expedition & going home just as this had been my first inclination but I put my point of view to him and he decided to stay". The next day they left for Grytviken but called into Leith Harbour for coal. Unfortunately, the coal ship had not arrived as expected and so they decided to go to Husvik and get coal from the whaling transportation ship *Orwell*. On 14 January the crews of the *Orwell* and the *Quest* both worked to refill the coal stores. Wilkins "stood on the deck house & emptied the bucket which was not a hard job but an awkward one. I soon got the knack of it & we soon loaded 40 tons". The crew of *Orwell* eventually refused to load any more coal even though the *Quest* could hold a lot more.

Again, Wilkins' frustration about the Expedition's organisation came to the surface:

> What riles me is that we need such a lot to be done. All sorts of things that could have been done in London or Rio were not done & tons of stores & much clothing has been purchased from here. Why come right down this far south trusting that we may get something from the whaling stations rather than making sure of them in early action.

With the coal restocked, the Expedition proceeded back to Grytviken. Wilkins prepared photographic negatives and prints to send back to the *Daily Mail*:

> I could see from the beginning that the general organisation & arrangements were a hopeless unproductive muddle & that if I thought of doing anything to guide their actions into what I thought to be the right ones that it would only lead to more trouble & bad feeling so I interfere as little as possible, have as little as possible to do with anybody & do my own work to the best of my ability under the circumstances which by the way are not at all comfortable & convenient.

By 19 January it became evident to the crew that the *Quest* was headed for Southern Thule and from there to Bouvet Island and then south towards Enderby Land:

> This to my mind is the perfectly ridiculous outcome of alcoholized incompetency. Why on earth go traipsing around these sub-antarctic islands if you want to go south to new land & if we don't want to go south, why not do all the South Sandwich & Clerke Rocks ... We are not so terribly late in the year but with this old hulk doing 4 or 5 knots it will take us all our time to reach the ice, let alone getting any distance into it. We are said to have had 110 tons of coal when we started. Nobody seems to know how much we do burn or how much we can but it is guessed that we might use about 2½ to 3 tons daily.

To take his mind off the incompetence, on 26 January, Wilkins threw himself into his work but found it "practically impossible" to draw from the microscope because the boat was "so jerky" that he was unable to keep the camera and microscope steady even when there was light available. The first aurora seen on the trip was witnessed two days later. By February the *Quest* was working through pack ice, which Wilkins wrote she "handles fairly well". By 8 pm on 10 February 1922, there was heavier ice that "looked like the real thing" and Wilkins doubted if the *Quest* "will ever get through stuff like this". The sunset on 11 February lit up the sky but Wilkins deemed the conditions not suitable for colour photography. Instead, he wrote some poetry:

> While waiting for the sun to disappear I thought of this timely line with which to describe the scene. "Glittering crystals & gold gleams, Shimmering o'er the icy streams, And softened

rays of the sun going down, clothed the Western sky in a shot-silk gown." Some day I may add to it for I rather like the sentiment, but why I should take to writing poetry I don't know.

This is an amusing observation given his proficiency in so many other areas.

Wilkins' diaries are peppered with disappointment that *Quest* did not stop in Cape Town and collect the airplane. On 12 February, he observed that "if we climbed to 7000ft even directly above the ship I daresay we could have seen land. I am so disappointed at not having the aeroplane that I had decided to say nothing at all about it but can't help thinking about it today". Flying was never far from his mind and as the *Newcastle Sun* reported, under the heading "Shackleton's Grave: Antarctic Snow", on 7 February 1922, "Captain Wilkins is filming the flight of albatrosses for aeroplane designers".

Quest continued heading west and northwards due to the pack ice. Wilkins would have preferred to "hang on here a little & see if the pack would open & let us get a little further south for I fully believe we are not far from land and although this cold snap has made things look bad I believe that it won't last & that we could afford to wait here for a week". He kept himself busy by making meteorological observations, recording any birds and fish, and collecting plankton samples in a scrim net. Also, from the same *Newcastle Sun* article, Wild records a change in appearance: "Wilkins, with a view to stimulating the laggard hairs on his crown to more active growth, shaved the top of his head, and looked like a monk. He was growing a beard, as were a number of the men". There were other amusing episodes on the ship. On 22 February, Wild celebrated his birthday. Green, the cook, "had made him a cake in the middle of what he put a 56lb [approx. 25kg] iron weight. It caused a good deal of amusement".

On 28 March 1922 *Quest* visited Elephant Island in the South Shetlands. This visit must have brought back many memories for Frank Wild, now in charge of *Quest*. Elephant Island was where Shackleton and his 27 crew members had landed after *Endurance* was crushed by ice and sank. Wild had been left in charge of the men remaining on Elephant Island when Shackleton and five of his men made the 800-mile voyage in *James Caird*, an open boat, to South Georgia seeking help. Those left behind spent more than four winter months here before the party was rescued and taken to Punta Arenas in Chile in early September 1916. Wilkins observed that animal life in this region was scarce.

Quest returned to Grytviken in South Georgia on 6 April. Before departing, the crew erected a cairn with a cross, in memory of Shackleton, at Hope Point overlooking the harbour. On 7 May, the expedition left for Tristan da Cunha.

The Cross at Hope Point, erected by the crew of the *Quest*, in 1922, in memory of Sir Ernest Shackleton. ©Ros Fletcher, 2003.[18]

---

[18] In 2018 the Hope Cross was removed in order to preserve it. A replacement was installed at Hope Point in 2021. In 2024 the Hope Cross travelled 7,000 miles across the seas and is now displayed at Discovery Point in Dundee, Scotland.

Boy Scout James Marr, on right, having just presented new flag to the Scout Troop on Tristan da Cunha. Mitchell Library, State Library of New South Wales. Series 06 Negatives of Shackleton-Rowett Expedition 1921-1922. Item FL561333.

It had been planned that James Marr and Norman Mooney, the Boy Scouts chosen in England, would present a flag to the Scout Troop on Tristan da Cunha. Unfortunately, Mooney had been sent home early, from Lisbon due to illness, so Marr did that duty. Wilkins and Marr also visited the other three islands in the Tristan da Cunha group, Gough, Nightingale and Inaccessible, to record their natural history. Rowett was honoured here as they identified a new species of finch, the Gough Finch (*Rowettia Goughensis*), introduced in 1923 by English ornithologist Percy Lowe. On Nightingale Island, a further two new species of finch were identified, named *Nesospiza questi* and *Nesospiza wilkinsi* after *Quest* and Wilkins himself.

Wilkins' frustrations with being on watch, in addition to all his other responsibilities, appeared again on 23 May 1922. "Douglas and I had to keep watch as usual although we had been out all day & had not nearly enough time to write up notes or prepare specimens at night". He was able to spend the next two days collecting specimens before *Quest* headed for Gough Island on 25 May. While sailing, Douglas and Wilkins spent the day getting gear ready so they could camp. Late on 26 May, Gough Island was sighted but it was too late to go ashore. When they did eventually go ashore they investigated two beach huts set back from the rocky beach. "There were some provisions but rotted through or destroyed by mice." They had packed tents so decided to use those for sleeping and the huts during the day. Wilkins collected bird specimens and observed the flora. He spent two days skinning the birds and commented that "It is a slow process with only one". He did get some help from the crew, including Marr, but "they take about 4 hours to do one bird so that's not much help".

Wilkins's finch (*Nesospiza wilkinsi*). ©Richard Gillam. 2013.

The weather became windy and on 1 June 1922, the crew lost their tent in the night. They gathered up what they could and went into the hut. "We were all wakened at intervals during the first night by mice running over our faces & hands. In the hut we thought they would be awful & last night we found that they were. We didn't get any sleep at all". Morning arrived and *Quest* arrived to pick them up, but the gusty weather caused the anchor to drag. They were able to board the ship the following day and sailed for Cape Town "via a shoal that someone told the skipper about that was somewhere NE of Tristan. It was the South Georgia whalers that have seen it I think". During the next few days *Quest* and her crew faced bad weather and heavy squalls. Unfortunately, because of the weather, on 9 June Query, the ship's dog, slid under the rail and into the water. "We will all be sorry to have lost Query for he was a nice companiable dog & clever if he had been given a chance but he was everybody's pet & considerably spoilt". The rough weather continued: "Rolling is getting frightfully monotonous & one can't do any work at all, couldn't even if one didn't feel so uncomfortable inside". And a few days later the sole entry in Wilkins' Diary is "Rolling Rolling Not a damn thing but roll".

There is an unsettling feeling on the ship. On 15 June the Expedition is a few days out from Cape Town. There is excitement about what news would be received when they landed but also apprehension about the direction of the expedition. "Wild & party apparently think we are going on. I hope to heaven we do not for there is no chance of doing any good work at sea on this ship." Wilkins cannot hide his frustration at being able to see Cape Town on 18 June but most of the crew were not able to go ashore. His "Home again. Home again. Hoorah!" is then contrasted with "We were sent out to sea so as 'to avoid the press' of all the damn silly rot". While they were anchored offshore the mail came on board. Wilkins noted that there was "no official correspondence but lots of personal letters. It is a wonder that John Q R [Rowett] or the Museum people didn't write but there you are – they didn't". In a roundabout way of finding out the expedition's direction, Douglas had received a letter from his sister who had been staying with Rowett and he told her that they would be in London in September. This ended the secrecy and speculation about their plans.

Two days later Wilkins had 16 cases ready to be dispatched to England including ornithological specimens, marine, biological, botanical, mammalogical, and entomological. He took the opportunity to get films developed and got leave from the ship to travel to Johannesburg for this purpose. "Wild gave me as he thought £27 for expenses but when I counted it I found it to be £32." He arrived in Johannesburg on 24 June and noted that most of the staff were away, so he would have to help develop the films. "The quality of all but 200ft was excellent much better than I expected." But it wasn't all work. Douglas travelled with Wilkins and he wrote to his mother "we have been having a most interesting time":

> Yesterday we saw a group of diamonds worth a million pounds. They had been set out for our inspection. Today we are going down a mine a mile deep to see the famous gold producing soil of the "Rand". On Thursday we have a drive of 150 miles to the Premier mine which is the other side of Pretoria so we will see Pretoria. Nearly every meal we are the guests of one or another of the big mining men of the country or the politicians or men of Science so you can imagine how interesting it must be.[19]

On 29 June, Wild sent a message to say that Douglas and Wilkins must be back in Cape Town by Tuesday, 4 July, when *Quest* would sail again. Wilkins replied and asked if that could be extended to 7 July as the film would not be finished by then. The reply came back:

> to report to Cook on arriving at Cape Town as the Quest will have sailed. This didn't worry me at all for it was reported in all the papers that the Quest was only going to Simonstown for a few days before leaving for home but I knew we would catch her there. They wouldn't go without us anyway & it was no use leaving this job just half done.

Wilkins need not have worried as Wild became ill with influenza and *Quest* was still in port at Cape Town when they arrived back by train on 6 July 1922. Cook met them at the station and bundled up the film and negatives to take back to London.

Quest arrived at Simonstown, a British Navy Dockyard, on 7 July and stayed for a week. The compasses were adjusted before leaving. *Quest* sailed for St Helena (not Rio as originally thought). Wilkins was, once again, frustrated with the change of plan:

---

[19] Letter dated 26 June 1922, on Rand Club letterhead, signed "I am your loving Son George". The original Rand Club opened in 1887, in the heart of Johannesburg. Rebuilt in 1904, modelled on one of London's leading clubs, it remains an icon of tradition, prestige and luxury.

This would be another sheer waste of time & more unnecessary expense as I believe 90% of the expenses at Cape Town to have been & that had I known that we were to go straight to St Helena & home instead of calling at Trinidad I should have asked Wild to allow me to go straight home so that I could have arranged my reports & get pictures in order for showing fast when the Quest arrived which would of course be the best time for exhibition. The public memory is so short that the Quest will soon be forgotten.

Throughout the whole expedition Wilkins recorded bird, turtle and fish observations, made notes on the local bird variations and had extensive records about weather, as well as other flora and fauna.

Before returning to the United Kingdom *Quest* also called in at Ascension, the Cape Verde Islands and the Azores before arriving at Plymouth on 16 September 1922. Rowett, who financed this expedition lost £15,000 and was "much affected by the death of Sir Ernest Shackleton".[20] He later sued Shackleton's widow in a "formal but friendly action" before committing suicide in 1924.

Wilkins' collections from the Shackleton-Rowett Expedition meant that on his return to London he spent a good deal of time at the British Museum (Natural History section). Never one to stay in one place for long, Wilkins agreed to spend two years in outback Australia sponsored by the British Museum (Natural History section). From January 1923 when he left London for Australia to June 1925, Wilkins journeyed through "Undiscovered Australia" keeping copious notes and taking a photographic record like no other. Although at this time he had not been knighted, he was by the time his book about this Expedition was published in 1928. It showed Capt. Sir G.H. Wilkins, M.C. as author.[21]

In 1925 Wilkins proposed what would have been his third

---

[20] "A Patron of Shackleton: Mr. Rowett Leaves £48,533", *Chronicle* (Adelaide), 6 December 1924, p. 42.
[21] Capt. Sir G.H. Wilkins, M.C., *Undiscovered Australia Being an account of an expedition to tropical Australia to collect specimens of the rarer native fauna for the British Museum, 1923-1925.*

Antarctic journey, if he had been able to put together enough money. Calling it the "Australasian Polar Pacific Expedition" his main purpose was to "explore and map out the at present unknown and unvisited 1500 miles of coast line at the base of the Pacific Ocean".

AUSTRALASIAN POLAR PACIFIC EXPEDITION
(CAPTAIN G. H. WILKINS, M.C., F.R.G.S., LEADER)

TREASURER TO THE EXPEDITION:
GEOGRAPHICAL SOCIETY OF
AUSTRALASIA
(S.A. BRANCH)

PRESIDENT: E. M. SMITH, I.S.O., J.P.
TREASURER: H. P. MOORE, J.P.
SECRETARY: F. L. PARKER

TELEPHONE CENTRAL 6644

ADDRESS COMMUNICATIONS TO THE
HON. SECRETARY
BOX 271, G.P.O.
ADELA[IDE]

16th September, 1925.

G. H. Fleming, Esq.,
South Terrace,
EAST ADELAIDE.

Dear Sir,

  Captain Wilkins of South Australia has become famed as the result of his war photography, his connection with various polar expeditions and recently because of his expedition to Northern Australia.

  Now, he plans to lead the Australasian Polar Pacific Expedition to explore and map out the at present unknown and unvisited 1500 miles of coast line at the base of the Pacific Ocean.

  £15,000 is needed for the venture.

  Mr. Napier Birks and Mr. Arthur J. Walkley were the first to come forward and offer substantial donations of £500 and £100 respectively. Others have intimated their desire to help, and Victoria, New South Wales and New Zealand are joining in.

  The S.A. Royal Geographical Society, in consenting to become Treasurers to the Expedition would be pleased to see the necessary funds raised in Australia, and will receive and acknowledge subscriptions that may be forwarded.

      Yours faithfully,

           Hon. Secretary.

P.S.
  Donations may also be sent to the 'Register' and 'Advertiser'.

OSU Box PA.2017.003.0001, Folder 1, Sir George Hubert Wilkins Papers, BPCRC, OSU.

According to *Australia in the Antarctic*:

> To raise funds Wilkins sought a loan of £15,000 which would enable him to purchase at least one plane plus all necessary stores and equipment. In his home state of South Australia the local branch of the Royal Geographical Society of Australasia set up a sub-committee in 1925 to help raise the required funds, but by October of that year it was clear that the sum required would not be raised. In the meantime Wilkins had gone to Europe to try to buy a plane, and had almost completed negotiations to get one of those used by Amundsen in the Arctic, when the shortage of funds, coupled with the lateness of the season forced him to cancel the project.[22]

During 1926-1928 Wilkins led the Detroit Arctic Expedition (1926), the first Detroit News Expedition (1927) and the second Detroit News Expedition (1928). On 15 April 1928, Wilkins as navigator, with pilot Ben Eielson, made the first trans-Arctic flight from Barrow in Alaska to near Spitsbergen, in Norway. In November that year they became the first people to fly in the Antarctic.

---

[22] Swan, *Australia in the Antarctic*, p. 169.

Wilkins and Douglas visited Premier Diamond Mine in the Transvaal (see page 72).

4

1928-1929 THE WILKINS-HEARST ANTARCTIC EXPEDITION

Newly knighted, with celebrity status following his flight from Alaska to Norway, Wilkins was sponsored by William Randolph Hearst for this Expedition. Richard Byrd had plans to be in the Antarctic about the same time. Everything worked well for Wilkins and on 22 November 1928, Wilkins and Eielson became the first people to fly in the Antarctic.

Not long after returning from his epic Arctic flight with pilot Ben Eielson in April 1928, Hubert Wilkins was preparing for his next Antarctic expedition. He and Eielson had been the first people to take a plane across the Arctic Circle, flying from Barrow, Alaska to Spitsbergen, Norway, crossing the Arctic ice cap and ocean. Wilkins was knighted by King George V on 4 June 1928, and his books *Flying the Arctic* and *Undiscovered Australia* were published later that year. He received many accolades for the Arctic flight and quickly became a 'celebrity'. Finding money for his next trip proved not to be too hard! Named the Wilkins-Hearst Antarctic Expedition, it was largely funded by William Randolph Hearst, a wealthy businessman and publisher whose life was loosely played out in the 1941 film *Citizen Kane*. Hearst, owner of Universal News Service, pledged US$25,000 for the exclusive newspaper and radio rights for this Antarctic Expedition.

The natural competition between fellow explorers was played up by the press. It was well-known US Navy Officer Richard Byrd (later Admiral) and Wilkins were both planning Antarctic expeditions at similar times. Correspondence between the two men, beginning as early as 1926, shows they were friendly and offered support to each other and discussed their future plans. In a letter dated 13 October 1927, beginning "My dear Wilkins" and concluding "With best of good wishes, Most cordially yours", Byrd says: "Do you wish me to keep your tentative plans confidential because I have a great many friends who are much interested in you. But, of course, if I tell one person they [his plans] will get all over the place".[1]

And they did! Fuelled by the press, rumours had started to spread, inferring there was animosity and competition between the two men. The president of the American Geographical Society, Dr Isaiah Bowman, took to *The Times*, to dispel "at once the foolish rumours that there will be any race between them to the South Pole. Captain Wilkins will not go to the South Pole at all but proposes to explore the unknown land extending from the Ross Sea to Graham Land".[2] Indeed, Byrd writing to Bowman in 1928 says of Wilkins:

> I do not for one single minute believe that Wilkins is anything but a high type gentleman, and that regardless of his contract with Hearst, whereby Hearst offers him $100,000 to beat us to the Pole, he will not make any effort to do so. He is not in a position to fly to the pole anyhow without extraordinary and unwarranted hazards. The last thing I said to him was that I would allow him to use my base for a landing place. He will get started flying long before we do.[3]

On 1 July 1928, the American Geographical Society wrote to Wilkins to forward some funds for the expedition. Bowman enclosed a cheque for US$1,000 to Wilkins. He noted that the cheque "was drawn at a time when we [the American Geographical Society] were informed through the newspapers that you had been knighted Sir George". Their contribution to the expedition is "made without any conditions attached and is an expression of our confidence in you, which has been unfaltering from the beginning". The American Geographical Society drew up a special new large-scale map of the Antarctic region built up from original sources.

---

[1] Letter on Byrd Antarctic Expedition letterhead, OSU Box 17, Sir George Hubert Wilkins Papers, BPCRC, OSU.
[2] Press clipping from *The Times* (London), 7 June 1928, AGSNY AC 1, Box 269, Folder 9, AGSL, UWML.
[3] Letter Byrd to Bowman, 1928, AGSNY.AC 1, Box 183 Folder 6. AGSL, UWML.

Bowman noted that it "will be ready for you by the time you take the field and sometime before you leave New York you ought to see it", a courtesy also shown to Byrd. He also recommended that Wilkins consult two cartographers, about a smaller scale map that could be used for navigation.

Wilkins had set up a headquarters for "George Hubert Wilkins Expeditions" in the Waldorf-Astoria in New York. From here, Wilkins wrote to Bowman on 17 September, to graciously accept the US$1,000 donation and gave detailed information about the planning, equipment and staff that was being gathered for the expedition:

> You will no doubt observe that our departure has been put forward almost two months. The Whalers are going very early this year and expect to return early. This suits me very well. We will have everything ready, I think. The two airplanes will be at Miller Field, Staten Island, set up on pontoons and ready for loading by Wednesday night. Most of my supplies are already at this hotel. The full staff, [Lieutenant Carl Ben] Eielson, Joe Crossan and Orval Porter are with me at this hotel. Joe Crossan is a Pilot with five years experience in Alaska, he flew our newspaper correspondent to Barrow in 1927. Orval Porter is the mechanic I had with me in 1927 [in the Arctic]. I think they comprise a capable staff. The machines are duplicates. One, of course is the one I used in the Arctic. It has been thoroughly overhauled in every part. The new one flew from Los Angeles in twenty-six hours flying time.
>
> My supplies for the Ross Sea have gone to Tasmania ... When I arrive at the Ross Sea I will radio the *Neilson Alonzo* and she will send a catcher to me with the necessary supplies. It is not possible to say what I will do after I reach the Ross Sea.
>
> Our equipment will go from New York to Montevideo on board the Munson Line *Southern Cross* starting 1 p.m. Saturday next. At Montevideo we will board the *Hektoria* and go to Deception Island. From there we will deposit supplies to some place on the Weddell Sea side of Grahams [sic] Land, about 500 miles south of Deception. We will take off from that depot for the Ross Sea. The second machine will stand by at the depot until we reach the Ross Sea, or, for assistance if necessary.

If we get through safely the second machine will return to Deception Island and home via South America. Each machine will be equipped with radio. There will be a competent operator on board the whaling ship which will really be our main base. We will, on the long flight, have a portable generator which should insure communication in case we come down on the way. Each of us will spend much time at radio practise on our way South. If everyone keeps their promises I should be clear so far as finance is concerned. Will know that by the end of the week. I am going to the Airplane Factory tomorrow.

Wilkins informed Bowman that he hoped to get back in time, the next day, to call and see him before 5 pm so that he could collect the navigation charts that had been produced by the American Geographical Society. Wilkins proposed to ring from the Waldorf-Astoria when he returned from Long Island where the airplane factory was located. He went to inspect the two Lockheed Vega monoplanes that they were taking on the expedition, one which had previously flown in the Arctic was to be renamed *Los Angeles* in honour of Hearst. They also had a duplicate machine named *San Francisco*, supplied by the Lockheed Aircraft Company at approximately US$10,000 less than the standard price.

Wilkins also mentioned to Bowman in his letter that he met Fred Walcott while in San Francisco who had promised US$1,000 towards the expedition. As a matter of courtesy to the American Geographical Society, who had provided funding and helped with logistics, Wilkins had asked the donor to send the cheque through the Society. The cheque arrived at the Society the next day along with a note from Walcott that read: "I am devoted to him as a man and admire him extravagantly as one of the world's great explorers".[4]

The Director of the American Geographical Society wrote again on 20 September 1928, not only to send the cheque from Walcott, but also to send encouragement to Wilkins. "I feel altogether confident that you will be successful and bring back a great quantity of plunder. Above all, I like the simplicity of your plans and believe

---

[4] Letter from Bowman to Wilkins, 20 September 1928, AGSNY AC 1, Box 269, Folder 9, AGSL, UWML.

that they are one of the surest guarantees of success. We look forward to thrilling reports from you as the expedition progresses".

Prior to his departure on the expedition, Wilkins wrote to Byrd. Despite the press rumours and speculation of a race to the South Pole, there was a cordial understanding between the two men:

> Should I by chance come down with my airplane on the way between Grahams [sic] Land and the Ross Sea, it is my desire that you do not interfere with your plans to come to my assistance or rescue, unless you receive my personal request. If I need your assistance I will not hesitate to ask because I know you would give it willingly but we both know that the public are likely to misunderstand the requirements in connection with rescue parties and in this letter I wish to relieve you, as officially as possible, from any responsibility in connection with rescue work which might interfere with the progress of your important plan. If I do not reach the Ross Sea at the expected time and no word is received from me, you can take it for granted that we are leisurely finding our way back on foot and probably, doing some useful work on the way. Wishing you complete success in your great undertaking.[5]

A few days later, on 22 September, Wilkins along with Ben Eielson, Joe Crossan, William Gaston and Orval Porter were given free freight and half fares on the Munson Line's *Southern Cross* and sailed from New York.

That same day, 22 September 1928, Miss Suzanne Bennett announced her engagement to Sir Hubert Wilkins. She had gone to the dock to farewell the expedition. Bennett was a Broadway actress who was born in Walhalla, near Melbourne, Australia. Wilkins had denied an engagement the previous month: "the matter of an engagement or marriage has never been discussed or suggested and the rumour is untrue".[6] Even in the same article, Wilkins says "we are very good friends but I cannot say anything at this time" while

---

[5] Letter from Wilkins to Byrd, 18 September 1928, AGSNY AC 1, Box 269, Folder 9, AGSL, UWML.
[6] "Sir George Wilkins: Engagement Announced", *Mercury* (Hobart), 24 September 1928, p. 10.

Bennett contradicts this and says "we became engaged three days ago". A few days after the announcement of his engagement, on either 26 or 28 of September, Mrs. Louisa Wilkins, Hubert Wilkins' mother died at the age of 86. By then, he was well on his way to Montevideo.

When they arrived at Montevideo, "At the request of the British Minister, the Hon. R. Scott and Mr. Parry, his first secretary, the Uruguayan Government gave us many facilities and much assistance, placing a guard over our machines during a temporary delay and giving us the facilities of the port".[7] The expedition was joined by Victor Olsen, the radio operator. The two planes and other equipment were loaded on board *Hektoria*, a ship of 15,000 tons supplied by the N. Bugge Hektor Whaling Company of Tönsberg, Norway.

On 15 October, the Secretary of State for the Colonies in London, sent the following confidential message to His Excellency the Acting Governor in Port Stanley:

> Please communicate following urgent and Confidential message from Casey representative of Prime Minister of the Commonwealth of Australia in London to Sir Hubert Wilkins on arrival begins Authorities here anxious to learn whether your expedition can rightly be described as a personal British expedition financing itself by sale of Press and similar rights. There is reason to suppose that Byrd expedition may intend claiming for United States any undiscovered territory in King Edward VII area. Would it be possible without interference your plans for you to plant or drop British flags on any Islands you may land or fly over in and between the Falkland Islands and Dependencies and Ross Dependency? Such action would be most helpful from the point of view of asserting British interests. If you are able to comply it would be appreciated if you would forward proof and statement of action taken to His Majesty's Government as early as possible. Please send reply through the Officer Administering the Government of the Falkland Islands. Good luck Casey ends.

---

[7] Hubert Wilkins, "The Wilkins-Hearst Antarctic Expedition, 1928-1929", *Geographical Review*, p. 375.

It is not clear when Wilkins actually received this message as his reply, via the Acting Governor is dated 29 October:

> Confidential. October 29th No.1 Your telegram of 15th October Confidential following for Casey from Wilkins begins Wilkins Hearst Antarctic Expedition is personal expedition commanded by me without obligation to anyone and is financed by personal effort including sale of press. I am honoured to accept official recognition by His Majesty's Government and will D V [God willing] drop or plant British flags in Weddell Sea area and between Falkland Islands and Ross Dependencies ends.

Along with this correspondence is an "authorisation" also dated 29 October 1928, signed by the Acting Governor for Wilkins to act as outlined in the area described further as "between 80 degrees and 150 degrees west longitude".[8] This meant he was given authority under his Majesty's Government to claim new lands and territories for the British Empire. Many of the files related to this instruction are held by the National Archives in England and are classified as "SECRET" or "PRIVATE". Most of the files are correspondence between the Secretary of State for the Colonies (based in Downing Street, London) and the Governor of the Falkland Islands, or members of their respective staff. The Government Telegraph Service in the Falkland Islands and Dependencies were also acting as an intermediary between Hearst's newspapers and Wilkins with Than Ranck, the Managing Editor at Hearst's Universal News Service, sending a message authorising them to collect press dispatches from Wilkins and send them directly to London or New York. On 24 October 1928, they sailed for Deception Island, part of the Falkland Islands Dependencies. During this voyage, on 31 October, Wilkins celebrated his 40th birthday. Wilkins noted that they were comfortably accommodated on the voyage.

Soon after leaving the Falkland Islands, the Wilkins-Hearst expedition met with snowstorms, high winds and rough seas, and, as they approached the ice, fog:

---

[8] File marked CONFIDENTIAL. 15 October 1928. ANT-GEN-1-7. National Archives, Falkland Islands File.

Our course took us between King George Island and Elephant Island, and as we entered Bransfield Strait we met with scattered ice and an occasional berg. We entered Deception on November 6 to find the ice thin and scattered and the land but lightly covered with winter snow. The whalers who had visited Deception Island for the last fourteen years proclaimed it to be an unusual season. The *Hektoria* was moored stern to the beach with her decks but a few yards from the shore.[9]

The expedition had arrived early but was hoping the ice would be thick enough for takeoff and landing the seaplanes. On 10 November 1928,[10] *Los Angeles*, the seaplane that Wilkins and Eielson had used on their Arctic flight, was unloaded from the *Hektoria*. "The machine floated daintily on the water as if afraid of getting its hollow feet wet".[11] This seaplane was the first complete airplane to touch Antarctic soil.

Sir Douglas Mawson had previously landed an airplane fuselage minus wings at Commonwealth Bay, Adelie Land in 1913. The Vickers plane had been supplied to Mawson for the 1911 Australasian Antarctic Expedition. On a practice flight at an Adelaide racecourse, the plane's wings suffered irreparable damage. "Mawson decided to use the flightless craft as Antarctica's first air tractor – a role in which it proved to be short-lived and fairly useless".[12]

As part of the sponsorship agreement with the American Geographical Society, Wilkins wrote a lengthy report for publication in their journal *The Geographical Review*. The Society had not only gone to "great expense and considerable trouble", but they had also produced the charts and curves and tables for aiding and simplifying navigation. Wilkins was clearly frustrated that they had relied on the existing records to predict the weather conditions

---

[9] Wilkins, "The Wilkins-Hearst Antarctic Expedition, 1928-1929", *Geographical Review*, p. 357.

[10] This is recorded by the Government Telegraph Service in Falkland Islands as 11 November 1928.

[11] Wilkins, "The Wilkins-Hearst Antarctic Expedition, 1928-1929", *Geographical Review*.

[12] David Burke, *Moments of Terror: The Story of Antarctic Aviation*, NSW University Press, Sydney, 1993. p. 12.

(most importantly, the thickness and rigidity of the ice) since this was misguided. In the article he details the weather that faced the expedition:

> We examined the flat bay ice and much to our consternation found it not more than two feet thick. ...
>
> The mildness of the season or the warmth from the volcanically influenced beaches surrounding it had melted the ice at its edges and honeycombed it in the center.
>
> Records show that for fourteen years this bay ice remained firm and solid until about Christmas Day.
>
> Extraordinary weather came but not of the kind hoped for! Rain and high temperatures continued for several days, and the snow disappeared. Water six to eight inches deep formed on the flat ice in the harbor.[13]

The two Lockheed Vega planes, *Los Angeles* and *San Francisco*. on Deception Island with *Hektoria* in the background.[14]

On 22 November,[15] Wilkins and Eielson made the first flight in the Antarctic region from Deception Island in the South Shetlands. It was an historic twenty-minute flight where Wilkins and Eielson "looked down through the clouds upon the runway we had built

---
[13] Wilkins, "The Wilkins-Hearst Antarctic Expedition, 1928-1929", *Geographical Review*.
[14] OSU Box 33_4_30. Sir George Hubert Wilkins Papers, BPCRC, OSU.
[15] This is recorded as 16 November 1928, in Wilkins' *Geographical Review* article, p. 358.

across the small peninsula on the western side of the whalers' anchorage".[16] It was a short reconnaissance flight as weather prevented them from going further. A longer flight was possible on 26 November when both planes went up looking for a better area to make a base.

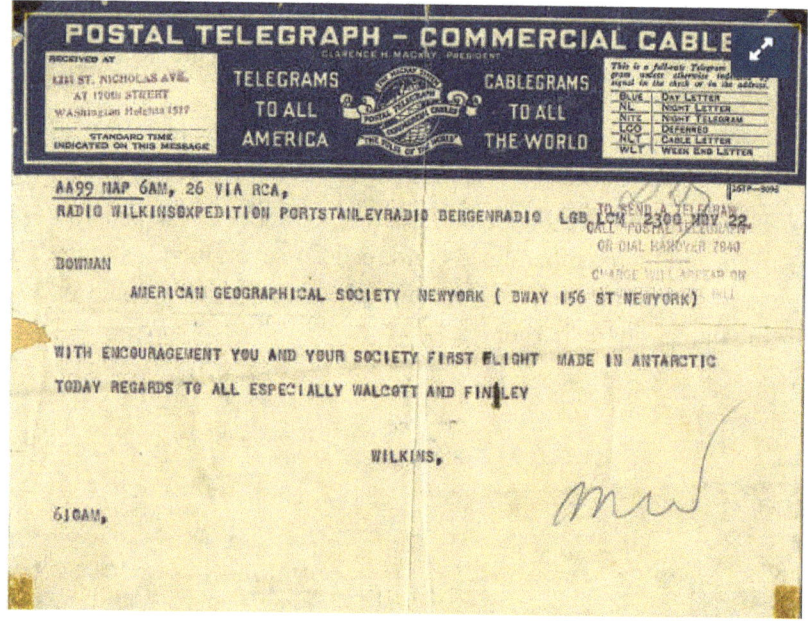

Telegram from Wilkins to Bowman to inform him of the first flight, sent on 22 November 1928.[17]

Wilkins recorded what it was like flying over the Antarctic ice on that momentous flight and the problems that they ran into:

> We flew for several hours about the cloud-engirdled mountains; then, as the midnight sun was sinking to its lowest level, we followed the shadowed coast to our base. There was nowhere else more suitable for our purpose, and so we carefully tested the bay ice at Deception and decided one clear morning to risk a landing on it. This nearly ended in disaster. The machine landed safely but ran far beyond the three-hundred-yard area we had tested into a soft patch in the ice and fell through. The

---

[16] Wilkins, "The Wilkins-Hearst Antarctic Expedition, 1928-1929", *Geographical Review*, p.358.
[17] AGSNY AC 1, Box 262, Folder 38, AGSL, UWML.

wings and fuselage held it from disappearing beneath the water. Eielson, who was piloting, climbed out unhurt; and with the help of twenty whalers and after several hours of difficult and extremely dangerous work we managed to raise the machine and drag it to a safe place on the ice. Attaching pontoons, the machine was brought back to the beaching place near the ship the next day. The machine was none the worse for its wetting, and we made many tests of it as a seaplane.[18]

Birds were attracted by the activities at the whaling station where Wilkins had based himself on Deception Island. This was a potential hazard while they were flying near the harbour:

Although we struck and killed several birds our machine was never out of control or badly damaged. It soon became evident, however, that our only chance of doing anything from Deception Island that season lay in using the machines as land planes. To make a runway half a mile long – the distance across the peninsula – through the mounds of lava, looked at first like an impossibility. With courage born of necessity we started the job and with hands, wheel-barrows, buckets, rakes and shovels, we cleared many tons of debris and had at last a runway forty feet wide and about two thousand five hundred feet long. A forced landing anywhere throughout the journey would mean disaster. The greatest danger, however, lay in the takeoff; the greatest difficulty for the pilot was to handle the heavily laden machine on the soft-surfaced runway. But something worse threatened. The weather could not be depended upon after December. We loaded two hundred gallons of gasoline into the tanks, filled our packs with our spare clothes, equipment, and food.[19]

William Randolph Hearst, the American Geographical Society and Walcott have been mentioned above as sponsors of the expedition but as Wilkins and the crew packed for the flights, other companies and contributors were recognised. There was chocolate given by Freia Chocolate Company of Norway, and malted milk, supplied by

---
[18] Wilkins, "The Wilkins-Hearst Antarctic Expedition, 1928-1929" *Geographical Review*, p. 358.
[19] Wilkins, p. 360.

William Horlick, sufficient for thirty days on a twelve-ounce-per-day diet. Other sponsors included a gift of $10,000 from the Vacuum Oil Company of Australasia who also provided adequate supplies of gasoline and "Mr. Henry Hughes of London presented me with special compasses and drift indicators for navigation". These were packed along with pemmican biscuits, a 'survival' food traditionally made from tallow and dried meat. They also packed nuts and raisins. Most of the supplies and equipment that had not been sponsored or donated were purchased at a discount from Abercrombie and Fitch and from Anthony Fialia,[20] New York. They had planned for emergencies and any eventuality they could imagine:

> There was ample room for our packs and alpine climbing gear, provided by Mr. Conway of Portland, Oregon, in the cabin of the plane. The Worumba Company of New York gave us splendid outfits made to our design in suitable camel's-hair cloth. Each man's equipment was separate and intact. It could be seized and swung upon our backs at a moment's notice or discarded with equal facility. In case of accident and a forced march home we should each have our own supply if one or the other happened to go through a crevasse. To each man's alpine rope was attached a pole and a small strong block and tackle with which he could, if uninjured, haul himself up the rope in a vertical position.[21]

On 14 December 1928, Bowman asked whether Ranck, the Managing Editor at Universal News Service, could send a message to Wilkins with Christmas greetings. Ranck advised that they were in contact by radio so Bowman then sent a message to the Director of the Radio Marine Department on 19 December to ask whether he would "kindly send the following message" to Wilkins and send the bill to the American Geographical Society at the rate discussed

---

[20] Anthony Fialia, *Fighting the Polar Ice*, Hodder & Stoughton, London, 1907. Anthony Fialia (1869-1950) an American Arctic explorer was photographer on the 1901-1902 Baldwin-Ziegler Polar Expedition's attempt to reach the North Pole. In 1903-1905 he was in command of the Ziegler Polar Expedition in a further attempt on the North Pole.

[21] Hubert Wilkins, "The Wilkins-Hearst Antarctic Expedition, 1928-1929", *Geographical Review*, p. 360.

on the phone of US$0.90c per word. The message read: "WILKINS INFINITE GOOD WISHES CHRISTMAS GREETINGS BOWMAN".[22]

The next day was deemed a suitable day for Eielson and Wilkins to fly again. In the morning "the weather was perfect, just a little wind, a clear sky, and sparkling atmosphere. The thermometer on the ground stood at about 38F., [3°C] a tolerable temperature" They were working in the camel-hair Worumba clothes and were "uncomfortably warm". In his article "The Wilkins-Hearst Antarctic Expedition, 1928-1929" Wilkins describes the flight:

> At 8.20 am, we were in the air heading south. The hazardous takeoff had been, with Eielson's skill and courage, successfully accomplished. We directed our course a little west of south, taking the peak of Trinity Island as a landmark. By 8.40 we were at 6000 feet altitude and beside Trinity Island. We passed Brialmont Bay. At Salvesen Bay, a few miles farther south, we turned and at 8200 feet decided to cross the plateau which we named Detroit Aviation Society Plateau. At 9.50 we could see Seal Nunataks and Robertson Island to the east. To the west were long ice-filled fiords almost severing Graham Land. These, named Hektoria Fiords, were not photographed until we were on our homeward journey. We were now flying above ice in Weddell Sea, the Nordenskjöld Shelf Ice. At 10 am I noted in my diary: "There appears to be a haze or a very low cloud ahead (we were flying at 8000 feet), or perhaps it is wind which over the Arctic pack ice I know from experience is indicated by milk-white sky upon the horizon." Later an entry reads: "Four hours out. Just struck the first bumpy air experienced today. We had come to the wind we had seen some hours before."

> At ten o'clock we were opposite a deep inlet, Evans Inlet, which appeared at first to cut right through Graham Land. In fact I actually made a note to that effect in my log but corrected it late when we could see the mountains at the end for the level ice. On our way south we passed between C. A. Larsen's "Foyn Land" and the coast and saw two conspicuous black mountains

---

[22] Letter from Bowman to Costigan, Radio Marine Department, 19 December 1928, AGSNY AC 1, Box 269, Folder 9, AGSL, UWML.

which we named Mt. Napier Birks. Just south of there we saw what we believe to be a circuitous channel dividing Graham Land. It was named Crane Channel.

South of Crane Channel we came near to the coast. I noted in my log that some of the peaks were of stratified material. The entry reads: "The islands have cliffs at their southern sides. The steepest exposures on the mountains face south... There are some black seams showing; perhaps they are coal." A mighty mass of mountains stretched far to the south westward from Crane Channel, and opposite was an island not marked on the chart until we named it Robinson Island. The most easterly point of the large island, which we concluded was South Graham Land, we called Cape Northrop; and the mountains we named Lockheed Mountains. From there a bay, Mobiloil Bay, extended deeply towards the west. The mountains flanking the northern half of the bay were deeply scarred with four huge glaciers, which we named Whirlwind Glaciers. The coast, which lies farther south than Nordenskjöld or Larsen had been and is opposite Fallières Coast, we named Bowman Coast.

By 12.32 we were opposite high steep mountains, one of which we named Mt. Ranck, and these seemed to terminate the second part of Graham Land. A channel, which narrowed in its center but appeared to hold only ice, widened again. We named it Casey Channel, and the island south of it Scripps Island.

At 12.50 I noted in my log "We are now quite certain that Graham Land is not connected with the mainland continent". We named the cape at the northern side of that channel Cape Walcott, the channel Lurabee Channel, and the islands to the south the Finley Islands. Dr John H Finley was the president of the American Geographical Society. There appeared to be a group of six or more of these islands scattered in a wide strait. We could not clearly define their outlines because we were then flying at two thousand feet. We called the strait Stefansson Strait, and the land beyond it Hearst Land.

The eastward edge of Hearst Land was marked a cape which I called Cape Eielson. When we reached a point estimated to be about latitude 71 20S, longitude 64 15W., we had used nearly half our supply of gasoline. Storm clouds that we had seen

Cape Mayo (left), Casey Channel Mt. Ranch and Cape Keeler. OSU Box 37_3_29. Sir George Hubert Wilkins Papers, BPCRC, OSU. A black and white photo similar to this appeared in *Geographical Review*, Fig. 28 "The Wilkins Antarctic Expedition, 1928-1929", AGSL, UWML.

developing behind us threatened to cut us off from our base; and so with the idea of returning safely with the information gathered we swung our airplane to face the north and hurried homewards. Meteorological conditions became interesting. Three cloud areas were developing. From 5000 feet above we saw through a hole in the clouds our landing field, and Eielson threw the machine into a sharp spiral nose dive and landed safely within ten hours of the time we started. Our ground speed on the return trip, helped a little by the wind behind us, averaged more than 130 miles per hour.

Following the second flight on 21 December, Hearst, in order to prepare for publishing Wilkins' reports under their exclusive rights agreement, wrote to Bowman requesting a 2,500-word article explaining the "significance of the discoveries made by Captain Sir George Wilkins in his airplane flights across the Antarctic".[23] Wilkins had recently made a discovery that showed Graham Land, previously thought to be part of the Antarctic Continent, was entirely cut off from it. So "what until now scientists and cartographers

---

[23] Letter from Ranck to Bowman, 21 December 1928, AGSNY AC 1, Box 269, Folder 9, AGSL, UWML.

have believed existed in that particular territory" had proved to be incorrect. Hearst asked Bowman to also explain "the mysteries that remain to be cleared up in that territory". The Universal News Service offered to pay $250 for the article and $50 for a map to illustrate the article with the details of Wilkins' explorations. While initially agreeing to the payment, Bowman later submits a supplementary bill for another $75 to cover the large amount of drafting of the map that was done over the weekend under "difficult conditions" to make the Monday deadline.[24] Continuing the conversation about the cost of the drafting, Bowman sends a letter to Hearst about the cost of two men that:

Hektoria Fiords, long ice-filled fiords almost severing Graham land. OSU Box 37 Group 3 Shackleton 58. Sir George Hubert Wilkins Papers, BPCRC, OSU. A black and white photo similar to this appeared in the *Geographical Review,* as Fig. 21 "The Wilkins-Hearst Antarctic Expedition, 1928-1929", AGSL, UWML.

> have worked on the map all day, with 15 minutes for lunch – one interpreting and plotting, the other drafting. The former has a salary of $18.00 a day, the latter $10.00. If we add materials (a $10.00 set of maps had to be wrecked to get this one sheet) it puts us behind about $50.00. I ought to charge $75.00 in all, because we used a very expensive base that cost us $3000.00 to

---

[24] Letter from Bowman to Hearst, 22 December 1928, AGSNY AC 1, Box 269, Folder 9, AGSL, UWML.

compile and draw during this past summer and I must get that money back in one way and another if the map department is not to go on the rocks. Sorry to bother about these small details, but I want you to understand that the bill doesn't represent a mercenary spirit. Maps cost like hell.

Bowman managed to write the article by the deadline the following day and sent a letter to Ranck with the article and a note to say that the draftsmen are working on the maps, and it should be completed by 11 o'clock on Sunday prior to the Monday deadline. Not long after, Ranck sent a radio message to Wilkins to inform him that his summary of the second flight was published under the first page headline by "Times and World and third page by Herald Tribune". While in the "New York American" the message was printed on the first page along with the article by Bowman interpreting the flight.[25]

In Australia the newspapers were following Wilkins' expedition. The *Sydney Morning Herald*, on 26 December 1928 (p.6), stated:

> Wireless and the aeroplane have revolutionized polar exploration. The scientific penetration of unknown Antarctica by this famous Australian explorer is of enhanced interest because Wilkins for the first time has enlisted these aids in a region for long attacked with the more familiar and primitive equipment of the dog-sleigh.

On 2 January 1929, Lura B. Shreck, Wilkins' secretary, wrote a message on "George Hubert Wilkins Expeditions" letterhead from the Waldorf-Astoria headquarters in New York to inform Bowman of recent radio communications. Wilkins had reported that "The whole of the magnificent coast south of Graham Land – an incontrovertible feature – we have named 'Bowman Coast' in honour of the great geographer and director of the American Geographical Society"[26]. This honour was also bestowed on other sponsors and crew (for instance, Cape Walcott, Hearst Land and Cape Eielson). Lura sent a separate letter to Bowman to ask whether they had an "accurate Antarctic map" as she has been asked for one on several occasions.

---

[25] Typed radio message from Ranck to Wilkins, [no date], AGSL, UWML.
[26] Letter from Shreck to Bowman, 2 January 1929, AGSL, UWML.

She noted that before Wilkins left, he said he would send her one from New York, but obviously his limited time precluded him doing so.[27] Bowman responded six days later to acknowledge her letters and included a copy of the American Geographical Society's "Map of Antarctic" and the Navigational Chart that had been supplied to Wilkins and Byrd. He suggested that any further map enquiries could be made to the American Geographical Society and would be charged at $10 each. He noted that "We should like to distribute the map widely and thus arouse as much interest as possible in the schools and elsewhere in the explorations of Captain Wilkins now under way".[28]

Concerns had been expressed about any further flights on this expedition. Hearst wired Wilkins on 4 January, to ask questions including "with smaller cheaper subsidiary whaler could this season locate suitable base for next season?" and "if such craft could carry airplane might not additional flights yield large harvest of scientific results supplementing discoveries already made?"[29] This was Hearst showing interest in future expeditions and putting actions in place to make them a success.

Back at Deception Island, by 6 January 1929 the weather had deteriorated and Wilkins reported to Hearst that:

> Every takeoff here now greatly endangers machine. Ross Sea flight my principal objective. Cannot jeapardize that by greatly risking present adequate resources. This may sound like cowards caution but expectantly idling here is more nervewracking than numerous flights. Can economically arrange for catcher with accommodation next season ... there is hope for this season yet but not much. We will try but believe postponement advisable.[30]

Hearst, understanding the situation the expedition now faced, responded on 7 January, over the radio, to say "Daring skill results your Antarctic achievements have already aroused profound

---

[27] Letter from Shreck to Bowman, [no date], AGSL, UWML.
[28] Letter from Bowman to Shreck, 8 January 1929, AGSL, UWML.
[29] Typed radio message from Hearst to Wilkins, 4 January 1929, AGSL, UWML.
[30] Transmission from Wilkins to Hearst, 6 January 1929, AGSNY AC 1, Box 269, Folder 9, AGSL, UWML.

Map of Wilkins' 20 December 1928 flight. Courtesy American Geographical Society Library, University of Wisconsin-Milwaukee Libraries.

admiration. Should you deem wise return America now and go back Antarctic next year ... such course will meet approval".[31] On the same day, Bowman wrote to Hearst to make sure that when

---

[31] Typed radio message from Hearst to Wilkins, 7 January 1929, AGSL, UWML.

the new map was sent out, the American Geographical Society was acknowledged and not the National Geographical Society as there had previously been a situation where they had been wrongly attributed. Ranck then sent out a wire message to the editors of all the Hearst newspapers to make sure the error did not occur again.

Plane at Deception Island preparing for another flight. Courtesy Dr David Larson Collection.

On 10 January, Wilkins made a second long flight over Graham Land. It was 250 miles out on more or less the same course as they had previously flown. On this trip they were able to confirm the observations made on the first flight. As discussed with Hearst, there were already plans being made for the next season and reflections on how the first Wilkins-Hearst expedition had gone:

> The N. Bugge Hektor Whaling Company has generously agreed to carry us again next season to Deception Island, where our machines and supplies are stored in a warehouse. We are expected to be ready to join the boat at Montevideo some time next September. The N. Bugge Hektor Whaling Company and its employees were always willing to help throughout the season.
>
> Everything except the earliness of the season was as we expected to find in the Antarctic. The season was no doubt three weeks or a month earlier than normal, and little snow had fallen throughout the preceding winter.

Another disappointment was the fact that a spare whale catcher, which is for use only in emergency and is the customary equipment of the Hektor Company at Deception Island, could not this year accompany us. I had planned to hire the spare catcher if necessary to help us in our work. It was not available; and it was not advisable from any point of view to hire at great expense, of nothing less than fifty thousand cash for transferring a 'working' catcher upon which the whole crew of the Company were dependent for their livelihood. The boat-for-hire problem will be solved next season, I hope, through arrangement with the Governor of the Falkland Islands Dependencies, who has promised to recommend that the Hektor Whaling Company be licensed to use an extra catcher with the understanding that it will be placed at my disposal if necessary. This is an arrangement to which I believe the Company will be agreeable.[32]

It is around this time that Wilkins sent another message to Hearst to clarify a few things about the plans for next season and about the way forward:

There is no certainty, even with a ship hired indefinitely, that we could reach suitable temporary base from which to make Ross Sea this season. The alternative is postponement, storing equipment here and returning for an early start when weather and other conditions more likely favorable. This would involve no further financial demands from Hearst and comparatively little extra expense anywhere. If we could leave here soon believe I could carry on work of interest and scientific value in Arctic this summer and in time to return with whalers next season. There is perhaps some valuable (copy) in Hearst's continuing Antarctic story next year. Beside hiring ship there are other indefinite uncertain possibilities of continuing here this season, yet would like frank comments on foregoing from Ranck, Bowman and Stefansson.[33]

Wilkins proposed a message be dispatched to the Director of the

---

[32] Wilkins, "The Wilkins-Hearst Antarctic Expedition, 1928-1929", pp. 371-372.
[33] Typed note from Wilkins, [no date], AGSNY AC 1, Box 269, Folder 9, AGSL, UWML.

Meteorological Service in Buenos Aires, to enquire whether there would be a ship visiting Laurie Island that could call in to carry Eielson and himself back to Buenos Aires. There was one and they joined the *Fleurus,* leased by the Falklands Island government as a mail and passenger ship, to begin the journey back to the United States. It was briefly suggested in 1928 that *Fleurus* be used to patrol territorial waters and prevent unlicensed whaling "but political problems arising from a Norwegian whaling company's ship carrying out British license enforcement rendered this impractical. *Fleurus* was also contracted to support the Wilkins-Hearst expedition in 1928-29".[34]

On 4 March 1929, Wilkins travelled back to Los Angeles arriving in the middle of the month. While on this trip, and nearing Havana on 7 March, he wrote an overview of the trip to Bowman as the basis for his longer report:

> After having made the initial mistake of not hurrying immediately on reaching Deception Island it soon became evident that we would have to postpone our flight to the Ross Sea. However, the weather upon our arrival was not at all favourable and I am not certain that we have not made the best use of our opportunities. Of course it is very disappointing to have to make two trys at a job but I think we shall have little trouble next season. The Governor of Falkland Islands has promised to allow the Hektoria Company an extra catcher on the understanding that it is placed at my disposal if necessary. This is the first season the company has been without a spare catcher and that was only because the British Colonial Office refused them the license. We hope that we will not have need to use a boat next year. The conditions at Deception are even better in normal years, than I anticipated. There are a few things I will do this season to provide for emergencies but very little that was not prepared for last year is necessary. In consequence I have hurried back with the idea that I might be able to interest the U.S. Navy in the possibility of crossing the Arctic in a submarine. I plan to go to Washington the night of

---

[34] Ian Hart, *Whaling in the Falkland Islands dependencies 1904-1931: a history of shore and bay-based whaling in the Antarctic*, Pequeno Press, Mexico, 2006, pp. 220-1, 343.

the 13th and see how the people there feel about it. If they are entirely unsympathetic I will catch a boat for London on the 16th and see what the British Navy thinks. My third string is the German Navy they were most interested in the idea when I mentioned it last year. If all that leads to nothing then – if it is going forward – I might join Nansen, Captain Bruns and Dr Berson on their Dirigible flight over the Arctic and if that fails I have another plan for occupying my time until September when we must go south again.[35]

With this letter, Wilkins attached some suggestions regarding the submarine plans to cross the Arctic Ocean, travelling from the Behring Sea to Spitsbergen or vice versa. He also sent a copy to Ranck and asked for his "criticism and advise" about his plans and whether he should publish the matter before he goes to Washington. Wilkins proposed that using a submarine "would afford the most efficient and most economical means of carrying a sonic depth finding apparatus across the Arctic Ocean".

On 12 March 1929, Wilkins wrote to Bowman to hand in his report and maps from the Wilkins-Hearst Antarctic expedition to the American Geographical Society. The negatives had been delivered to Universal News Service, Hearst Newspapers who, as part of their sponsorship agreement, had bought exclusive rights to the photographs. Wilkins regretted that "more work could not be accomplished last season" but looked forward "with confidence to the completion, next December, of the program originally outlined including the flight from Graham Land to the Ross Sea Barrier".[36]

An unsigned letter from Bowman was sent to Wilkins over a month later on 25 April 1929. It detailed the two cheques, both for US$100, which were to be presented to him. One was an honorarium for the lecture he provided to the American Geographical Society and the other cheque was for an article that was to appear in the July edition of *The Geographical Review*. It was noted that Wilkins gave a "first class performance" at the last lecture and the Society was

---

[35] Letter from Wilkins to Bowman, 7 March 1929, AGSNY AC 1, Box 269, Folder 9, AGSL, UWML.
[36] Letter from Wilkins to Bowman, 12 March 1929, AGSL, UWML.

eager to have him on the same platform again. The lecture included slides and motion pictures and was held at the auditorium of the Engineering Societies Building, where nearly a thousand people could be accommodated. Unfortunately, it was noted that the Society was unable to provide financial support for future expeditions as the patron that the Society relied on for support, Mr. James B. Ford, had died in April. There was also a personal request that Wilkins join the Bowman family at their home as the two children were "put out" that they were not able to talk to Wilkins personally, and "Rob's admiration is so great that he will not be satisfied unless he can talk with you for some time alone".[37]

Wilkins replied to Bowman's letter the next day to say that he had a definite offer of US$140,000 from Hearst for his Arctic submarine proposal. Wilkins would be "glad to pay another visit to your home and spend more time with young folks".[38] He also made a note that he had an invitation from Ellsworth asking him to visit his home in Switzerland, but he was sorry he would not have the time to do that. Wilkins was about to lose his headquarters base in the Waldorf-Astoria as it was about to close and be demolished to make way for the Empire State Building.

The Florence Nightingale Institute of Honorables wrote to Bowman on 28 December 1928, after reading Bowman's article in the *Los Angeles Examiner*. Georgia Bryton, the founder of the Florence Nightingale Institute of Honorables, asked for Bowman's advice:

> From your comment and deductions concerning Capt. Sir Hubert Wilkins' discoveries to date, and their important contribution to scientific and geographical knowledge, I have formed the opinion that Capt. Wilkins merits appreciation from this Institute in the form of a testimonial of honor, which should be shared by Mr. William Randolph Hearst, as the financial backer of the expedition who made the voyage possible, and also by Mr. Eielson and the others of Capt Wilkins's fellow voyagers.[39]

---

[37] Letter from Bowman to Wilkins, 25 April 1929, AGSL, UWML.
[38] Letter from Wilkins to Bowman, 26 April 1929, AGSL, UWML.
[39] Letter from Bryton to Bowman, 28 December 1928, AGSNY AC 1, Box 184, Folder 20, AGSL, UWML.

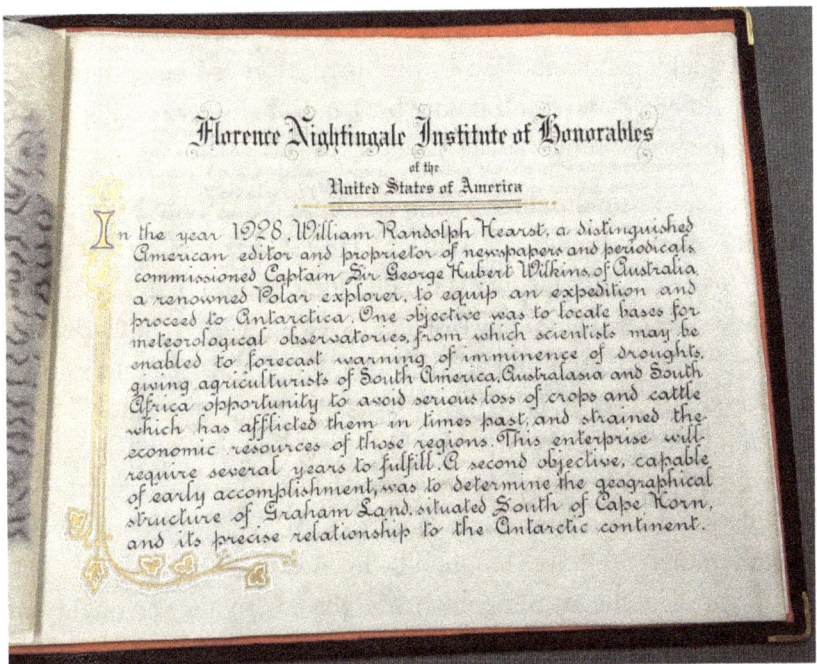

Page detail from Wilkins' Florence Nightingale Institute of Honorables testimonial. Box 1.2 Sir George Hubert Wilkins Papers, BPCRC, OSU.

The Florence Nightingale Institute of Honorables was conceived by Bryton in 1927. Bryton was a friend of Florence Nightingale, and Bryton's family had a close, forty-two-year friendship with her. She maintained the office in her home and contributed all secretarial work, postage, printing and general costs from her funds. An initial movement was to remember Nightingale's work each year on her birthday (12 May), then to award ribbons as insignia of honours which then became testimonials. Honours were awarded to people "of either sex or any nationality … who, during the calendar year last past, shall have contributed the highest service to the Greater Glory of Almighty GOD, and … the person whose contribution of service shall be, by a Supreme Council of the Institute, pronounced inestimably beneficial to mankind"[40]. Bryton wanted to acknowledge Wilkins and the crew of the Wilkins-Hearst expedition. Bryton wrote to Bowman and described in detail how the testimonials would be presented. They "will be engraved and written on parchment in the

---

[40] Florence Nightingale Institute of Honorables, 1928-1931, UWML.

form of books, bound in purple Morocco leather with solid gold corner shields, and enclosed in silk lined Morocco envelopes. The books will be 23 and a half inches by 9 and a half inches when open, and exquisite examples of art".[41]

Identical testimonials were created by the Florence Nightingale Institute of Honorables for Wilkins, Hearst, Eielson, Crossan and Porter and were endorsed by sixty-eight international organisations. To make the presentations, Bowman was appointed "a Colleague of the [Florence Nightingale] Institute, and Special Commissioner in charge of the Wilkins-Hearst expedition presentation". The testimonials were dated 12 May 1929 to coincide with the 109th anniversary of Florence Nightingale's birth. There was a delay in completing the books as they were "spoiled by penman's errors".[42] Bryton aimed to have the books to Bowman by 1 May. She reiterated that "the art of penmanship, the engraving, the quality of workmanship of the gold lettering on the Morocco leather covers, the delicate illuminated initial letters done in gold and bright colours, will combine to produce a result which, as shown by the preliminary work submitted by the manufacturer, is impossible of surpassment by the world's leading craftsmen". The cost to produce one of the testimonial books was US$155.

The presentations were delayed as Wilkins was abroad and due to return on the LZ 127 *Graf Zeppelin*, the 200 yard long, German hydrogen blimp. Also on board on that trip was a female gorilla for the Chicago Zoo,[43] but on 16 May 1929, on the first night of its second trip to the US, the Zeppelin lost four of its engines and was unable to be controlled. It made an emergency landing near Toulon, France. Wilkins took it all in his stride saying:

> I am rather accustomed to being battered about in a plane, but never underwent such an experience, or one quite so thrilling. The airship was bucking in a heavy wind all day long, with

---

[41] Letter from Bryton to Bowman, 14 April 1929, AGSNY AC 1, Box 184, Folder 20, AGSL, UWML.

[42] Letter from Bryton to Bowman, 28 December 1928, AGSNY AC 1, Box 184, Folder 20, AGSL, UWML.

[43] "Graf Zeppelin – Wilkins as Passenger", *Canberra Times,* 15 May 1929, p. 5.

hardly any power, and tossed backwards and forwards ... We continually faced the fear that our last motors would break down under the strain ... many of the passengers were seasick, and that added to the horrors of the situation ... I would rather fly over the North Pole any time than go through another such experience.[44]

The breakdown of the airship meant further delay to the testimonial presentation and still greater uncertainty as to when Wilkins would return to the United States. Hearst had also changed his plans and returned to the Pacific Coast. Bowman proposed posting the testimonial to him or waiting until the autumn when Wilkins might also be going to the Pacific Coast.

Shortly after the *Graf Zeppelin* landed safely back in the United States, on 30 August 1929, Sir George Hubert Wilkins and Miss Suzanne Bennett were "quietly" married. They were then known as Sir and Lady Wilkins and they travelled, shortly after their wedding, on 1 September, on the *Graf Zeppelin* from Lakehurst, America to Fredrichshafen, Germany. According to Lady Wilkins, the trip was a wedding gift from Hearst and she remarked that "we are sailing on a magic ship betwixt heaven and earth".[45] According to Sir Hubert, he was asked by Hearst to cover the technical details of the flight!

The presentation of the Florence Nightingale Institute of Honorables testimonials was eventually made at a private Society dinner at the University Club, New York City, on 26 September 1929 to both Hearst and Wilkins. Franklin Roosevelt, who was then Governor of New York but became President of the United States in 1933, wrote to Bowman with an apology for the dinner. He said "I am particularly sorry not to have the pleasure of meeting Sir Hubert Wilkins, as I have followed his explorations with very keen interest, especially as they have been conducted with such thorough care for the scientific data and information".[46]

---

[44] "Graf Zeppelin", *Sunday Times* (Sydney), 19 May 1929, p. 1.
[45] "Sir G.H. Wilkins: Honeymoon on Zeppelin", *Newcastle Morning Herald and Miners' Advocate,* 5 June 1930, p. 8.
[46] Letter from Roosevelt to Bowman, 17 September 1929, AGSNY AC 1, Box 125, Folder 18, AGSL, UWML.

Certificate of Marriage

United States of America
State of Ohio

This is to Certify that by virtue of a license duly granted under seal of the Probate Court of Cuyahoga County, Ohio, authorizing the solemnization of the marriage contract between Mr. George H Wilkins and Miss Suzanne Bennett they were on the 30th day of August One Thousand Nine Hundred and twenty nine by me duly joined in Marriage.

In Witness Whereof I have hereunto subscribed my name the day and year above written.

R J Barnwell
J T Caine

J. E. Chilek, Cleveland, Ohio

OSU Box 2 Folder 12 Sir George Hubert Wilkins Papers, BPCRC, OSU.

5

1929-1930 THE SECOND WILKINS-HEARST EXPEDITION

With the help of Prime Minister Bruce's "political agent" in London, R.G. Casey, Wilkins secured support from the "Discovery Committee" of £10,000 and the use of the ship RRS 'William Scoresby'.

As mentioned previously, George Hubert Wilkins was knighted on 14 June 1928, at Buckingham Palace in London, by King George V, for services to aviation and exploration. Less known is that he was also knighted by King Emmanuel II of Italy. And he received many other tributes and awards. He became a celebrity and one with a long list of things he still wanted to achieve. He found getting sponsorship became much easier. Following the 1928-1929 Wilkins-Hearst Antarctic Expedition and the excitement of becoming the first people, again with Ben Eielson, to fly in the Antarctic, Wilkins was still planning to return south as soon as possible. He also wanted to take a submarine under the Arctic ice to the North Pole.

From the end of April until early August 1929, Wilkins spent time in England and the Continent with several aims including seeking a ship (RRS *William Scoresby*) for his next Antarctic venture; to find a submarine to take under the Arctic ice; and to organise a motor car (Austin Seven) to take to Deception Island. During this visit he had several meetings, in May and July, with R.G. Casey (later Lord Casey, Governor General of Australia, then Baron Casey of Berwick), at that time Liaison Officer at Australia House and Prime Minister Bruce's "political agent" in London.[1] Archives held

---

[1] See Chapter 4. Casey hosted at least two lunches for Wilkins. Casey and Wilkins probably met towards the end of World War I, either in France or London. Over the next twenty years they met or communicated on many occasions and in 1939, by which time Casey was Treasurer in the Australian Government, *Wyatt Earp* was sold to the Australian Government. See Chapter 9.

by the Australian Department of Foreign Affairs and Trade, known as DFAT files[2] reveal some of Casey's daily "PERSONAL AND CONFIDENTIAL" letters to Prime Minister Bruce. Although dated 11 April 1929, this one is marked (Due to arrive Canberra 10.5.29). Casey remarks first "The Antarctic Expedition arrangements are going ahead fairly satisfactorily, although with the inevitable squabbles between your Committee in Australia and Mawson and myself here. However, we seem to be prevailing. I like Mawson much better on further acquaintance, but he unfortunately has not the gift of clearness of thought or expression which a scientific training usually engenders.

Casey continues:

> I am glad Wilkins has given up his idea of his submarine polar enterprise for this year at least. I have just had a long letter from him in which he sets out his reasons for thinking that it is a practical possibility and justified by the scientific results that would accrue. However, his most useful role in the coming Antarctic season is to try and complete his contemplated flight from Graham Land to the Ross Sea – and to do so before Byrd can do it in the reverse direction.
>
> He has written a most extraordinary article in one of the Hearst papers, in which he queries the validity of Antarctic claims in general, ridicules the idea of anyone claiming territory by having flown over it – and generally seems to have forgotten that he accepted with enthusiasm the formal authority of H.M.G. to drop flags and claim territory in the name of the King, prior to his past season's enterprise.
>
> He is coming to London shortly and I will have to have it out with him and see where he stands before we suggest his being entrusted with such a formal commission again.[3]

Casey to Bruce on 16 May 1929 reveals:

---

[2] DFAT (Australian Department of Foreign Affairs and Trade) Historical Documents, Volume 17, R.G. Casey's Letters to S.M. Bruce, 1924-1929. All further quotes in this chapter from Casey to Bruce come from these files.

[3] See "Very Secret" telegram dated 3 October 1929. Between Secretary of State and Governor of Falkland Islands, in the Falkland Islands and Papers held in the British National Archives, 29 October 1928.

I saw a good deal of Wilkins while he was here, and to my great surprise, was able to be instrumental in getting him a virtual promise of 10,000 [Pounds Sterling no doubt] from the 'Discovery Committee towards the funds for his coming season's operations in the Antarctic. Before I started work on them, I should have said that there wasn't a hope of squeezing anything appreciable out of them – but they fell for the idea, and morally committed themselves in quick time. This will mean that instead of doing the long flight (2,000 miles) from Graham Land to the Ross Sea in one jump and with no support, he will now be able to have a ship in the offing to come to his aid if necessary – in other words, he is able to assure himself of another chance of life.[4]

Following his meetings with Casey, on 28 May 1929, Wilkins writes two separate letters to the Under Secretary of State at the Colonial Office. In the first he gives a short report of what his "Antarctic summer 1928-29" expedition achieved and how, where the equipment from that expedition is stored (Deception Island), and his plan of operation and costs for the 1929-1930 season. Funnily enough the estimated costs add up to exactly £10,000! He adds:

> In view of the fact that the Wilkins-Hearst Antarctic Expedition is a private expedition under my undivided and personal control financed last year almost entirely from my own personal resources, and that this year I propose to contribute my private equipment and machines valued at £20,000 to the expedition, I respectfully request that my application be favourably considered for a grant of £7,500 to be made available, if possible, by June 15th and a further grant of £2,500 to be made available by January 1st, 1930 in order to meet the cost of operation and cover the expense for providing for possible emergency.

In his second letter of the same date to the same person Wilkins

---

[4] The Discovery Committee was appointed in 1924 by the Secretary of State for the Colonies to carry out recommendations made in *A Report of the Interdepartmental Committee on Research and Development in the Dependencies of the Falkland Islands*. Much of this work related to whaling in Antarctic waters and was carried out by the Discovery Investigation's ships, *Discovery* (Scott's ship), *Discovery II* (see Chapter 8) and *William Scoresby* (see this chapter).

"respectfully request you to consider the possibility of having your research vessel, "William Scoresby", operate from November 15th to the end of December 1929, in the vicinity of Deception Island, South Shetlands." Wilkins gives details of modifications that would be required to the ship including adding "a derrick 38 feet long" in order to transport or salvage his aircraft.

And the response didn't take long. On 6 June 1929, Casey writes to Bruce:

> To my increasing surprise Wilkins is managing to get all he wants from the Discovery Committee. I have been shepherding him and doing all I could for him with them – and to my great surprise they have agreed to let the "William Scoresby" (a whale catcher converted to scientific work which used to work with the 'Discovery') be at his disposal during the period of his activity in December and January next, for conveying his aeroplanes and personnel from Deception Island to the farthest south base that he can establish. And, over and above this, they are, I believe about to agree to a contribution of 10,000 from their funds towards the general purposes of his efforts!
>
> They have, of course, got very considerable funds on which to draw – something approaching 100,000 a year from whale oil taxes from the Falkland Islands. We put it to them with the bait that Wilkins' work in the coming season was likely to add to the knowledge (and sovereignty) of the Falklands Islands sector of the Antarctic mainland – this happened to be the right button to press. On the usual principle, we asked for much more than we expected to get – and look like getting the lot!

And on 20 June 1929, in response to a letter Prime Minister Bruce had forwarded to Casey, from Dow, the Official Secretary to the Australian Commissioner in the United States, Casey comments:

> I note the letter you sent me from Dow (Official Secretary to Australian Commissioner in the US) in New York with regard to Wilkins. This does not give me much pause. Dow knows only a part of the story. I have never thought Wilkins was a very thorough or inspired scientific man, but his usefulness lies in the fact that he has the initiative and courage to open up new areas and do a little rough but useful scientific work

which gives the lead to the more scientific but less hard individuals who follow in his footsteps. He is the tin-opener. In his Antarctic work I would almost disregard the scientific side and look on merely as an individual who can do a good deal to keep our end up in the way of straight discovery. As regards his connection with the Hearst Press, I do not blame him in the least. He has never been able to raise money in Australia and until this last month he has never been able to raise money here. The Americans came at him with their purses open and did not impose conditions – other than that he should write a good deal of rather monotonous rubbish for their papers. I am delighted that our efforts to help Wilkins with the Discovery Committee have been successful – and (as I report in another letter) he is getting 10,000 and the use of the small ship 'William Scoresby' from the Discovery Committee.

Casey's final comment to the Prime Minister on Wilkins is contained in his letter of 4 July 1929, where he says "I have managed to get five or six hundred pounds more money for Wilkins, and he has himself got another thousand, so that his financial worries in respect of the coming season's work are behind him."

On 29 June 1929, following the various exchanges of correspondence noted in Chapter 4, between the Governor of the Falkland Islands and the Secretary of State for the Colonies in London, there is a "SECRET" letter from Lord Passfield, Secretary of State for the Colonies, to the Governor enclosing "copies of [five] items of correspondence with Sir Hubert Wilkins regarding certain aeroplane flights which he proposed to undertake in Antarctic areas in or near the Falkland Islands Dependencies during the Antarctic summer of 1929-30." Passfield tells the Governor "The aspects of the matter affecting British territorial rights should not be made public but you are at liberty to announce,[5] when you think fit, that arrangements have been made with Sir Hubert Wilkins for undertaking certain aeroplane flights in order to add to geographical knowledge of the areas referred to." The Secretary of State continues that it was not practicable to consult the Governor before the arrangements were made and that "I shall be glad to

---

[5] Underlining in pen in original document.

receive in due course a report from you upon the work done by Sir Hubert Wilkins and your views upon the question whether similar arrangements should be made for a second season."[6]

Captain J.K. Davis was Master of the *Discovery* for the first of Douglas Mawson's 1929-1931 BANZARE (British Australian New Zealand Antarctic Research Expeditions). Mawson would join the ship in Cape Town. *The Times* of Monday 29 July 1929 (p.9) reported under the heading "Australian Antarctic Expedition – Reception on Board the Discovery" that:

> The Master, Captain J.K. Davis, and the officers of the steamship Discovery entertained about 300 British, Australian, and New Zealand guests on board on Saturday [27 July] to mark the departure, on August 1, of the Commonwealth Antarctic Expedition. ... The guests included several members of previous Antarctic expeditions. Among them was Sir Hubert Wilkins, who had arrived the previous night from the United States, and announced his intention of going on to Germany, where he hoped to join the Graf Zeppelin on her projected flight across the Atlantic and, if possible, round the world, after which he would prepare for his return to the Antarctic in the autumn.

So many Antarctic heroes together, it was widely reported in British and Australian newspapers. Wilkins greeted Hurley saying "Good Lord! Fancy meeting you again" on board *Discovery*. Also present was Dr Leonard Hussey who had been on both Shackleton's expeditions, 1914-1917 and 1921-1922, with Hurley on the former and Wilkins on the latter. "Boy Scout" Marr who had also sailed with Hussey and Wilkins on the 1921-1922 voyage was also on board as he was sailing on the Mawson Expedition, as was Hurley. And "Captain Davis, who received the guests on the gangway, is very proud of his new chart of the Antarctic. It is a rare old print of

---

[6] Sheet No.80 Falkland Islands files. COLONIAL OFFICE – FALKLAND FILES: An extensive set of papers in the National Archives. Many of those quoted in this chapter are classified "SECRET" or "PRIVATE" and are between the Secretary of State for the Colonies (based in Downing Street, London) and the Governor of the Falkland Islands, and/or members of their staffs. These are covered in Chapters 4 and 5.

1850, which was dug out of an antique bookshop by two brothers Richard[7] and Dermont Casey, who presented it to Captain Davis."[8]

Wilkins' Diary of the same year shows that he did go to Germany and returned to the United States in time to board the *Graf Zeppelin* round-the-world flight from Lakehurst on 8 August.[9] The airship flew to Germany, across Russia to Japan, to Los Angeles and returned to Lakehurst on 29 August. Away for three weeks the actual flying time was 12 days, 12 hours and 13 minutes!

Given the excellent publicity that Wilkins received for his earlier expeditions and the *Graf Zeppelin* flight and for his marriage to Australian actress Suzanne Bennett in August 1929, it is not surprising that Hearst was prepared to sponsor another Antarctic expedition, this one with Wilkins' name firmly in the title.

Helping to plan the Second Wilkins-Hearst Expedition, the American Geographical Society listed several topographical suggestions to assess, observe and describe. These included the "relative position of the east and west coasts of Graham Land". They also asked for photographs and topographical details of South Bay, Livingston Island, the southern part of Snow Island and the West and South East sides of Low Island, all located in the South Shetlands, as well as the West and North sides of Trinity Island, Charcot Bay, Larsen Channel, Biscoe Islands and Coronation and Powell Islands in the South Orkneys and their relation in size and location to Laurie Island.[10]

The Expedition left for Montevideo on 24 October 1929, aboard the Hektoria Whaling Company's transport ship *Melville*. This time Wilkins was accompanied by two pilots, Parker Cramer and

---

[7] R.G. Casey had been supporting Wilkins through the previous months in fundraising and his successful efforts to obtain the use of a Discovery Committee ship, *William Scoresby*.

[8] *Queenslander Illustrated Weekly* (Brisbane) 1 August 1929, p. 26.

[9] The airship *Graf Zeppelin* flew over a million miles on nearly 600 flights from 1928 to 1937, before it was retired following the Hindenburg disaster. From 1933 it provided passenger and mail service between Germany and Brazil.

[10] Suggestions by the American Geographical Society for the Wilkins-Hearst Antarctic Expedition 1929-1930, 26 September 1929, AGSNY AC 1. Box 269, Folder 9, AGSL, UWML.

Al Cheeseman, as well as Orval Porter, the aviation engineer from the previous Wilkins-Hearst expedition, and Vigo Holt, the wireless operator. The *New York Times* later reported that the party of aviators and explorers was "cruising about in the icy seas of the Antarctic aboard the research vessel, RRS *William Scoresby*, built specifically for the British Discovery Committee in 1925". The British Government had also contributed £10,000 to this expedition. Wilkins also had with him a caterpillar tractor and the first car taken to the Antarctic, an Austin Seven, one of Britain's automotive "Babies".[11] The car could be fitted with eight wheels for use when "crossing soft ground or deep snow" with the ability to fit a "caterpillar track" on four sprocket wheels if necessary.[12]

Fig. 2 Preparations for the season's work at Deception Island.[13]

---

[11] "'Babies' in Antarctic: Wilkins-Hearst Antarctic Radios", *Nelson Advocate* (New Zealand), 24 January 1930, p. 5.
[12] "'Baby' in Antarctic: Capt. Wilkins' Expedition", *Examiner* (Launceston), 12 February 1930, p. 4.
[13] Wilkins, "Further Antarctic Explorations", *Geographical Review*, 20:3 (1930) p. 359.

Discharging Austin car at Boasochen Bay, December 1929. National Library of Australia, George Rayner: P2249296.

In the Falkland Islands files (Sheet No.87) is a handwritten decoding of a "Very Secret" telegram dated 3 October, signed SofS (Secretary of State). Given Casey's comments to Prime Minister Bruce in his correspondence dated 11 April 1929, the telegram makes interesting reading: "His Majesty the King has issued to Sir Hubert Wilkins commission empowering him to take possession in the King's name of such hitherto unknown territories as may be observed in the course of his expedition between Falkland Islands and Ross Dependency."

However, with even more evidence of questioning whether the left hand knew what the right hand was doing, it appears that the Commission, very similar to the one for the previous expedition, was "signed with Our Royal Hand" on 21 August 1929. It was only communicated to Sir Hubert Wilkins in a letter dated 24 September 1929, from the Colonial Secretary, by which time Wilkins, with his pilots, had sailed from New York for Montevideo to start his 1929-1930 expedition. And thus, a flurry of Secret telegrams on how to contact Wilkins ensued!

An undated, handwritten note (Sheet No.88) with the printed heading "Draft Despatch From the Honourable the Colonial Secretary to His Excellency the Governor" appears to be an outline of how the Governor should report to the Colonial Secretary. The first line is "<u>Secret</u> <u>Type yourself</u>". It gives five points to be addressed, all of which then appear in the first report by Arnold Hodson, the Governor of the Falkland Islands, to the Secretary of State on 13 November 1929, and showing the first comments of some antipathy towards Wilkins. He reports that Wilkins arrived on the "floating factory *Melville*" on 6 November and left the following day for Deception Island. And that he was accompanied by two pilots, "one a Canadian and one an American, and an engineer. Neither of the pilots has been in the Antarctic before." He continues:

> For some reason unknown to me the third aeroplane mentioned in Section 5 of Sir Hubert's plans, ... has not been brought. I mention this matter to Your Lordship as it would appear to create a breach of the agreement under which Sir Hubert has received a grant of £10,000. From what I have heard of the machines stored at Deception Island I do not consider they will be able to perform the ambitious programme he wishes to undertake."[14]

This comment proved misguided as upon arrival at Deception Island:

> Our machines, which had been stored without attention or watchmen throughout the winter, were found to be in good shape. The wings were under cover but the bodies of the machines had remained out in the open. They had not been snowed under. The tail surfaces of one were partly covered with snow, which, melting in the early spring, had fractured a small part of the stabiliser. It took us but a few hours to make the slight repairs necessary and, after waiting for a spell of fine weather, to place the wings in position.[15]

---

[14] Sheet No. 89 Falkland Files.
[15] Wilkins, "Further Antarctic Explorations", *Geographical Review*, p. 357.

Preparations for the season's work at Deception Island. The planes after wintering in the open.[16]

Wilkins and his team spent several weeks at Deception Island preparing the planes but conditions were against them. They made some test flights but it was not until 12 December that they loaded one plane on the *William Scoresby* and started a search for ice suitable to fly from.

The Falkland Island files are silent until 23 November 1929, when there was a communication from the Whaling Officer, South Shetlands, to the Colonial Secretary, Stanley, reporting "CONFIDENTIAL My telegram 15th flights of 15 minutes duration were successfully carried out by both pilots yesterday afternoon. WHALING OFFICER." This was followed on 27 November by "When landing after test flight 25th November slight damage done to tail skid necessitating repairs which will take about 4 days to complete. WHALING OFFICER." And on 8 December 1929, "From "COMMANDING. WILLIAM SCORESBY. To COLONIAL SECRETARY, STANLEY." came the following message:

---
[16] Wilkins, p. 359.

PRIVATE. Both aeroplanes have now flown satisfactorily. One is now on board Scoresby with all necessary fuel and gear for flight to Ross Sea. Proceeding South 8th December if weather permits. Wilkins proposes flying to Ross Sea if good taking off ice field can be found, if not he will survey south of Graham's land using floats for landing. He cannot rise with full load using floats thus precluding long flight if flat ice field cannot be found by us. COMMANDING OFFICER. WILLIAM SCORESBY.

Wilkins records that on the way to Port Lockroy they "passed through the spectacular Neumayer Channel. Mountains reaching to ten thousand feet rise almost sheer from the water. About their sharp peaks is an almost constant whirl of snow. Halfway up their sides the massive cliffs are so steep that snow cannot cling to the surface."

Entrance to Neumayer Channel, OSU Box 37_3_29. Sir George Hubert Wilkins Papers, BPCRC, OSU. A black and white photo similar to this appeared as Fig. 10 "Further Antarctic Explorations", *Geographical Review*, p. 362.

Port Lockroy on the western side of Wiencke Island. OSU Box 37_3_54. Sir George Hubert Wilkins Papers, BPCRC, OSU. A black and white photo similar to this appeared as Fig. 13, "Further Antarctic Explorations", *Geographical Review*, p. 365

And lest anyone was left out of the messages the Whaling Officer confirmed on 10 December that "Scoresby left here noon G.M.T. in search of suitable place to commence trip". After a week of silence, the telegrams recommenced on 18 December 1929. The Commanding Officer led with:

> PRIVATE
>
> Have been South as far as Marguerite Bay off Alexander Island without finding taking off ground for aeroplane which could be reached owing to heavy pack ice. Wilkins has made one flight with floats over Graham's Land reporting Bescochen [Boasochen] Bay now suitable and moderately clear of Pack Ice. Am again attempting to make this.

While on the same date the Whaling Officer, South Shetlands reported:

After unsuccessful attempt to penetrate pack ice Scoresby returned to Port Lockroy 17th December. Taking off from water immediately on arrival at Port Lockroy Wilkins succeeded in locating flat ice suitable for starting place for Ross Sea Voyage. Crossing Graham's Land at 10,000 feet he verified last year's work. BRECHIN.

But on 29 December 1929, the Commanding Officer, *William Scoresby*, reported "Ice in Boasochen Bay proved unsuitable. Wilkins has made two flights from position 88 degrees South 75.5 degrees West over Charcotland Southward. I am proceeding North for flight from Adelaide Island."

On 5 January 1930, the Whaling Officer updated what was happening: "Scoresby arrived here (Deception Island) 2200 4 January. Wilkins has succeeded in adding about 300 miles new coast line to map besides verifying last year's observations."

William Scoresby in the ice, plane on aft deck, December 1929. George Rayner: P2249291 National Library of Australia.

Lowering Lockheed Vega Float Plane from Ship, Wilkins Hearst Expedition Port Lockroy, Antarctica, circa 1929 by George Rayner, Museums Victoria Collection: https//collections.museumsvictoria.com.au/items 394614

Then there was silence from the Whaling Officer and the Commanding Officer from 5 to 25 January, presumably as they stayed on the *William Scoresby* while she went to Port Stanley for fuel and provisions, returning via Grytviken in South Georgia. Wilkins and his team remained on Deception Island.

From the Wilkins' team viewpoint, we have Wilkins' Report "Further Antarctic Explorations".[17] Here he comments that when he first visited Deception Island in December 1919, "the ice on the water was six feet thick. In 1928, when we arrived on November 11, it was less than three feet. This year it was not even two feet thick, an unexpected condition that upset our calculations and made it necessary for us to fall back on our emergency plan".

The two Lockheed Vegas, *San Francisco* and *Los Angeles*, had

---

[17] Wilkins, "Further Antarctic Explorations", *Geographical Review*, pp. 357-391.

been left at Deception Island through the winter with the wings under cover but the bodies in the open. The only damage was a fracture on a small part of a stabiliser, which was quickly fixed, and as soon as there was fine weather the wings were attached. Using the Cletrac caterpillar tractor and the Austin Seven car they endeavoured to improve and enlarge the runway used the previous year. They made some test flights in mid-November but it became clear that the runway would not allow the fully-loaded plane to take off for the flight to the Ross Sea. They needed to head further south. One of the aircraft was loaded on board the *William Scoresby* and they were ready to leave to search for suitable areas, either along the coast or in the pack ice. But bad weather "held us prisoner in the harbor for two days". On 12 December they sailed and two days later reached Port Lockroy. They spent the next six days trying to find suitable sites but the "ice was extremely far south this season" and when they did find the edge "the ice surface was rough and broken, a condition that made it impossible even to land the machines from the deck. It was a great disappointment."

They did have two successful flights: on 27 and 29 December. Wilkins told the story in *The Times* in April 1930.[18] On the first they were fighting with the weather and the Lockheed plane "sprang from wave to wave like a hunted kangaroo. The pounding of the pontoons on the water sounded like artillery fire". On the second flight on 29 December, they took off and flew due south for 20 miles over scattered pack ice managing to get accurate bearings from Mt. Havre on Alexander Island and E. de Rothschild Island. Eighty minutes of flying got them to the north coast of Charcot Land, which revealed itself to be a large island. Wilkins dropped a flag and document proclaiming the land in the name of King George V.

Wilkins continued actively sending out news messages by radio. Many were picked up in Australia, often by perhaps unexpected publications. The *Casino and Kyogle Courier and North Coast Advertiser* of 4 January 1930, under the heading "New Antarctic Coastline – Wilkins Active", reported:

---

[18] "Flying in the Antarctic: Sir H. Wilkins's Exploit", *The Times* (London), 15 April 1930, p. 17.

Three hundred miles of coastline have been added to the maps of the world in the last days of 1929. The first attempt to penetrate the unknown region lying south of us was baulked by an impenetrable wall of falling snow. After going 200 miles we came within sight of Charcot Land, when we were forced to return with nothing accomplished, says Sir H. G. Wilkins, the Australian explorer, in a message from Deception Island.

The second attempt, however, met with complete success. We started with a small vessel, the William Scoresby, which hove to near the edge of the ice pack, 115 miles from the nearest land. Charcot Land was found to be an Island. We flew over Hearst Land and succeeded in charting the coast for 300 miles along the edge of the Antarctic Continent. We returned safely, but at the loss of a camera, as when lifting the aeroplane on board the vessel the sling broke, and the plane crashed into the sea, but it was only slightly damaged.

His report to *The Times* continued:

Far to the east we could see the western sides of two islands, one large and one small. They lie apparently between latitude 69.30 and 70.30. The large one seemed to be about 30 miles long, crossing latitude 70, in longitude between 68 and 69. These two new islands may be part of the group of which we saw the eastern-most last year and named the Finley Islands. We were too far away to chart them accurately. Near the two new islands and south of them we could see a few icebergs fast in the ice-shelf ... We judged that this shelf continues until it joins that part of Stefansson Strait which we crossed last year on our flight to Hearst Land.

Travelling further he described what they saw:

We could see the south-western termination of Charcot Land, which we discovered was an island. We could see it was shaped like a ham with the narrow end pointing south-west. At about latitude 70, longitude 76, south-west of Monique Peak, there is a sharp cape. I propose for this the name of Cape Byrd in honour of Admiral Byrd [Wilkins proposes later that the other cape he discovered on opposite sides of Charcot Island be named Cape Mawson, after Sir Douglas Mawson]. The western distance called us. In that direction lay the Ross Sea and our longed-for goal. But, because we could not find one clear mile of flat ice, we were not likely to be able to make that flight. We had really done quite a lot of exploration. We had seen three new islands, extended the coast of Hearst Land and Stefansson Strait a distance of 250 miles, and had outlined 150 miles of the coast of Charcot Land that had never before been seen; and we had discovered that it was not part of the mainland but an island ... A little more than four hours had been spent on the flight. With the last few tons of oil swishing about at the bottom of the tanks we headed the Scoresby northward ... At Deception Island we found everyone excited about an earthquake that had occurred two days before. A part of the harbour bottom near the beach had suddenly dropped 15ft., carrying with it the end of the wharf and a section for the light railway ... With the aid of our wireless we got permission from the Colonial Office for the Scoresby to visit the Falkland Islands to re-provision and re-fuel.

Wilkins and his pilots, engineer and radio operator must have had a break while *William Scoresby* visited Stanley and then called at Grytviken in South Georgia on the return voyage to Deception Island. Then:

Again leaving Deception Island on the William Scoresby on January 25, the expedition was able to pass south of Peter I Island, the pack ice lying about 20 miles south. In spite of heavy winds and seas, the edge of the pack was followed westward to about 69° 20′ S. and 100° E., when the vessel turned south. Here an attempt to fly south was frustrated by heavy snow squalls and a course along the edge of the pack was resumed to 70° 10′ S. Bad weather and failure of the radio made this position almost untenable, but finally on February 1 the plane was launched and a course set for the south. Flying through a snowstorm over scattered ice floes and sighting large icebergs which at first appeared to be land, the aviators penetrated to 73° S at 101° W. Here, although their range of vision was greatly limited by a heavy storm bank, no indications of land could be observed over an area where previously land had been thought to exist. Failing another break in the weather, the William

Scoresby turned towards Deception Island and continued her oceanographical research en route. At Deception Island a quick shift put the party on a Norwegian whaler bound for Montevideo, which was reached on February 22.[19]

By February 1930, Hearst and Bowman are in discussions about distributing the new Antarctic Map, produced by the American Geographical Society and drawn from Wilkins' observations, to schools. To accompany the map, a pamphlet would be made to describe the sources of the map, describing the flight, and how to interpret the results. The initial distribution was a minimum of 15,000 copies. Bowman clarified that a 'pamphlet' did not mean a "cheap contrivance that looks like a circular. I mean a well printed document somewhere between ten and sixteen pages long, with photographic and map illustrations".[20]

Wilkins' base at Deception Island was about 2,300 miles from that of Byrd at Little America on the Ross Sea. The two expeditions communicated with each other over the radio by way of San Francisco. Direct communication was impossible, Wilkins said, because "signals cannot be sent in a westerly direction in Antarctica. Intervening mountains probably interfere". He also said that his radio had worked perfectly nearly all the time he was in the Antarctic except when he wanted it most. The radio brought sad news when word arrived that (Carl) Ben Eielson, Wilkins' pilot on his two most historic flights, the crossing of the Arctic continent and the first flight in the Antarctic, was dead. The body of Eielson was found in February 1930, after his plane had disappeared on 9 November 1929 when flying from Alaska to the ice-bound Nanuk with Earl Borland. Eielson was found 200 ft from the fuselage of his wrecked plane, and 90 miles south-east of Cape North, Siberia. It was about 150 ft from where the body of his companion, Borland, had been found a week before.[21]

---

[19] Letter from Bowman to Ranck, 18 March 1930, AGSNY AC 1, Box 269, Folder 9, AGSL, UWML.
[20] Letter from Bowman to Ranck, 7 February 1930, AGSL, UWML.
[21] "Lieutenant Eielson: Body Found Buried in Snow", *The Times* (London), 23 February 1930.

The 1929-1930 Expedition saw the completion of one of the tasks Wilkins had set for himself in the Antarctic. This was the selection of numerous sites suitable for meteorological stations, which he believed could forecast weather conditions "more accurately than at present and avoid severe crop and cattle losses in South America and Australia".[22] The discoveries on this second Wilkins-Hearst expedition also "pushed back" the Antarctic continent about 8 degrees of latitude.[23]

Wilkins told the *New York Times* that the longest flight on this expedition lasted six hours and covered about 900 miles.[24] Although prone to embellishment, Wilkins had relayed that the flying conditions were the worst he had ever experienced in the Antarctic, and blinding snowstorms, and gales which reached a velocity of from 80 to 100 miles an hour, were common. Wilkins said that it was not unusual to be overtaken by such storms in the air and it was often impossible to land because of the rough and jagged ice. "There was nothing to do, but fight it out with the storm. Each storm was thrilling. There was more danger than I ever encountered before."

The *Sydney Morning Herald* of 24 February 1930, reported, citing news from New York dated 22 February, that:

> Sir Hubert Wilkins has arrived at Montevideo by 'plane with his pilot, Captain Cheeseman. They left the steamer Henrik Ibsen when about 125 miles from port, and completed the trip in little more than an hour. A reception was given for the explorer by the staffs of the United States and British Embassies and the Uruguayan authorities. The steamer is expected later in the day with other members of the expedition.

On the way home, at the end of this expedition, the two Lockheed Vega aeroplanes which had been stored at the N. Bugge Hektor Whaling Company on Deception Island and used on two expeditions, were sold to the Argentine Government. There was

---

[22] "Wilkins Returns. Quits Polar Flying", *New York Times*, 20 March 1930, p. 3.
[23] "Wilkins Arrives from Antarctic", [undated], AGSNY AC 1, Box 269, Folder 9, AGSL, UWML.
[24] "Wilkins Returns. Quits Polar Flying", *New York Times*, 20 March 1930, p. 3.

no need to bring the planes back because Wilkins announced, on arriving back from this second Wilkins-Hearst expedition, that he was "through with flying" in the Arctic or the Antarctic. He made this observation "casually amid a nonchalant discussion of his plan for a submarine voyage under the polar ice from Spitsbergen to Alaska". This interview, in the *New York Times* of 19 March 1930, also stated that Wilkins was due to arrive that day in New York from Montevideo, on the steamship *Eastern Prince* of the Furness Prince Line.

Fanefjord, soon to become *Wyatt Earp*. Courtesy Romsdalsmuseet, Norway.

6

1933-1934 THE FIRST ELLSWORTH TRANS-ANTARCTIC EXPEDITION. *WYATT EARP* ENTERS THE SCENE

Lincoln Ellsworth engaged Wilkins to find a ship, crew, a plane, stores and equipment and take all to the Antarctic so that he, Ellsworth, could fly across the continent. The plan for the flight was to fly from the Ross Sea across the continent and back. After lengthy preparations and one trial flight in 1934 the plane was damaged, the expedition was over.

After announcing he was giving up flying, Wilkins turned his attention to taking a submarine under the Arctic ice to the North Pole. He was already talking about this when interviewed by the *New York Times* in March 1930.

In the spring of 1930, Wilkins with Suzanne, as part of a delayed honeymoon, spent six weeks with Lincoln Ellsworth and his wife at Lenzburg Castle in Switzerland, which Ellsworth had inherited from his father. At that time Ellsworth agreed to support Wilkins' plans for a submarine expedition. He offered more than US$70,000, and with his backing, the expedition was officially named Wilkins-Ellsworth Trans-Arctic Expedition. Although reaching the Arctic ice pack, it was not successful and left Wilkins with very little money and a moral debt to Lincoln Ellsworth who had added an extra US$20,000 to his original support to help pay the crew at the end of the voyage.

Ellsworth was a wealthy man who had not only supported polar explorations but had also been on expeditions himself. He had travelled to the Arctic with Roald Amundsen, he had flown across the Arctic reaching 88° latitude, and in May 1926, he was co-leader of the Amundsen-Ellsworth-Nobile North Polar flight from Teller,

Alaska to King's Bay, Spitsbergen.[1] As a polar explorer, there was still only one "first" that needed to be achieved and that was to fly across the Antarctic continent. Wilkins agreed to take charge of this project. For Wilkins, this meant finding the right men and equipment, the support needed and a suitable vessel to provide the ship-based support. He also agreed to Ellsworth's constraints, including that all recognition for this expedition be focussed on Ellsworth, and that Wilkins would not have his photograph or name in any publicity material.

The planning for the first expedition, officially named the Ellsworth Trans-Antarctic Expedition started in 1930, almost certainly when Ellsworth and Wilkins were also putting together the plans for the Arctic submarine expedition. Indeed, Wilkins wrote to Dr Isaiah Bowman, the Director of the American Geographical Society, on 'Wilkins-Ellsworth Trans-Arctic Submarine Expedition' letterhead to edit the official press statement that he suggested should start with "Ellsworth will lead an expedition etc". In this press statement, the program for the Antarctic trip was carefully laid out including what was to be expected:

1. Plan as to ice conditions at specific points and specific months (e.g., November).
2. Secure for the expedition support at a given mid-way point at a given time.
3. Secure the assistance of whalers a year later than now planned and when they have already agreed to cooperate with the management of the Second International Polar Year.
4. Guarantee success by representing the United States in a meteorological program of international importance.
5. Limit cost of shipping by chartering one boat only in order to reach Coates Land, the entrance and exit on the Ross Sea side to be dependent on the cooperation of the whalers, a matter to be arranged through Sverdrup and others.
6. Get in and out in one season, the wintering of the second

---

[1] "Antarctic Wastes", *Daily News* (Perth), 19 April 1932, p. 5.

division being arranged to accommodate the meteorological and geological programs, which can only be carried with provision for more extended time.²

Two days after Ellsworth had drafted this outline, Bowman was trying to secure support from the Norwegian whaling ships so that the expedition could take place in 1932, during the Second International Polar Year.³ The goal for the Second International Polar Year was to investigate how observations in the polar regions could improve the accuracy of weather forecasts and the safety of air and sea transport. As part of this concerted effort, in which 44 countries took part, 27 weather observation stations were established in the Arctic but the Great Depression hampered efforts to erect further stations.

Initially there were thoughts that Ellsworth and Wilkins could use *Discovery* but a response came back that she was "as wide as a barn, [had]... a relatively blunt bow, and rolls on the slightest provocation" not to mention that she would have been expensive to refit.⁴ Bowman then wrote to Dr Harald Ulrik Sverdrup, Norwegian oceanographer and meteorologist who had been the scientific leader on the Wilkins-Ellsworth Trans-Arctic Submarine Expedition. Bowman appealed to him for advice because he had:

> the program of the Second International Polar Year very much at heart. It would be greatly to the advantage of this program to have a meteorological station maintained at Little America in 1932-1933 and to have the United States represented in the manner proposed, through the cooperation of Lincoln Ellsworth. May I ask what assurance you can obtain that the cooperation of the whaling companies will be forthcoming during the autumn of 1932? If they were willing to help the plans of the New Zealand government they would certainly be willing to help similar plans for an American station which would have the double purpose of satisfying the meteorological

---

² Ellsworth Papers, 7 March 1931, AC.1.Box 269, Folder 2 AGSNY, UWML.
³ The First International Polar Year took place in 1882-83 and carried out intensive research in polar regions in a coordinated international effort.
⁴ Letter. 18 July 1931, AGSNY, AC.1. Box 269, Folder 2.

progress and at the same time enable Lincoln Ellsworth in his flight from the Weddell Sea to reach an established base at the end of his flight on the Ross Sea as well as to reach the starting point of his flight on the Weddell Sea side. We have been in communication with Lars Christensen who is especially well disposed toward this Society and could be counted on to help; but he answered me from Cape Town that he could give no help in the autumn of 1931 because his whalers were not operating in that vicinity. This was to enable the expedition to get off this year. It is now thought that a delay of one year would greatly increase the chance of cooperation from the whalers and at the same time take a part of the work of the expedition as a contribution towards the completion of an international meteorological program.[5]

Sverdrup replied on 25 March 1931, having received a reply from the Association of Whaling Companies. He translated the message and relayed it to Bowman:

> We ask you already now to inform him that there in the season 1931-1932 [because of the production of whale oil] probably not will be sent any whalers to the Antarctic waters. At present we do not know whether or not the whaling industry will be resumed in 1932-33, but it is probable that this will be done at present it is very difficult to indicate which assistance Mr. Ellsworth can obtain from Norwegian whalers, but, considering the interest which the whaling companies always have shown such expeditions, we assume that Mr. Ellsworth can rely upon that he will receive the assistance which possibly can be rendered him, and on reasonable terms ... However, I may add that a postponement of the expedition to the year 1932-33 will not decrease the value as far as the co-operation in the plans for the Polar Year are concerned. This co-operation is supposed to take place between February 1931 and March 1933 – in the southern hemisphere.

This letter raised the possibility of hiring a ship and crew, for a relatively small sum, given that the whaling vessels would not be

---

[5] Ellsworth papers, 9 March 1931, AGSNY, AC.1. Box 269, Folder 2.

actively engaged in whaling during that period. In trying to solve the problem of no whaling support for the proposed expedition, Ellsworth asked confidentially, through Bowman, to polar scientist Gunnar Isachsen for advice on a fair price to charter or purchase a vessel. Bowman received a letter back from Isachsen proposing some solutions:

> As we know in Norway have no suitable wooden ship of sufficient size, the best advice is:
>
> A.1) To buy or charter Amundsen's "Maud" (now "Bay-Maud" of the Hudson Bay Co.) or [Byrd's] the "City of New York". Besides such a mother-ship, I consider it necessary:
>
> 2) to buy or charter a wooden ship of 200-300 tons burden, a steam sealer with sails. Such a ship may be bought in Norway for about L 5,000-/-.
>
> B.1) To buy one of our floating whaling factories which will not go out again because they are too small – 5 to 8000 tons d.w. Price will be, I think, about L10,000-/-.
>
> 2) Besides this a ship as under A.2).
>
> ... Captain Wisting [Norwegian Arctic explorer who accompanied Roald Amundsen], whom I have seen yesterday, agreed with me on what I have written above, was much interested to hear about the expedition, and he is willing to engage himself for the expedition.

Ellsworth, writing from Lenzburg Castle, his estate in Switzerland, proposed that the expedition be called "Ellsworth American Norwegian Antarctic Expedition"!

Bowman, who was clearly still trying to help organise a crew for the expedition, a ship and supplies, sent a telegram to Ellsworth on 14 July 1931, offering the services of an enthusiastic George Thorne, the surveyor who had accompanied Byrd on his Antarctic expedition in 1929, and Bernt Balchen, the Norwegian-born, later US citizen, aviator who accompanied Admiral Byrd on his flight to the South Pole in 1929. He suggested that they visit him at Lenzburg Castle to discuss plans further. Ellsworth replies "Prefer Thorne and Balchen do not come have no future plans and do not desire to be forced into any decision such as proposed meeting would do".[6] It seems Ellsworth was feeling pressured into arrangements and wanted to make the decisions himself.

Two days later, Ellsworth received unsolicited correspondence from a ship broker called A L Burbank & Co.:

> We note from the Norwegian papers that you are interested in the purchase of a vessel suitable for an expedition to the Ross Sea and take the liberty of placing the S.S. "ELEANOR BOLLING" before you for sale.
>
> You are undoubtedly aware of the splendid condition into which Admiral Byrd put this vessel before she proceeded on the Byrd Expedition ... they are willing to dispose of her at $28,000 with delivery St. Johns, Newfoundland.
>
> P.S. This vessel is extremely well fitted in every respect. She is sheeted for ice, has wireless and direction finder on board, together with a number of auxiliaries which are quite unusual on a boat of her size.

Although Ellsworth's response is not available, if indeed he did reply, we know that he did not accept this offer as it is *Fanefjord/Wyatt Earp* that was acquired in 1933 for this expedition. Things started to become clear for Ellsworth. He cabled, on 21 July 1931, having come up with a plan to invite Balchen and Thorne to visit. Then, two days later, he sends a message to Bowman asking him, confidentially, whether he thought Hearst newspapers would offer $50,000 for exclusive rights to the expedition content.[7]

The delay in finding a suitable vessel and crew meant the expedition could not leave as originally planned in 1932. It is in 1933 that Wilkins made a visible appearance in this particular

---

[6] During much of this time of letter-writing by Ellsworth, Wilkins was in the submarine *Nautilus,* travelling from New York in June to Devonport Royal Navy Dockyard in England and arriving in Bergen, Norway. They sailed from there on 5 August, arriving at the pack ice on 19 August and finally giving up on 4 September to return to Bergen.

[7] Letter from Ellsworth to Bowman, 23 July 1931, AGSNY, AC.1. Box 269, Folder 2.

expedition. He returned to Norway to look for a suitable vessel. He was adamant that it was to be a wooden vessel and entered into discussions with shipping companies. He found *Fanefjord* and entered into negotiations through an agent. The initial offer of 55,000 kroner was "simply laughed at"[8] considering the asking price was 75,000 kroner and the seller also wanted assurance for the sale otherwise it would be used for herring fishing in Iceland in August. An agreement was reached, over a number of hours between the owners and the agent, and the *Fanefjord* was purchased for 67,500 kroner (at the time the equivalent of US$12,000) with further negotiation to include the fishing gear and two boats and an initial settlement of 1,000 kroner. The agent finalised the sale with the words "Well, Sir Hubert, I wish that the "Fanefjord" may bring you continued good luck and that neither of us will ever regret that you have bought her".[9] It was hauled out of the water at Ålesund and inspected by representatives of the Norwegian Veritas, the Norwegian Ship Control and representatives of three ship building companies to make sure that it complied with Norwegian laws relating to vessels leaving for the polar regions. Many recommendations were made to ensure that the vessel was suitable. Over the next two months it was refitted and it was then that Wilkins realised that it had an old engine. The agent tried to reassure Wilkins that it had been rebuilt and modernised prior to being installed into the vessel and they even claimed, as Wilkins had assumed, that they thought it was new.

Also, it was during the refitting that it became known that Ellsworth had decided not to go in that year and that Wilkins had bought the boat on his "own responsibility and may find that I have the 'horse on my hands and no cart'". Consequently, it seemed obvious that the ship would be laid up for at least the next year. As a safety precaution, a watchman was hired to look after everything.

---

[8] Letter from Aksel Holm to Hubert Wilkins, OSU Box 15, Folder 15, Sir George Hubert Wilkins Papers, BPCRC, OSU.

[9] Letter from Aksel Holm to Hubert Wilkins, Sir George Hubert Wilkins Papers, BPCRC, OSU.

Fanefjord/Wyatt Earp. Bergen, July 1933. Courtesy Magnus Johannessen's photo album, Romsdalsmuseet, Norway.

The letterhead designed for the Expedition.[10]

Wilkins described the expedition's plans at an address to the annual dinner of the Explorers Club in New York. In part, he said, one of the main reasons for going was to make a flight that will be the "last big geographical discovery it is possible to make".[11] The plan was to base the ship on the Ross Sea side of the Antarctic continent, fly to the Wedell Sea and return without stopping, a distance of 3,000 miles, 1,300 of which have never "been seen by human eyes". It was described as a bold and daring plan and Wilkins told the 200

---

[10] Box PA2017.003.001, Folder 4. Sir George Hubert Wilkins Papers, BP-CRC, OSU.

[11] "Polar Flight Plan", *The Mercury* (Hobart), 8 March 1933, p. 5.

members at the dinner that a forced landing in the centre of the flight "would mean that the two fliers could not return to base safely without outside help".

The aeroplane to be used was the *Polar Star*. It was a Northrop all-metal low-winged monoplane, which was specifically built for the expedition. Northrop Corporation had verbally agreed with Balchen and the particulars were sent to Ellsworth in April 1932.[12] It took them four and a half months to build, weighed 3300 pounds and was equipped with a 500-horsepower Wasp engine, capable of 230 miles an hour and of lifting a load of nearly two tons. The price was quoted at $25,000.

> While Sir Hubert Wilkins is on shore studying meteorological conditions, the aviator Balchen, accompanied by Lincoln Ellsworth will essay a flight of 3000 miles over the uncharted Antarctic at the end of the year. The steamer Fana Fjord [*Wyatt Earp*] will take them to the edge of the ice. They will use an automatic camera, taking a shot every minute. Their aeroplane will be fitted with air brakes, which can reduce the speed of the machine to 23 miles an hour. At that speed they can land in case of emergency. The flight will occupy 20 hours, and the whole expedition a week, but the party will take sufficient provision to last them a whole winter in case of mishap.[13]

This was to be done by means of two Zeiss cameras for horizontal and oblique exposures and an aerial camera operated by a clock that could take a vertical picture every ten seconds throughout the journey and thus provide a continuous strip record of the route traversed. The cameras were supplied by Fairchild Aerial Camera Corporation at a cost of $1,625 and were mounted with the shock absorber cord around the rear part of the camera to hold it in place when not in use.

---

[12] Letter from Northrop Corporation to Lincoln Ellsworth, 27 April 1932, Box 15, Folder 15, BPCRC, OSU.
[13] "Sir H. Wilkins", *Maryborough Chronicle, Wide Bay and Burnett Advertiser*, 9 May 1933, p. 5.

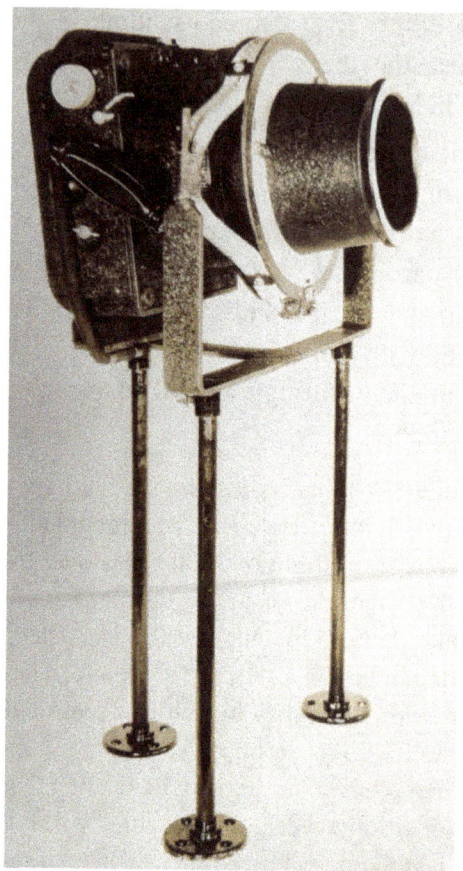

One of the cameras that was mounted in the plane.[14]

When it was clear that the expedition would not take place until 1933, Ellsworth wanted to ensure that he kept the skilled crew that had been selected for the expedition. It was in May 1932, a month after securing the contract with Northrop, that Ellsworth wrote to Balchen and offered him US$800 a month until after the plane was manufactured and then he was to be kept on a retaining fee of US$300 a month until practice flights were undertaken, when his salary would again be increased to US$800 (until the end of the expedition itself). This was on the condition that Balchen would not participate in "any unusual or hazardous flying".[15] It is in the

---

[14] Box 15 Folder 17, Sir George Hubert Wilkins Papers, BPCRC, OSU.
[15] Letter from Lincoln Ellsworth to Bernt Balchen, 12 May 1932, Box 15, Folder 15, Sir George Hubert Wilkins Papers, BPCRC, OSU.

same month that Richard Byrd wrote to Ellsworth as he felt that the depression had hit hard, and he didn't believe that the public would look favourably on two explorers going to the Antarctic unless Ellsworth could get "outside sources" for support. Byrd felt strongly that "it goes mightily against the grain to be in this competition with you" but he believed that "I must attempt to do this thing or give up entirely any further trip to the Antarctic ... I cannot go into all my reasons for the necessity of my doing in a letter. I just want to get this point over to you and want you to remember it".[16]

Ellsworth wanted to keep his private finances separate from those of the expedition and so he set up a Norwegian company for registration of the ship. This helped with the concerns the agent had about difficulties arising if it was transferred to another nationality.[17] Ellsworth renamed the ship *Wyatt Earp*, after his childhood hero, the legendary lawman whom he greatly admired. Wyatt Earp A/S Ltd, had ten thousand shares at one kroner per share issued with Aksel Holm, their shipping agent holding 6,000 shares, Ellsworth 3,000 shares and Wilkins 1,000 shares.

Initially, Wilkins was tasked with sailing the *Wyatt Earp,* to New Zealand. In April 1933, he again went to Norway from the United States, via London, "whence the expedition's ship is scheduled to leave for New Zealand about August 1. About November 1 she will leave New Zealand for her base, the Bay of Whales,[18] arriving about December 15".[19] The cost for the expedition was estimated at $139,931 (including the wages and all the ship expenses). Of this, $15,000 was to be recovered from the news agreement with *The Times*. The supplies that were reused from the *Nautilus*

---

[16] Letter from Richard Byrd to Lincoln Ellsworth, 21 May 1932.
[17] Letter from Aksel Holm to Hubert Wilkins [n.d.].
[18] The Bay of Whales was an ice harbour at the front of the Ross Sea. It was named by Shackleton in 1908. Amundsen had a base here in January 1911-February 1912. Byrd's Little America I was here in 1928-1930, while Little America II was close by in 1933-1935. The latter was used by Ellsworth and Hollick-Kenyon in 1936 (see Chapter 8). The Bay of Whales had disappeared entirely by 1987 when a 154 km iceberg broke off into the Ross Sea.
[19] "Sir Hubert Wilkins' Explorations", *Queensland Times*, 11 November 1933, p. 5.

were estimated at $15,550, and would otherwise have had to be purchased.

In July, Ellsworth received correspondence, presumably from Bowman, to say "I hear from Miller,[20] who saw quite a little of Wilkins in Ålesund, Norway, that Wilkins is in high spirits and that the ship is all that could be desired. I was so glad that Miller could get a look at the Wyatt Earp before she sailed". On 11 August 1933, Ellsworth reached New Zealand and there he waited for *Wyatt Earp* which had left Bergen, Norway, on July 30. On board *Wyatt Earp* with Wilkins was Bernt Balchen, the pilot, Dr Jørgen Holmboe, a meteorologist who was to make upper air observations and forecast flying conditions and the Captain, Baard Holth along with a crew of Norwegian whaling men. Wilkins was reporting the whole expedition by wireless for the *New York Times*.

Hubert Wilkins, in the front, second from right. On his right are Lincoln Ellsworth, Leader, and Bernt Balchen, Pilot with the Crew of *Wyatt Earp* in Dunedin Harbour, c. December 1933.[21]

---

[20] Possibly Osborn Maitland Miller, cartographer with the American Geographical Society.
[21] Members of the Ellsworth Expedition to Antarctica. Ref:1/2-112426-F. Courtesy Alexander Turnbull Library, Wellington, New Zealand./records.22807737.

En route to New Zealand, *Wyatt Earp* was delayed in Cape Town, as Bernt Balchen, the pilot, had appendicitis and needed an operation. When writing to Suzanne about the delay, Wilkins told her that he stayed in the operating room and assisted the doctor.

Much of Wilkins' correspondence highlights the purpose of the Second International Polar Year and pressed the need, as is common in his work, for meteorological research to obtain data for forecasting the weather weeks, or even months, in advance. This was one of the principal objectives of his polar exploration work and he referenced the "ravages of drought in South Africa, resulting in great loss of livestock and cereals".[22] Wilkins proposed a chain of meteorological stations linked with posts in the Arctic, the tropics and the Antarctic that were in daily radio communication with a central bureau where reports would be assembled and correlated, making long-distance weather forecasts possible.

From the ship, between Cape Town and Dunedin, in October 1933, Wilkins sent a radio message to congratulate Sir Charles Kingsford Smith on his record flight from England to Australia.

Wilkins had hoped he would make it to Australia as part of this expedition, by changing to a passenger ship at an intermediate port and rejoining the expedition at Dunedin. Consequently, the Australian Prime Minister, Joseph Lyons, had invited him to visit Canberra as the guest of the Government to attend a luncheon to be given in his honour. Lyons received a cablegram from Wilkins expressing appreciation of the Government's invitation but explaining that circumstances had arisen which now made it impossible for him to be in Australia during September.[23]

Wilkins sent a radiogram to Bowman on 8 November 1933, relaying the good news that the "plane ship and reliable crew will reach Ellsworth in good order and condition. Expect he will plan leave Dunedin about seventh December". *Wyatt Earp* had

---

[22] "Sir Hubert Wilkins", *Sydney Morning Herald*, 20 October 1933, p.17.
[23] "Sir Hubert Wilkins: Unable to Visit Canberra", *West Australian*, 9 September 1933, p.15.

encountered severe gales but Wilkins was able to deliver her safely to New Zealand. The ship had arrived on Thursday 8 November, but were asked by Ellsworth to stay out of the port until the following day, which did not go down well with the crew who had to wait another 24 hours after such a long journey. The journey to New Zealand had taken them 101 days. Ellsworth and his new wife, Marie Louise then met them at the harbour entrance. On 10 November the *Polar Star* was unloaded and overhauled before being stowed away again in the hold for the journey south. It was noted that *Wyatt Earp* was the smallest Antarctic expedition ship to visit New Zealand, even described by one correspondent as "a surprisingly small vessel on which to make the hazardous trip south from Dunedin, which port has gained some measure of world notoriety as the 'hopping off' place for Antarctic expeditions".[24] Bowman, on hearing of the safe arrival, sent a message to Ellsworth wishing him a "hearty congratulations". During the time the ship had been sailing from Norway, Ellsworth and Mary Louise had been honeymooning around New Zealand.

The ship headed south on 5 December, with Wilkins consoling a distraught Ellsworth who cried on leaving Mary Louise, and musing to Suzanne in a letter that Ellsworth had taken, for personal use, 40 bottles of whisky: "How he will consume it I don't know", and wrote that as a comparison, the boat crew of 15 men drank 2 bottles of whiskey in the 3 months it took them to get from Norway to New Zealand.

By 13 December 1933, *Wyatt Earp* had entered the pack ice as it headed to the Bay of Whales where they planned to establish the headquarters for the expedition. However, it was a slow voyage with pack ice holding them up.

---

[24] "Long Voyage Ended", *Evening Star* (Dunedin, New Zealand), 10 November 1933, p. 12.

ELLSWORTH'S SHIP CAUGHT IN PACK ICE

Wyatt Earp Two Hundred Miles from Open Sea

(Special to "The Daily News" by Mr. Lincoln Ellsworth, Copyright)

AT SEA, Dec. 17.

We are about 200 miles inside the great Polar ice-pack, held up by wide, heavy floes. Snow is driving up with a southwest wind and the whole pack is in motion. To be locked in there without means of propulsion would be a serious affair, but we expect that the wind and current will soon make rifts in the ice and leave lanes of open water, of which we may take advantage and proceed.

Our entry into the pack was sudden and dramatic; our only warning was a quick drop in the temperature to two degrees below freezing, and a light fog. Three hours later two huge icebergs loomed in sight, one to port and one to starboard. Fitting guardians they seemed to the realm of the ice king.

We passed between them, and two hours later, and 180 miles to the north of where Rear-Admiral Byrd found it in 1930, we entered the Polar pack, a world apart from the one we left, and where silence and desolation reign supreme. Lifeless and unfriendly it may seem, yet it holds a fascination all its own.

WORK CONTINUES

Amidst such surroundings men are drawn closer together, so within the four walls of our little ship there exists a comradeship that can make us forget the dreary outside. To work in these latitudes we must eat often, and we look forward to our mess every four hours, which brings us together from our work.

None on the exploring ship can afford to be idle. There are sledges to make, sewing to do, films to take, and everyone takes a turn at watch on deck.

Occasional ivory gulls, fulmar and black and white Antarctic petrels, are to be seen. Yesterday morning I saw the first sea crab-eater and last night Mr. Bernt Balchen shot one, which we had today for dinner.

COLORFUL SCENES

Notwithstanding the first impression, there is much color in Polar scenes, for drifting ice is tinged with yellow, red and green. The yellow is a microscopic vegetable matter known as Diatoms, and upon it the tiny red and green shrimp life feeds. The shrimp in turn is food for seals and whales. Interesting phenomena seen in these latitudes are iceblinks and water sky. Iceblinks are indicated by white or pale greyish streaks upon the clouds, while water sky is represented by a heavy streak of dull tarnished lead-grey color.

[25]

As soon as they arrived at the Bay of Whales, on 7 January 1934, they conducted a test flight and planned for another trial flight on 13 January to test the radio but disaster struck at 4.30 am.

After the trial flight the *Polar Star* had apparently been moored on what was thought to be firm ice. Later messages received by wireless from the expedition contained the startling news that on January 13 the ice had broken up suddenly in consequence of the wind, and that the ship had been cast adrift and the plane wrecked. It appears that when the break up occurred, the plane slipped through the crack in the ice, sustaining considerable damage. Fortunately,

---

[25] *Daily News* (Perth), 18 December 1933, p. 7.

the wings prevented the machine from sinking, and a party of ten men directed by Mr. Balchen succeeded in rescuing it, and re-embarking it on board the *Wyatt Earp*.[26]

Alongside the ice, *Polar Star* assembled and unloaded in the Bay of Whales, 1934. Courtesy Magnus Johannessen, Romsdalsmuseet, Norway.

The damaged *Polar Star*, Bay of Whales, January 1934. Courtesy Magnus Johannessen, Romsdalsmuseet, Norway.

The realisation dawned on the crew that repairs were needed and that the proposed Trans-Antarctic Flight must be postponed. Frustratingly, Wilkins believed it would only take ten days to repair

---

[26] "Ellsworth Antarctic Expedition, 1933-34", *Polar Record* 1:6 (1933) pp. 123-124.

but the expedition did not have the appropriate tools.[27] Having only taken one plane on the expedition, the main objective of the expedition was not possible, necessitating *Wyatt Earp*, and her crew, to return to New Zealand. Admiral Byrd, on board *Jacob Ruppert*, was also near the Bay of Whales and offered to lend Ellsworth one of his planes. It is unclear why Ellsworth or Wilkins were reluctant to accept. Writing on his way back to New Zealand, Ellsworth remarked that "It is tough to build dream castles only to have them shattered, but I am not dismayed, realising that success in these latitudes means a battle".[28]

Initially Ellsworth believed they could ship the plane to Los Angeles, have it repaired and then have it flown the 8,000 miles to Punta Arenas in Chile, on the Strait of Magellan, to pick up *Wyatt Earp* and reach winter quarters at Deception Island. This would have allowed them to try and fly from the Weddell Sea across Antarctica to the Ross Sea.[29] However, *Wyatt Earp* arrived back in Dunedin on 28 January 1934 and Ellsworth's feelings were palpable: "It was the bitterest moment of my life to come so near success and have it snatched from us at the last minute".[30] When Wilkins wrote back to Suzanne on 5 February, there is still uncertainty. "Ellsworth doesn't know what he wants to do or what he wants me to do except wait and it is uncertain that he will go on even if I wait for two months here so I am in a fix ... It is such a muddle. I wish he would make up his mind".[31] At the time Ellsworth said he wasn't sure if he should go back to Antarctica but his perseverance to conquer this last bastion continued for a few more seasons.

While that was playing out and while waiting for Ellsworth's decision, Wilkins arranged a series of lectures in New Zealand in

---

[27] "Ellsworth Expedition: Damage to Aeroplane", *Maryborough Chronicle, Wide Bay and Burnett Advertiser*, 30 January 1934, p. 5.
[28] "Dream-Castle Fades", *Herald* (Melbourne), 20 January 1934, p. 7.
[29] "Knights of Adventure Still Roam the Wide World", *Daily News* (Perth), 20 January 1934, p. 10.
[30] "How Ellsworth's Plane was Damaged: Ship at Dunedin", *Advertiser* (Adelaide), 30 January 1934, p. 14.
[31] Letter from Wilkins to Suzanne, 5 February 1934, Box PA2017.003.001, Folder 5, Sir George Hubert Wilkins Papers, BPCRC, OSU.

February and March 1934. He was not a person to either give up or sit down to wait and do nothing. By now he had learned a lot about Ellsworth and he was probably confident that there would be another expedition. Wilkins, despite often appearing as slightly shy did not back away from the limelight and he was used to lecturing to large groups so that a tour in New Zealand,to raise some money, was something he felt he could do.

Bernt Balchen (pilot), Lincoln Ellsworth and Sir Hubert Wilkins in Dunedin, New Zealand, 1933, at the start of the first Ellsworth Expedition. Courtesy Magnus Johannessen's photo album, Romsdalsmuseet, Norway

7

1934-1935 THE SECOND ELLSWORTH EXPEDITION. AND THE WEATHER DEFEATS THEM AGAIN, AND AGAIN

Wilkins set up a demanding schedule in New Zealand, raising funds by giving lectures and showing his films not only of the Antarctic but also of the Arctic and his submarine expedition. He briefly visited Adelaide. The plan for the flight was changed, to a one-way crossing from Deception Island to the Ross Sea. But the plane's engine was damaged, spare parts had to be obtained. Then the weather was too mild!

Lincoln Ellsworth's first Trans Antarctic Expedition finished unsuccessfully, with an unflyable plane. *Wyatt Earp* returned to Dunedin, New Zealand on 28 January 1934.

Unloading *Polar Star* in Dunedin, New Zealand, after the accident on the First Expedition, 1934. Courtesy Magnus Johannessen's photo album, Romsdalsmuseet, Norway.

The plane, *Polar Star*, was shipped back to the Northrop factory in America for repairs before being returned to Auckland, New Zealand. *Wyatt Earp* also needed maintenance and repairs to the engine, which were carried out in Dunedin, where she stayed until August. The gears had been badly worn by the effort of backing up and crashing forward against pack ice, trying to make a way through.

Ellsworth returned immediately to San Franciso on the luxury liner SS *Mariposa*, while Wilkins, still hoping to take another submarine under the Arctic ice, made a trip to England before returning to New Zealand, via Australia. But first, probably needing funds, he organised a whistle-stop tour mostly in the south of the North Island and in the South Island of New Zealand with a much advertised showing of "Personal Film Record of his Experiences in the Artic and Antarctic".

Appearing widely in many New Zealand newspapers, advertisements promised "THE PERSONAL APPEARANCE OF SIR HUBRT WILKINS ON THE STAGE", "More Than a Travel Picture – A Thrilling, Exciting Story of Amazing Events in the Far North and South – And as Timely as Today's Newspaper" and "See the Most Amazing Adventure of the Century – the Journey Under the Ice in the Submarine "NAUTILIUS". With more equally descriptive and exciting words – "Thrills above and beneath the Ice – The North Pole – The South Pole – Polar Bears – Eskimo – Walrus – Whales – The Famous Submarine "Nautilus – The Aeroplane "Southern Cross. 6,000 FEET OF EXCITEMENT!

Wilkins arrived in Christchurch on 27 February 1934, after spending most of that month organising his impressive and busy tour. Starting at St James's Theatre on 3 March, giving two shows daily for six days, it was a demanding schedule. Newspapers also reported other events that he included in his programme. In Timaru on 10 March, he gave a lecture at the Theatre Royal.

Papers of Elizabeth Chipman.

He met up with Sir Charles Kingsford Smith at Rongotai Aerodrome (now Wellington International Airport) on 14 March.[1] Several days later Sir Hubert was the guest at the Wellington Rotary Club luncheon and the same day the Wellington Philosophical Society entertained him at an "informal afternoon tea". On 27 March he addressed the Auckland Travel Club, and appeared at the Gisborne Opera House on 31 March. He then addressed the Palmerston Rotary Club on 9 April, and appeared in two performances at the Plaza Theatre in Stratford on 16 April. The following day, 17 April, he was guest at the Wanganui Rotary Club luncheon, followed by a Civic Reception at the Majestic Theatre that same day. He was interviewed in New Plymouth on 16 April, when he told the reporter he would be returning to Dunedin on 20 April, before leaving "on 5 May for the United States to see Lady Wilkins and thence to England".

New Zealand to New York in 16 days! That is all it would take said Sir Hubert Wilkins, who told a reporter that he would be leaving the country on 5 May for the United States and England. His ship would arrive in Los Angeles on 20 May, and he would be taking a trans-continental airlines flight and be in New York the next day. "And yet it takes two whole days," added the visitor, "to travel from one end of New Zealand to the other!"

Sir Hubert said that what he would do next was unclear until Mr. Lincoln Ellsworth announced his future plans. "If he decides to go to the Antarctic and needs me," said the explorer, "I shall no doubt return in August to take the Wyatt Earp to Valparaiso."[2]

On 8 July 1934, he left Croydon, near London, by air for Singapore, and it was reported he would fly from there to New Zealand.[3] It appears from other newspaper reports that when he

---

[1] Wilkins sold his plane *Detroiter*, used on his 1926 Arctic Expedition, to Charles Kingsford Smith and Charles Ulm who renamed it *Southern Cross*. In 1928 Kingsford Smith and Ulm made the first flight across the Pacific Ocean from California to Brisbane in that plane. Kingsford Smith died when his plane crashed into the sea off Burma in November 1935. Ulm died when his plane crashed into the Pacific Ocean in December 1934.

[2] "Explorer's Plans", *Dominion* (Wellington, New Zealand), 17 April 1934, p. 4.

[3] *Press* (Christchurch), 9 July 1934, p. 11.

arrived in Singapore he boarded the steamer *Mineroo*, arriving in Derby, Western Australia, on 27 July. He continued on that ship to Broome, from where he flew to Perth and then on to the Parafield Aerodrome in Adelaide. Wilkins spent only two hours in Adelaide with friends and relatives on his way to New Zealand to join the Ellsworth Antarctic Expedition. Still reverting to his favourite theme, Wilkins told a reporter from *The Mercury* (Hobart) of 2 August 1934 (p. 7) that he hopes:

> that investigations in the Antarctic may secure more certain weather information which may help to solve the problem of droughts in Australia. He will spend six or eight months in southern snows, compiling data, mapping and surveying, and learning all that is possible in this time, of the mysterious continent. Then he plans for another North Pole voyage.

Under the heading "Sir Hubert Wilkins – Meets His People in Two Hours' Stay", a home town newspaper described his very brief visit there:[4]

> Sir Hubert Wilkins, the South Australian explorer, spent two hours in Adelaide last week. He is on his way to the South Pole; and by train, ship and car, but mostly by plane. He is making a rushed trip to New Zealand to join the Ellsworth Antarctic expedition and, although it would have hastened his trip to have taken the direct route from Singapore, he came down south, instead, to see his people.
>
> Sir Hubert Wilkins will spend six or eight months in the south, compiling data, mapping and surveying. Then he has plans for another North Pole voyage.
>
> Last week, however, he forgot all these things for two hours. After nine years he was back in the land of his birth with his family. From Parafield aerodrome, where he landed after a flight from the West, Mr. Napier Birks drove him to the city, where five brothers and a sister were awaiting his arrival. Then they climbed to the top floor of a city café and exchanged memories over cups of tea.

---

[4] *Chronicle* (Adelaide), 9 August 1934, p. 41.

While in Adelaide Wilkins also managed to spend some time with Sir Douglas Mawson and they discussed Antarctic matters before Wilkins caught the express train to Melbourne. The *Sydney Morning Herald* of 7 August (p.9) reported that he would leave Sydney that day for New Zealand. Further it stated that yesterday (6 August), Wilkins was guest of Sir Edgeworth David "at luncheon at the University Club. Others present included the Chancellor of the University of Sydney (Sir William Cullen), the Commonwealth Official War Historian (Dr. Bean) and Father O'Leary of Riverview Observatory."

Wilkins travelled to Port Kembla, south of Sydney, where he boarded the *Port Nicholson*, which arrived in Timaru on 12 August 1934. "As soon as he left the ship, Sir Hubert Wilkins hurriedly caught a service car to Christchurch, being unable to outline his plans."

The plan for the forthcoming trip differed from the previous year. Instead of flying from the Ross Sea and back, Wilkins and Ellsworth decided to make a one-way flight in the other direction. *Wyatt Earp* would take the plane and crew to Deception Island. The ship would then head for the Bay of Whales, on the other side of the continent, to meet the fliers after their flight to 'Little America' on the Bay of Whales in the Ross Sea. This was a shorter route than the previous plan, so required less fuel. This in turn would allow them to carry extra supplies – a sledge, tent, more food and camping equipment.

Polar Star, now repaired, was loaded on *Wyatt Earp* in August and the ship visited Wellington to collect scientific equipment and Wilkins, who had returned from England and Australia. *Wyatt Earp* returned to Dunedin where Ellsworth embarked. They sailed for Deception Island on 19 September 1934, still chasing Ellsworth's dream to be the first to fly across the Antarctic. Wilkins was designated as Manager and Technical Assistant, with Ellsworth as Leader and Bernt Balchen again the pilot. The party included the doctor, radio operator, meteorologist and mechanic along with nine Norwegian crew again commanded by Captain Holth.

The 6,500 km voyage was never easy. This year it was particularly nasty. The weather, gales, blizzards and hurricanes, were extremely wild almost every day. The voyage took twenty-six days to reach Deception Island. The ordeal was not over as the worst weather, including exceptionally low visibility, hit *Wyatt Earp* as she approached the island. They eventually entered the harbour and arrived at the abandoned Norwegian whaling station, Port Forster, on 14 October 1934. Next day they were frozen in for five days with more rain, sleet and high winds. Nothing could be done to start assembling *Polar Star* until the weather improved. Eventually the plane was unloaded and dragged up the steep beach. On the evening of 29 October:

> They deemed it advisable to run the Wasp engine a little and after a half-turn of the propeller, there was a terrific jar and a loud snap as the engine stalled. The engine broke a connecting rod and despite boxes of spare parts taken along, none were included, though everything else was there.[5]

Organised by radio, spare rods were flown to the Chilean port of Magallanes.[6] Ellsworth and four others remained on Deception Island and Wilkins on *Wyatt Earp* left on 31 October, returning on 16 November with the required part. Australian newspapers kept a close eye on what Sir Hubert was doing in the Antarctic and with the heading "Ellsworth Plane Damaged" it was reported:

> VALPARISO. Nov. 7. – The antarctic exploring vessel Ellsworth, [sic *Wyatt Earp*] base ship for the expedition financed by Mr. Lincoln Ellsworth, arrived today at Magallanes (South Chile) from Deception Island.
>
> "We have come to get repairs to our plane, which was damaged during a south polar storm," said Sir Hubert Wilkins, the Australian explorer, who is co-operating in the expedition. "No one was hurt. Mr. Ellsworth remained at the island with Mr. Bert Balchen, the pilot, Dr Dama and two other explorers.

---

[5] Trish Burgess, *Wyatt Earp: The Little Ship with Many Names*, Connor Court, Brisbane, 2020, p. 26.

[6] The town of Punta Arenas was renamed Magallanes in 1927 but returned to its previous name in 1938.

We are remaining at Magallanes at least long enough to secure repairs and the needed fuel oil. We expect to continue our explorations until March next".[7]

They planned to use the snowfields on Deception Island for takeoff but during the time Wilkins was away they melted, exposing patches of rock. By the time the engine was repaired the weather was against them again. Fog and mild temperatures continued.

Wyatt Earp tied up at the former whaling station, Port Foster, in the harbour at Deception Island, October or November 1934. Courtesy Magnus Johannessen's photo album, Romsdalsmuseet, Norway.

On 27 November, *Polar Star* was reloaded on to *Wyatt Earp* and they sailed south searching for another area from which the plane could depart. They moored to the ice shelf at Snow Hill Island on 3 December 1934. On 18 December *Polar Star* made a short test flight and everything was ready for departure the following morning. Overnight, once again, the weather deteriorated. The flight was postponed. Another test flight was made and, again, on 31 December/1 January 1935 the weather was unsuitable for flying. On 3 January 1935, Ellsworth, with Balchen as pilot, made

---

[7] *West Australian* (Perth), 9 November 1934, p. 23.

a flight of 2 hours and 28 minutes, before the weather forced them to turn back.

Pack ice was beginning to close in and gales and blizzards made loading *Polar Star* on to *Wyatt Earp* impossible until 9 January 1935. Ellsworth was disappointed again, but he recalled in *Beyond Horizons* his thoughts on leaving Snow Hill Island: "Defeat by the weather I could accept philosophically and try again".[8] They started north but found the Antarctic Sound blocked with ice and had to wait in shelter for a northerly wind to clear the passage. Five days later and after some nasty experiences with wind, pack ice and cliffs *Wyatt Earp* stopped briefly in Hope Bay before arriving back at Deception Island on 20 January. *Polar Star* was dismantled and stowed below and on 21 January, disappointed, but well aware of the consequences of weather on their plans, *Wyatt Earp* sailed from Deception Island to Montevideo, Uruguay, arriving on 2 February 1935 where the aircraft was stored and the ship laid up. Ellsworth returned to New York via Buenos Aires and the west coast of the United States.

Wyatt Earp alongside ice at Snow Hill Island, December 1934. Courtesy Magnus Johannessen's photo album, Romsdalsmuseet, Norway.

---

[8] Lincoln Ellsworth, *Beyond Horizons*, Doubleday, Doran & Company Inc., New York, 1938, p. 291.

The Australian press recorded many short items about Sir Hubert (and Lady) Wilkins during 1935. The majority related to his plans to again take a submarine under the Arctic ice. Lady Wilkins' announcement that she would be going as cook made some headlines! But amongst these were notes to the effect that the couple were in Oslo en route to London on 27 June, where Sir Hubert was "recruiting for the Wyatt Earp expedition next winter".[9] Under the heading "SIR HUBERT WILKINS' PLANS, New York, July 24" it was reported that "Sir Hubert Wilkins who arrived here today from Germany en route to South Africa [South America?] to join the Antarctic expedition, gave further details of the plans for his submarine exploration to the North Polar Seas in 1937".[10] His long-held desire to establish meteorological stations around the world also received coverage in May that year when he gave a lengthy interview:

> Sir Hubert Wilkins, that Australian Polar explorer, passed through Toronto en route to Winnipeg last week. He said that he had two expeditions in view, one for an Antarctic flight, and the other for the establishment of meteorological stations in the Arctic regions. He interviewed air pilots here, and he will interview others in Western Canada with the view of finding two to accompany him and Mr. Lincoln Ellsworth on what may be the first non-stop 2,900 mile flight across the Antarctic continent. He said that he favoured Canadian pilots as they were the only ones with the possible exception of Russians with sufficient experience of flying in similar climatic conditions. The party would leave the United States early in October, and their plans would be practically the same as for the first attempt in 1933 when the plane was crushed in an ice fissure.
>
> The flight would be from the base in the Weddell Sea across the South Pole to the opposite side of the continent for the purpose of determining whether Antarctica was one continent.[11]

Funds from Wilkins' public lecture tour in New Zealand at the start of 1934 allowed him to make an around-the-world trip from New Zealand to the United States and on to England. Here he spent

---

[9] *News* (Adelaide), 28 June 1935, p. 5.
[10] *Central Queensland Herald* (Rockhampton), 1 August 1935, p. 57.
[11] *Australasian* (Melbourne), 11 May 1935, p. 43.

time trying to find another submarine suitable for another voyage to the Arctic. Ellsworth eventually asked Wilkins to "manage" his second expedition in *Wyatt Earp*. Wilkins returned to New Zealand, via Australia, where he spoke with several long-time Antarctic acquaintances. Perhaps it was from them or perhaps having the time to think about the planning but he was able to make a number of changes for this expedition, which could have proved successful had it not been for the weather. Both Ellsworth and Wilkins were well aware that they just had to accept this. Wilkins focussed on planning for another submarine trip and, as requested by Ellsworth, the third voyage in *Wyatt Earp*. In October 1935, the Third Wilkins-Ellsworth Antarctic Flight Expedition set forth.

Hubert Wilkins on board *Wyatt Earp* in Dunedin, 1934. Courtesy of Colin Monteath, Polar and Mountain Archive.

Wilkins with camera at Deception Island on board *Wyatt Earp*. Courtesy Olaf Dahl's photo album, Romsdalsmuseet, Norway.

8

1935-1936 THE THIRD ELLSWORTH EXPEDITION – SUCCESS! AND RESCUE!

Wilkins' support and management allowed Ellsworth, with Hollick-Kenyon, to be the first people to fly across the Antarctic Continent. When 'Polar Star' went missing Wilkins took Wyatt Earp to the Ross Sea participating in the rescue.

Before the Third Ellsworth Expedition could set off a new pilot had to be found. Having given up two years to Antarctic exploration, Bernt Balchen[1] resigned to go back to Norway and work in commercial flying. Wilkins found two pilots, both working for Canadian Airways, who agreed to join the expedition. Herbert Hollick-Kenyon (born in London, he moved to Canada with his parents when he was about 13), and J.H. Lymburner (from a farm in Ontario, Canada). Hollick-Kenyon joined the Canadian Army as a trooper in 1914 and then, in 1917, joined the Royal Flying Corps. He flew for Western Canada Airways from 1928. In 1937 he piloted Sir Hubert Wilkins' long-range aircraft for several months in the search for a missing Russian plane across Alaska, the Northwest Territories and to within 120 miles of the geographic North Pole.

In May 1935 Lincoln Ellsworth and his wife Marie Louse made their annual visit to Switzerland and then took the *Graf Zeppelin* airship to Rio de Janeiro. Marie Louise returned to the United States and Ellsworth boarded the Italian ship, *Augustus,* to Montevideo. Wilkins, *Wyatt Earp*, the plane *Polar Star* and the new pilots were awaiting his arrival. On 18 October, *Wyatt Earp* sailed from Montevideo to Magallanes, where she had been almost twelve

---

[1] In 1931 Balchen became a US citizen. He joined the US Air Force in 1941 and served until his retirement in 1956, but continued to serve on special assignments until his death in 1973. He and Wilkins became close friends over many years and much of Balchen's Air Force work related to work Wilkins did in Alaska.

months previously collecting the spare connecting rods for *Polar Star*! With a new captain, Captain Hartveg Olsen, *Wyatt Earp*, refuelled and with stores for two years, left port on 28 October, arriving five days later at Deception Island. Despite ice around the island and in the harbour they made it to Whalers Bay, on 4 November. Here the *Polar Star* was assembled and lashed to the deck.

On board *Wyatt Earp*, going South. Wilkins filming Ellsworth and the Meteorologist Jørgen Holmboe. Courtesy Harald Holmboe's photo album, Romsdalsmuseet, Norway.

On 11 November 1935, they left Deception Island for Dundee Island, off the north-east tip of the Antarctic Peninsula. They based themselves at the north-west end of Dundee Island, on a sheltered passage between that island and Joinville Island. They found an ideal site for takeoff – a gently sloping, snow-covered area more or less triangular in shape which offered a runway 1,200 feet long in each of three directions.[2] On 12 November. *Polar Star* was put over the side on to the sea ice and dragged half a mile to the shore. By 18 November, *Polar Star* was prepared, tested and ready for their third attempt to cross Antarctica. With good weather continuing,

---

[2] Kenneth J. Bertrand, 'Ellsworth's Transantarctic Flight' in *Americans in Antarctica 1775-1948*, American Geographical Society Special Publication No.39, New York, 1971, pp. 362-394.

exploratory flights took place on 20 November (3 hours and 11 minutes) and 21 November (10 hours and 27 minutes) around the Peninsula. With hopes high for the trans-Antarctic flight, 22 November was spent servicing, loading and checking *Polar Star*.

At 4.20 am local time, on 23 November 1935, THE flight took off from Dundee Island, with Lincoln Ellsworth, and Herbert Hollick-Kenyon as pilot. For detailed information on their flight read 'Ellsworth's Transantarctic Flight'.[3] Abridged from that are the following details. After taking off *Polar Star* headed southwest over the Prince Gustav Channel. Across the Weddell Sea they maintained an altitude of 7,500 feet and an indicated air speed of 126 mph. They crossed the Larsen Ice Shelf, went higher and were able to see glacier-filled valleys. They crossed George VI Sound and the English Coast and lost use of the radio (later determined to be a defective switch on the antenna lead). After 13 hours they decided to land as visibility was poor. They made camp and stayed for 19 hours. Before noon, on 24 November, they took off again but had to land after 30 minutes because of bad weather. Unable to fly they stayed there for three days and late on 27 November, were in the air once more with this flight lasting 50 minutes. They landed with just enough time to tie the plane down and pitch their tent before a blizzard hit them. Another three days passed including a storm, which nearly buried *Polar Star*. Days were spent clearing the snow from the plane. The engine was started on 3 December 1935, and then before takeoff another storm. It was 11.38 am on 4 December, when they managed to get airborne again. They took off towards the Bay of Whales. Four hours later they landed to check their position and fuel and stay the night. On 5 December, at 8.58 am they took off again, now only 150 miles from the Bay of Whales. A little over an hour later their fuel ran out and they glided to a landing at 10.03 am. They spent the rest of the day securing the plane and setting up camp. They were about 16 miles from 'Little America' but did not reach it until 15 December, after several false starts and returns to the plane. On 16 December Ellsworth (with a foot badly infected from frostbite) and Hollick-Kenyon settled in

---

[3] Bertrand, *Americans in Antarctica 1775-1948*, pp. 362-394.

to the relatively comfortable base to await *Wyatt Earp*, which they expected to arrive in the Bay of Whales, as had been planned, about a month later.

When *Polar Star* lost radio contact with *Wyatt Earp*, on 23 November, only eight hours after departure, two plans were put into action. George Deacon (later Sir George), then a scientist on the R.R.S. *Discovery II,* tells what happened in his "Report to the Royal Geographic Society" at a meeting of the Society on 9 January 1939:

> In spite of careful preparations, Ellsworth's flight was ambitious, and when his wireless messages ceased after eight hours' flying from the Weddell Sea towards the Ross Sea, there were graves fears for his safety. Sir Hubert Wilkins came northwards with Ellsworth's ship, the *Wyatt Earp*, to get another aeroplane from the United States, and the world's press rang with the news of a search for the missing fliers. It was then that the Australian Government approached the Governments of Great Britain and New Zealand with a view to assisting in the search, and the action taken was so swift that we were sailing from Melbourne with two aeroplanes, seven airmen, and three months' stores less than three weeks after we had received the first telegram at the ice-edge in 98°E.

As *Discovery II* raced to Melbourne to load extra stores, a small plane and other items needed for her dash to the Bay of Whales, Wilkins had already put his plan into action. Three days after constant efforts failed to contact *Polar Star*, he ordered *Wyatt Earp* to Deception Island and then to Magallanes. Mrs. Ellsworth, who was in contact with Wilkins by radio, was also organising a relief party. A plane was chartered to fly them to Magallanes but crashed in the US before it could leave. The Texaco Company offered another Northrop plane and it flew to Chile and it was loaded on *Wyatt Earp*, which sailed on 22 December for Charcot Island, in the Bellingshausen Sea, en route to the Ross Sea and the Bay of Whales. Supplies had previously been left here in case *Polar Star* had problems. Pack ice again impeded their progress and weather made it impossible for the plane to be used. After waiting several days Wilkins put *Wyatt Earp* on a course directly to the Bay of

Whales. She arrived on 19 January 1936, three days before she was expected under Ellsworth's original plan!

Discovery II reached the Bay of Whales at 9.30 pm on 15 January, several days before *Wyatt Earp*. George Deacon, in charge of the Scientists on the ship, describes the scene:

> Soon we were able to make out a tent on the top of the ice-cliffs ... To make sure that the two fliers, Ellsworth and his pilot, Hollick-Kenyon, were safe, Douglas and Murdoch flew over Admiral Byrd's old base camp at Little America, some 5 or 6 miles away. Soon after, Hollick-Kenyon came off, very fit and well, and we learned that Ellsworth was well except for an injured foot.[4]

Ellsworth was brought aboard *Discovery II* the following day and later that day, 17 January, the ship left the Bay for scientific work in the region north of The Barrier.[5] *Discovery II* returned to the Bay on 20 January, in company with *Wyatt Earp* now arrived on the scene. From on board *Discovery II*, F.D. Ommanney describes the *Wyatt Earp*:

> The little ship now forging southward through the ice after us bore the illustrious name of this legendary figure. We met her after a short scientific cruise in the Ross Sea. It was a cold, grey, foggy day and we could see through glasses, when she was still a long way off, the words 'Ellsworth Expedition' blazoned in huge white letters on her black sides. She was a sealer and had a stout wooden hull, a fine, sturdy little ship. Her diesel engine shot upwards little sharp puffs of smoke from her funnel and amidships she carried the *Texaco 20*, a Northrop monoplane, which also wore its name in huge letters on its fuselage.[6]

---

[4] G.F.R. Deacon, "The Antarctic Voyages of R.R.S. *Discovery II* and *R.R.S. William Scoresby*, 1935-37", *Geographical Journal* 93:3 (1939) p. 190.

[5] 'The Barrier' is the Ross Ice Shelf, the largest area of floating ice in the Antarctic. Originally called 'The Barrier' as it barred ships sailing further south. Currently (2024) it is about 970 miles long and 500 miles wide. The ice above sea level varies in height from 15 meters to over 50 meters. It was discovered in 1841 by Captain James Clarke Ross.

[6] F.D. Ommanney, *South Latitude*, Longmans Green & Co, London, 1938, p. 211.

On the night of 21 January, *Discovery II* gave a farewell dinner to those on board *Wyatt Earp* and sailed very early the next day, at 12.40 am (almost 24-hour daylight in January). Lincoln Ellsworth decided to return to Australia on *Discovery II*. Some scientific work, landings and surveys, in the Balleny Islands, were conducted en route. They arrived in Melbourne on 16 February 1936. All the Melbourne, and many other Australian, newspapers carried stories of the successful mission with headlines such as 'Epic Battle in Icy Wastes', 'Month in Hut Under the Snow', and 'Thousands Greet Ship'. *The Herald* on 17 February (p.1) had stories on several pages as well as a full-page spread of photographs:

> The Royal Research ship *Discovery* II, flying the American flag from her track and the flag of the Falkland Islands from her stern, berthed at Nelson Pier, Williamstown, at 10 am today, bringing with her Lincoln Ellsworth, the American aviator-explorer of the Antarctic and members of the R.A.A.F. detachment who rescued him from Little America.

And on page 2 of the same paper:

> Australia's welcome to Lincoln Ellsworth was extended officially by the Minister for Defence (Mr. Parkhill), representatives of the State Government, the Services, the University, learned societies and leaders of former Commonwealth expeditions to Antarctica.
>
> Thousands of people, including the pupils of local schools, surged round the barricades placed on the ramps and ... leading to Nelson Pier, and the impatience with the police control that barred them from the official enclosure, from which the addresses of welcome were broadcast, broke down when the explorer came into view on the bridge of the *Discovery*.
>
> When *Discovery* tied up, crowds boarded her, despite the rule of the service which debars visitors unless by special invitation, and the crew were embarrassed in their shore tasks.

Sir Douglas Mawson came from Adelaide to welcome Ellsworth and Captain John King Davis, Captain of Mawson's 1911-14 expedition ship *Aurora*, looked after Ellsworth during his stay in Melbourne. On 20 February Ellsworth flew to Canberra where he was welcomed by the Prime Minister, Joseph Lyons, and the Minister for External Affairs, Sir George Pearce, at a luncheon given by the Commonwealth Government at Parliament House. This probably turned out to be a useful occasion for Ellsworth, as Lyons was still Prime Minister in February 1939, when Ellsworth and Wilkins were intent on selling *Wyatt Earp* to the Australian Government!

Back in the Ross Sea, Ellsworth's pilot Hollick-Kenyon joined *Wyatt Earp* with the hope that *Polar Star* could be salvaged. Wilkins and the crew managed to get one of Byrd's abandoned tractors going and took a load of fuel to the plane. It was flown to the Bay of Whales and loaded back on *Wyatt Earp*. Wilkins remained on board and the "List or Manifest of Aliens Employed on the Vessel as Members of Crew" provided to authorities on arrival in New York, shows him listed as "Purser". The Manifest shows Captain Hartvig Olsen to be the oldest man on board at 48, with Wilkins a year younger at 47! The ship left the Bay of Whales on 30 January 1936, via Valparaiso (12 March), Port of Balboa (30 March) on the Pacific end of the Panama Canal, and arrived in New York on 19 April. Ellsworth, having sailed from Australia on the *Mariposa* was there to greet the ship. *Wyatt Earp* stayed in New York until 17 June when she left for England, arriving in Barrow on 8 July.

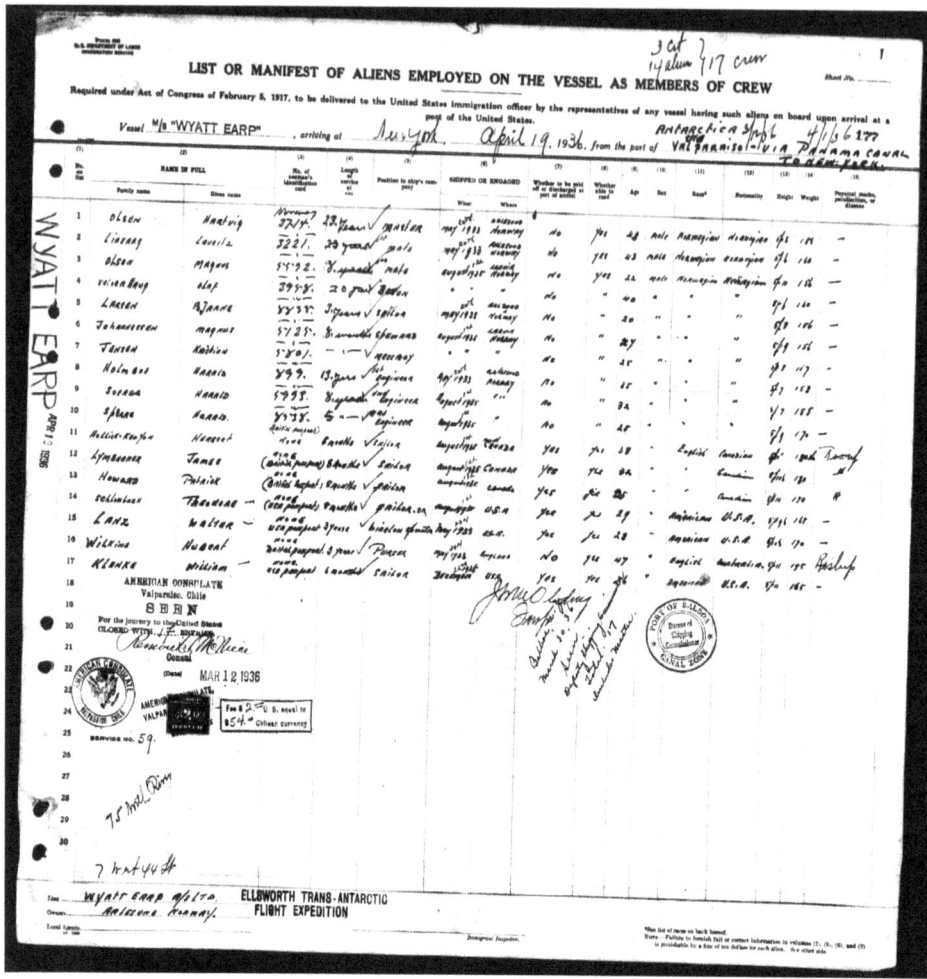

The National Archives in Washington, DC; USA; *Passenger and Crew Lists of Vessels Arriving at New York, 1987-1957*; Microfilm Serial or NAID: T715; RG Title: *Records of the Immigration and Naturalization Service, 1787-2004*; RG: 85.

The Flying Inn, by G.K. Chesterton, was taken from 'Little America' in January 1936. It is signed by Lincoln Ellsworth, Herbert Hollick-Kenyon and Sir Hubert Wilkins. More details are shown on the inserted note shown opposite on 'Discovery Expedition' letterhead. (Trish Burgess personal papers.)

Lincoln Ellsworth
Bay of Whales
16 Jan. 1936.

Discovery II 16 Jan to 17 Feb.

Hollick Kenyon

Little America Dec 15 1935 to Jan 16 1936

Hubert Wilkins

This book was taken from the hut at 'Little America' (Admiral Byrd's Base Camp at the Bay of Whales) in which Lincoln Ellsworth and his pilot Hollick Kenyon lived from the 15th December 1935 to the 16th January 1936 after their successful Trans-Antarctic Flight of 2,300 miles, and until the arrival of the Royal Research Ship "Discovery II" which had gone to their relief.

The signatures are those of:-
    Lincoln Ellsworth.
    Hollick Kenyon.
    Sir Hubert Wilkins.

71.45 S. 177.42 W. *Discovery II* in the Ross Sea when searching for Ellsworth and Kenyon. Personal papers Trish Burgess.

Discovery II in the ice, probably in the Bay of Whales when searching for Ellsworth and Kenyon. Personal papers Trish Burgess.

9

1938-1939 THE FOURTH ELLSWORTH ANTARCTIC EXPEDITION – CLAIMING LAND

The final voyage of Ellsworth and Wilkins on the 'Wyatt Earp' – taking a different approach to the Antarctic and both claiming land for their respective countries.

Once again Casey is seen supporting Wilkins. In June 1938 the then Australian "Treasurer (Mr. Casey) said to-day that Sir Hubert Wilkins may lead an aerial expedition covering some part of the Australian section of Antarctica during the coming season."[1] He continued:

> On Tuesday, Cabinet will deal with a proposal that an Australian expedition should go the Antarctic to consolidate Australia's position.
>
> Several Ministers believe that Australia's claim to this territory will be enhanced by an expedition whether by air or sea.

Casey followed this with further comment at the end of August under the heading "Ingenious Plane to be Used":

> Plans for a visit to Antarctic by Sir Hubert Wilkins who will arrive in Sydney on September 5 from America were indicated to-day by the Commonwealth Treasurer (Mr. Casey), who was associated with Sir Hubert Wilkins in connection with the former expedition.
>
> Mr. Casey said that he understood that Sir Hubert Wilkins planned to travel to Capetown, whence he would proceed to about 80 degrees east longitude, and passing through the pack ice, follow westward along the coast with the hope of finding a point where he could land his Northrop Delta plane.
>
> The machine was an ingenious one, said Mr. Casey. It

---

[1] *Canberra Times*, 25 June 1938, p. 1.

could be used on wheels, skis or on floats as circumstances required.²

This became the final trip by Ellsworth and Wilkins on the *Wyatt Earp* and it was different to the previous three. With war looking inevitable and Ellsworth lacking a real purpose in his life, he still wanted to fly across the Antarctic continent via the South Pole. He was persuaded by Wilkins to focus his attention on American interests in the Indian Ocean sector of the Antarctic. Having spent some time in the Arctic searching for missing Russian fliers, Wilkins' reputation and his appeal to newspaper readers had risen again. Ellsworth was unhappy with this. As in his three previous expeditions, however, he asked Wilkins to organise the journey and he financed it, the last Antarctic expedition of any country to be funded entirely by private money. First in Norway, then in Cape Town, Wilkins did what was asked of him. He organised the Expedition, while Ellsworth spent five weeks on safari in Kenya!

The official plan for this voyage was:

> To launch a number of triangular flights into the Indian Ocean sector of Antarctica, an area of 750,000 square miles, the interior of which was then practically unknown. Of secondary importance, only because it was less certain of achievement, was Ellsworth's plan for a second transcontinental flight. If ice conditions allowed them an early start and if weather permitted, he hoped to fly from the Indian Ocean sector over the South Pole to the Bay of Whales, a distance of approximately 2,000 miles. Here he and his pilot would wait until the *Wyatt Earp* picked them up later in the season.³

Wyatt Earp had been berthed at Ålesund in Norway, her home port, following Ellsworth's third expedition. In May 1938, Wilkins visited the ship to arrange for the necessary maintenance for the forthcoming voyage and to obtain a new crew. Once again all were Norwegian whaling men with Antarctic experience. The Captain, Londer Johansen, had been a gunner and captain of a whale catcher

---

² *Canberra Times*, 31 August 1938, p. 4.
³ Kenneth J. Bertrand, 'The Ellsworth Antarctic Expedition, 1938-1939' in *Americans in Antarctica, 1755-1948*, p. 395.

in the Antarctic. Several of the crew had been on previous Ellsworth expeditions. J.H. Lymburner, reserve pilot on the previous voyage joined as chief pilot and Wilkins was again Technical Adviser and Manager. On this trip Ellsworth was titled Organiser, Leader and Aerial Navigator.

After her refit *Wyatt Earp* returned, on 12 August 1938, to New York from Norway, to the Floyd Bennett Field seaplane base in Brooklyn. Stores were loaded as well as two aircraft, a Northrop 'Delta 1D' and a smaller Aeronca Model K, a two-seater scouting plane. Both planes had wheels, pontoons and skis and two-way radios giving them alternatives for takeoff and landing options and better communications than on previous expeditions. *Wyatt Earp* sailed on 16 August for Cape Town, via Pernambuco, Brazil. Ellsworth joined the ship in Cape Town, from his hunting trip in Kenya.

Being away from New York, home to his wife Suzanne, much more than he was there, Wilkins took the opportunity to take his wife to Australia, and they arrived in Sydney on the SS *Monterey* on 6 September 1938. The following day *The Sun* (Sydney), reported on page 3:

> Many of Sydney's leading public men, including the Minister for External Affairs (Mr. W.M. Hughes) were present at a luncheon "welcome and farewell" to Sir Hubert Wilkins at the Hotel Australia to-day. Guests of Mr. E. Allan Box, a personal friend of Sir Hubert, they wished him "god-speed" on his adventurous trip to the South Pole. Sir Hubert left for Melbourne this afternoon by the Monterey.

William Hodgson (Lieutenant Colonel, who served at Gallipoli), then Secretary of the Department of External Affairs, came from Canberra to meet with Wilkins. "... they had a serious discussion regarding Antarctic. Mr. Hodgson gave Sir Hubert charts of the Australian Sector prepared from the latest information from all sources."[4] Department of External Affairs files record a letter from Hodgson to Wilkins, dated 22 September and addressed to

---

[4] "Southward Ho! Sir Hubert Wilkins, Polar Explorer", *Sydney Mail*, 14 September 1938, p. 10.

him at the Menzies Hotel, Melbourne, in which he refers to his conversation with Wilkins of 5 [sic 6?] September and Wilkins' "interview with the Minister for External Affairs (W.M. Hughes) on 6th September".[5] Attached to this is a copy of a letter to Captain Sir Hubert Wilkins M.C., dated 8 September which says:

> You are hereby authorised to enter upon, explore and report upon that part of the territory in the Antarctic Seas which comprises the islands and territories, other than Adelie Land, situated south of the 60th degree South Latitude, and lying between the 160th degree East Longitude and the 45th degree East Longitude, which territory has been accepted by the Commonwealth of Australia as a Territory under the authority of the Commonwealth. (Sd.) W.M. HUGHES. MINISTER FOR EXTERNAL AFFAIRS.

Hodgson's letter explains it is not necessary for Wilkins "to perform such as acts…as the hoisting of the Australian flag and the reading of proclamations" and gives the reasons. He says:

> The interests of the Commonwealth can best be furthered by the Minister, who is in charge of the administration of the Antarctic Territory Acceptance Act, issuing to you a general authority to enter upon, explore and report on the Australian Antarctic Territory. In other words you are given official status as a representative of the Commonwealth Government to carry out work which would demonstrate that the Commonwealth Government has not been content merely to make a formal claim to territory in the Antarctic, but has taken action to enhance the probability of international recognition of that claim by the exercise of additional acts of sovereignty over the territory.

Sir Hubert and Lady Wilkins arrived in Adelaide by train from Melbourne on 16 September 1938, on Wilkins second visit there since 1925. They were met at the station by his brothers, Tom and Fred, and Sir Douglas Mawson. The family gathered at dinner that night where Wilkins also saw his brothers Harry and Frank

---

[5] Document 1-BB-AU-791, Antarctic Documents Database, Special Collections, University of Tasmania.

and sister Mrs. J.H. Cockshell. He drove out into the country, to Burra, Mount Bryan and Hallett, places that figured largely in his childhood. He addressed a luncheon at the Commonwealth Club on 20 September, highlighting once again his never-ending wish for weather observation bases in the Antarctic. Four days later they sailed on the SS *Anchises* to Durban, from where Wilkins flew to Cape Town.

About this time the State Department of the United States of America decided that they should start claiming land in the Antarctic. Unknown to Wilkins, the American Consul in Cape Town asked Ellsworth to claim any unexplored land for the United States, whether or not it lay in territory already claimed by another country! Ellsworth, in a face-to-face meeting with the Consul, was told that the American government's role must remain secret and that it would not admit to being involved should it become known. "Ellsworth was not even given a copy of the instructions for fear they may become known to a foreigner. It is clear they meant Wilkins, for the land in question had already been claimed by Australia."[6] Ellsworth was apparently enthusiastic despite knowing Wilkins regarded their proposed destination as Australian-claimed territory. In fact, in relation to Ellsworth, Wilkins stated:

> Before leaving New York he had published a statement (which I had helped to prepare) in which it was said that he would not while on this expedition claim any land. He left New York with a definite understanding with me that he would make only one flight of not more than 500 miles inland from the coast of the Antarctic, starting from some point near Enderby Land and would leave the coast on the return journey not later than January 15th, 1939.[7]

The Fourth Ellsworth Expedition sailed from Cape Town at noon on 29 October 1938, for the Kerguelen Islands. Just over two weeks later, after worse than normal rough weather was encountered in the

---

[6] Simon Nasht, *The Last Explorer*, p. 271.
[7] Wilkins, "Report of the Ellsworth Antarctic Flight Expedition, 1938-39" to the Australian Minister for External Affairs dated 6 February 1939, National Archives of Australia A 1838 1495/1 ANNEX D, p. 2.

'Roaring Forties', *Wyatt Earp* moored in Royal Sound. Three days were spent here while work was done on the engine and the fresh water tanks were filled. Fuel oil that had been carried on deck was transferred to the bunkers in the expectation of even heavier seas and storms. Plenty of rabbits, teal (ducks) and even some Ross seals were added to the food supplies. Despite the relatively sheltered harbour, several gales hit them with snow and winds of more than 60 miles per hour. Both anchors and three heavy mooring lines, both bow and stern, were required. On 17 November *Wyatt Earp* left the Kerguelen Islands for Heard Island but three days of still more severe weather made it impossible to land there. On 20 November *Wyatt Earp* reached the edge of the pack ice, meeting it much further north than expected. It took 45 days to pass through this 800-mile-wide barrier, sometimes drifting with the pack, sometimes making no progress at all. During one drifting phase, two hardwood planks were found missing from the outer sheathing on the bow, ripped off by the ice. The Norwegian crew knew what to do and how to do it, even on a 400-ton ship at sea in the Antarctic:

> With a sling about a heavy mass of ice and a block and tackle to the mast head, the ship was careened, and by shifting oil and supplies from one side of the ship to the other we brought the damaged part above the water line and undertook repairs.
>
> Standing on a convenient ice floe the carpenter chiseled out the damaged parts and fitted in new planks and now the ship is as sound as she was when we entered the ice.[8]

Finally on 1 January 1939, they reached the Antarctic coast – well almost. The details of what occurred over the next 10 days were recorded on the spot by Wilkins in the Meteorological Log which was kept on board the *Wyatt Earp*. On the voyage from the Antarctic and/or immediately on return to Hobart he also wrote, for the Australian Government, the "Report of the Ellsworth Antarctic Flight Expedition, 1938-39".[9] The ship arrived in Hobart on 4 February. The Report is dated 6 February 1939. Further and differing

---

[8] In Kenneth J. Bertrand, "Ellsworth's Transantarctic Flight" in *Americans in Antarctica 1775-1948,* p.400, from *New York Times*, January 3 1939, p. 5.

[9] Australian Archives, A1838, 1495/1 ANNEX D, p. 6.

details can also be found in "The Ellsworth Antarctic Expedition" article.[10] And they are particularly confusing when comparing dates and or landing places. More information has come to light in 2024 regarding landing sites and this is recorded later in this chapter.

According to the Meteorological Log[11] Lymburner, the pilot, in the Aeronca made a scouting flight after which the ship had a "lay to" for New Year's Day lunch. On 3 January they were able to moor the ship against the ice in Prydz Bay and two short scouting flights were made. There was plenty of ice that looked good for the plane to use for takeoff, but it was only one year old and Wilkins worried it would not take the weight of the Northrop Delta plane. Ever hopeful, on 4 January, the plane was brought on deck and assembly began.

Reconnaissance flight in the Aeronca. Courtesy Oluf Dahl's photo album, Romsdalsmuseet, Norway.

The ship steamed among the many small islands in the area (both Rauer and Svenner groups), and sometimes drifted with the ice and sometimes was moored to it. All the time they searched for areas suitable for the larger plane, the Northrop, to take off. They needed the right site and the right weather before a flight could take place.

---

[10] Kenneth J. Bertrand, "The Ellsworth Antarctic Expedition, 1938-1939", pp. 400-403.

[11] Transcript of Meteorological Log. Sir George Hubert Wilkins Papers, BP-CRC, OSU.

Wyatt Earp moored to the ice with both planes on deck and an inquisitive visitor. Courtesy Oluf Dahl's photo album, Romsdalsmuseet, Norway.

Ellsworth, Wilkins, Lymburner and, at least, the First Mate Liavaag, all landed on several islands and collected geological specimens. *Wyatt Earp* moved to the Rauer Islands and on 5 January, was moored to level ice which, with nearby islands, made a protected harbour. About 200 yards from the ship was a huge, grounded iceberg, broken off from a nearby glacier tongue. Ellsworth decided to try the ice for takeoff calling it "the only possible flying field in this vicinity". The big plane assembled on deck was now made ready for flight but as they prepared to lift her from the ship on to the ice the weather turned against them. Both planes were secured.

On 7 January the weather was still not good enough for flying. Early that morning they became alarmed when the big iceberg, presumed grounded, began moving, threatening the ship. *Wyatt Earp* moved urgently astern, away from possible disaster. Ellsworth could no longer keep his secret and told Wilkins that he intended to set foot on and claim the land Mawson had only seen from the coast. This put Wilkins in a difficult position as a paid adviser to Ellsworth – but he also had loyalty to his own country. And he too had a secret! He had his own instructions from the Australian

Government. In Wilkins "Report of the Ellsworth Antarctic Flight Expedition, 1938-39"[12] to the Australian Government he tells how he achieved Australia's claims:

> January 8th. With Pilot J.H. Lymburner as a witness I landed on the northernmost island of the group marked as Rauer on Lars Christensen's chart. It is the highest of the Group and near the highest part at the southern end close to the topmost nest of a penguin rookery, I flew the flag of the Commonwealth of Australia and then deposited the flag and a record of the visit in a small aluminium container.
>
> The container is placed at the foot of a rock about three feet high and covered with small stones. A small cairn of stones was erected about 25 yards to the southward of the deposit.[13]

Ellsworth meanwhile had to wait until he could fly inland. Still waiting for suitable flying conditions, they had to move again on 9 January as a large and heavy ice floe was forced upon them by several icebergs. The new mooring had no suitable flying area, weather conditions were not good enough and more waiting ensued. Waiting time allowed Wilkins, Ellsworth and Lymburner to make another landing:[14]

> Landing in first bay to northeast of glaciers edge. I climbed to second highest peak south of landing place and deposited in a hole in a weathered boulder due south from a large isolated boulder and south of a fractured collection of rocks which resembles a small tumble down hut a record and a small Australian flag in an aluminium container. The huge, isolated boulder is conspicuous from the sea near shore. The hole in which the record is placed is plugged by a small round rock about 4 inches in diameter. I made some pick axe marks beside it.[15]

---

[12] Australian Archives, A1838, 1495/1 ANNEX D, p. 6.
[13] In 2024 this was identified as on Skips/Skipsholmen Island in the Svenner Islands. See page 178.
[14] In 2024 this was identified as Macey Peninsula in the Rauer Islands. See page 178.
[15] Meteorological Log Transcript, Sir George Hubert Wilkins Papers, BP-CRC, OSU.

Photo courtesy ©Simon Harley, 1 February 2007. "Taken from a site that is a few tens of metres to the north and downhill from the location, shown on the Macey air photo image in my Aurora article, from which the Wilkins landing party (Wilkins, Ellsworth and Lymburner) took their film there on 9th January 1939. The image looks across eastwards towards my 'Dragon Peak', the unmistakeable landmark that I saw in the OSU film footage that Sue sent me to check out. There is absolutely no doubt that they landed on Macey (though precisely where the motorboat docked is still not defined) and walked up and across to near the point from which the attached photo was taken by me in 2007."[16]

With a wind change the ship returned to their first mooring to discover the fast ice had broken loose and the bay ice, from which they planned to fly, had broken up. Using the scouting plane on 10 January, Lymburner in the Aeronca was able to take off from the sea for a flight of 1 hour and 40 minutes. He found a small fjord which he thought might be suitable for takeoff for the larger plane. With the small motor boat they were able to lead *Wyatt Earp* to a mooring against flat ice. On 11 January they finally found an ice edge suitable to land their Northrop airplane and it was unloaded,

---

[16] Personal email Simon Harley to Trish Burgess, 13 November 2024.

test flown and left on an inland flight at 6 pm. And again, Wilkins took the opportunity to make another claim for Australia:[17]

> Meanwhile I proceeded to near the eastern end of the snow-free land at the edge of the continental ice-cap – presumably the mainland – and at the top of a dyke which appears black against the surrounding granite and which extends vertically from sea level – where it is four inches wide – to the top of the hill where it is about four feet wide., I flew a large Commonwealth of Australia flag and then deposited it together with a record.[18]

He goes on to record that he has "put foot on the Antarctic mainland in several places and upon several islands" and "having flown the flag of Australia, leave it with this record". This place was identified in 1957, when the cache was found. It is now known as Walkabout Rocks. and is an Antarctic Heritage Listed Site. It was given this name because Wilkins' "Record of Visit" was rolled inside a copy of the Australian magazine *Walkabout*.

Wilkins filming on board *Wyatt Earp*. Courtesy Oluf Dahl's photo album, Romsdalsmuseet, Norway.

---

[17] Australian Archives, A1838, 1495/1 ANNEX D, p. 9.
[18] In 1957 this site, in the Vestfold Hills, was identified and has been named "Walkabout Rocks".

On the copy of Wilkins' Report in the Australian Archives there is a hand written note in the margin on page 9 of this document which states: "This is the cairn discovered by the Davis party on 8/5/1957".

On 21 May 1957, the Australian Ambassador in Washington, Sir Percy Spender, wrote to "My dear Sir Hubert" on behalf of the Minister for External Affairs, Mr. R.G. Casey. Noting the finding of the cache in the Vestfold Hills, he asked: "Mr. Casey would be most grateful if you could tell him the details of this action, and if you could also let him have any information concerning other similar action which you may have taken within the Australian Antarctic sector in pre-war years."

Under the heading 'Explorers Find Wilkins' Flag in Antarctica' the *Canberra Times* on 21 May 1957 (p.1), recorded the finding:

> An Australian flag, and a message left by the well-known Australian explorer, Sir Hubert Wilkins, 18 years ago, has been discovered by Australian explorers at the new Australian Antarctic base at Davis.
>
> This was announced yesterday by the Minister for External Affairs, Mr. Casey, who said the message and flag were in a small container beneath a boulder surmounted by a cairn of small rocks.

Starting in 2021 considerable research by Sue Hilliard and her colleagues has led them to conclude that the other two sites where Wilkins deposited his caches are on Skipsholmen/Skips Island[19] in the Svenner Islands and Macey Peninsula in the Rauer Islands. Film footage taken by Wilkins that Sue sent to Professor Simon Harley, at Edinburgh University, was identified by him as being the same place that he had photographed in 1986, when he was carrying out research in that area. By reversing a frame from Sue's film, he was able to see his photo was the same place as one of the stills taken from the Wilkins' film – on Macey Peninsula. Having

---

[19] First mapped in 1937-38 by the Lars Christensen Expedition. Australia adopted the name Skipsholmen in 2011, and changed to Skips Island in 2021 when the coordinates were corrected to match the location on Norwegian maps. See Australian Antarctic Data Centre.

identified the two landing locations, it remains for the needles in the haystacks to be found. As demonstrated by Sue Hilliard, the 8 January landing and proclamation site is located at Skipsholmen/Skips Island in the Svenner Islands. "To conclude, the Wilkins January 9th proclamation and record of landing is located on the main summit block of Macey Peninsula in the southernmost Rauer Group".[20]

The takeoff site for the big Northrop was short and would not allow a full load of fuel but on 11 January, about noon, it was lowered to the ice ready for a test run, having not been flown since New York! The return of the test flight confirmed the poor condition of the ice and the weather was clouding up in the north. It appeared clear to the south so Ellsworth and Lymburner took off with fuel for three hours and stores for two men for five weeks.

Crew of *Wyatt Earp* watching/helping loading of the Northrop for the big flight. Courtesy Oluf Dahl's photo album, Romsdalsmuseet, Norway.

Details of this flight can be found in "Ellsworth's Last Antarctic Expedition".[21] After half the fuel supply was used Ellsworth estimated they were 210 miles from the coast. At this point they had

---

[20] Simon Harley, "Walking in the Footsteps of Wilkins", *Aurora* (Journal of the ANARE Club Inc.) 44:1 (2024), pp. 16-18.

[21] Kenneth J. Bertrand, "The Ellsworth Antarctic Expedition, 1938-1939", pp. 402-404.

to turn back. And at this point Ellsworth made the formal claim to the territory which he had just discovered. Being unable to land and place his foot upon it, he dropped a brass cylinder containing the following words:

> To whom it may concern: Having flown on a direct course from latitude 68:30 south, longitude 79:00 east, to latitude 72 degrees south, longitude 79 east, I drop this record, together with the flag of the United States of America, and claim for my country, so far as this act allows, the area south of latitude 70 to a distance of 150 miles east and 150 miles west of my line of flight and to a distance of 150 miles south of latitude 72 south, longitude 79 east which I claim to have explored, dated Jan. 11, 1939. Lincoln Ellsworth.[22]

Lymburner and Ellsworth flew back over their outward course and arrived directly over the ship. They circled a few times before landing. High winds were causing the *Wyatt Earp* to bash against the ice, from which pieces were breaking off. It was clear this flying field would not be used again. The plane was loaded on the ship and the moorings cast off.

On 12 January Wilkins radioed a confidential message to government officials in Canberra, urging Australia to establish a winter base in order to challenge Ellsworth's claims. He sought £150,000 to purchase all Ellsworth's equipment and offered ... to set up the base himself. The government found the idea of bases too expensive, but at Wilkins suggestion agreed to make an offer to purchase the *Wyatt Earp* to raise the Australian flag over Antarctica in a more permanent sense.[23]

The storm lasted for two days and then the First Mate Liavaag had an accident. He and two others were chipping pieces of ice from a small iceberg to put in the fresh water tank. He was caught between two large blocks of ice and his knee was crushed. He needed surgery of a kind not available on the *Wyatt Earp*.[24] Ellsworth gave

---

[22] *New York Times*, 13 January 1939, p. 21.

[23] Simon Nasht, *The Last Explorer*, p. 272.

[24] When they reached Hobart Dr J.H. Gaha, MLC, the Tasmanian Minister for Health, operated on First Mate Liavaag assisted by the *Wyatt Earp*'s doctor

up further hopes of flying and directed the ship to head for the nearest hospital – in Hobart. The return voyage started well with clear seas until the afternoon of 15 January when they found heavy pack ice. The previous night *Wyatt Earp* had met very heavy seas which stove in the bridge and did other damage. After five days through the heavy pack with snow squalls and poor visibility they were in open sea again and on 4 February 1939, *Wyatt Earp* arrived in Hobart.

"First Mate Lauritz Liavaag tries to catch a penguin." Courtesy Oluf Dahl's photo album, Romsdalsmuseet, Norway.

The attention of the Australian Government and the Australian public was focused on *Wyatt Earp* through Australian newspapers. Throughout January newspapers, as diverse as the *Recorder* in Port Pirie and the *Kalgoorlie Miner*, were printing stories of 'Sir Douglas Mawson's Plea' that the Australian Government should purchase the *Wyatt Earp* on her return from the Antarctic. On 19 January under the heading 'Constant Contact with Antarctic', it was reported that Sir Douglas had asked the Commonwealth Treasurer, Mr. R.G. Casey to buy the ship as part of a wider plan for annual scientific trips to the South and to build meteorological

---

Dr Harmon Rhoads Jr. Despite the three-week delay between accident and operation and the severity of the injury the operation was successful. *Mercury* (Hobart), 7 February 1939, p. 9.

stations on the Antarctic continent as well as at Macquarie and Heard Islands. It was further reported that "Mr. Ellsworth would sell to the Commonwealth the ship at less than £4000, a fraction of her real value".[25] Wilkins kept in contact with people in Australia by radiograms during the voyage and submitted his Report to the Australian Government after his return.[26]

The *Chronicle* in Adelaide, on 2 February 1939, under the heading "Quick Decision Needed" says that the *Wyatt Earp* "is expected to reach Hobart within a fortnight". The ship was returning as fast as possible with an injured crew member in need of urgent medical treatment. The article continued that Sir Douglas Mawson had earlier suggested the Commonwealth Government should purchase the *Wyatt Earp* for use in the Antarctic and survey work on the Australian coast. He suggested that a quick decision was needed because Lincoln Ellsworth would put the ship up for sale in the United States if Australia did not want it.

When *Wyatt Earp* reached Hobart, Ellsworth lost no time in publicly reasserting his claim, on behalf of the United States of America, of the land over which he had flown on 11 January. And he increased the area involved, to cover all that he could see as well as that he had flown over, from his original claim of 80,000 square miles to 430,00 square miles! The Australian Government immediately rejected the claim and Mawson had another reason to urge the government to buy a ship capable of visiting the Antarctic continent. Australia needed a permanent presence there.

On 8 February 1939 Lincoln Ellsworth wrote to "The Hon J.A. Lyons, Prime Minister, Commonwealth of Australia", on Ellsworth Antarctic Expedition letterhead, confirming the arrangements "set out in your letter under date February 7th in connection with the sale and purchase of the M/S WYATT EARP". As well as setting out how much and to who the payments should be made, he notes that:

---

[25] *Recorder* (Port Pirie), 19 January 1939, p. 4.

[26] "Report of the Ellsworth Antarctic Flight Expedition, 1938-39" from Sir Hubert Wilkins, to the Minister, Department of External Affairs, Commonwealth of Australia. Australian Archives, A1838, 1495/1 ANNEX D.

It is understood that permission will be granted to discharge and remove through the Naval authority premises the property on board, such as 10 sets polar clothing, pemican, biscuits, ovaltine, special chronometers, etc. the personal property of Sir Hubert Wilkins and which is not included in the sale.

From early in February 1939, Australian newspapers ran frequent short articles over the next few weeks concerning *Wyatt Earp*. "Wyatt Earp Before Cabinet" (*Daily Telegraph*, Sydney, 6 February), "Cabinet and The Wyatt Earp" (*News*, Adelaide, 6 February), "Purchase of Wyatt Earp Sir Douglas Mawson Delighted" (*Advertiser*, Adelaide, 9 February), "The Wyatt Earp – Exploration Value" (*The Age*, Melbourne, 9 February). And in *The Mercury*, also on 9 February, "Wyatt Earp – Departure for Sydney" with the information that "In the half darkness of last evening the Wyatt Earp, Lincoln Ellsworth's exploration ship which has been purchased by the Commonwealth Government, left Queen's Pier, Hobart, for Sydney". Again, the *Kalgoorlie Miner* seemed to be quick with the news:

'Mr. Lincoln Ellsworth has made a generous gesture to assist Australian scientific investigation, and I am delighted that the Commonwealth Government has taken the opportunity of purchasing so valuable and fully equipped a vessel as the Wyatt Earp,' said the professor of geology and mineralogy at the University of Adelaide, Sir Douglas Mawson yesterday.

The purchase price from Mr. Lincoln Ellsworth is about £4400. 'I am convinced that it was a first-class purchase,' said Sir Douglas Mawson. 'I believe that it has been sold on the understanding that the vessel will be used for scientific investigation. The aircraft bought with the vessel, a Northrop all metal low wing, and a small Aeronca scouting machine, are of recent design and, when new, were valued at £17,000.'[27]

The report continues, still quoting Sir Douglas Mawson:

Previously, the obtaining of a suitable vessel and brining [sic bringing] it to Australia has been a most expensive item and crippled previous explorations before they left for the Antarctic.

---

[27] *Kalgoorlie Miner*, 10 February 1939, p. 1.

However, the future proposals for the use of the Wyatt Earp eliminate the biggest expenditure.

The Wyatt Earp is an inexpensive vessel to run and the monthly cost would be not more than half of that of vessels used previously on Australian Antarctic expeditions. The reasons are that the ship is driven by Diesel engines, requiring a small staff to handle fuel. The sails are rigged fore and aft with no spars, and are handled from the deck, obviating the employment of high skilled seamen.

Various newspaper reports noted the arrival of *Wyatt Earp* in Sydney on 12 February. The Brisbane *Courier-Mail* reported on 3 March that Sir Douglas Mawson had spent the two previous days in discussions with "Mr. Lincoln Ellsworth and Sir Hubert Wilkins and made a thorough inspection of the Wyatt Earp and the two aeroplanes which were included in the equipment purchased by the Commonwealth Government from Mr. Ellsworth". Sir Douglas Mawson commented, on 6 March, that he had visited the ship in Sydney, and that no plans for Antarctic exploration would be considered until the report of the marine surveyor was received.

Under the heading "Navy Will Use Ship Wyatt Earp" several newspapers reported very similar news: "Immediate use for the motor vessel Wyatt Earp, which was engaged in Antarctic exploration, is to be found by handing the vessel over to the Defence Department. The Naval Board has applied for the ship for the work to which she is specially adapted".[28] The report continued: "The Treasurer (Mr Casey) said today that these arrangements need not interfere with plans for Antarctic exploration during the summer. He was not in a position to say exactly what defence work the vessel would be engaged in". While these discussions were taking place, Sir Hubert Wilkins decided to become further involved and submitted his ideas directly to the Prime Minister. He suggested that the *Wyatt Earp* should:

> undertake a two months' cruise between Sydney and Fremantle, starting about the middle of May, and experimenting en route

---

[28] *News* (Adelaide), 5 April 1939, p. 1.

in handline fishing at various points of interest to the fishing industry.

It is then suggested that the Wyatt Earp should undertake a cruise to the edge of the Antarctic pack ice, to make meteorological observations. 'Later in the year a meteorological base might be established at Macquarie Island',[29] says Sir Hubert Wilkins ... whose plan will be referred to Cabinet.[30]

Slowly more information became available. On 9 May, the *Kalgoorlie Miner* hinted:

> The Antarctic exploration vessel, Wyatt Earp, may be used as a munitions transport. At present interstate steamship services are used to convey munitions and explosives between Australian ports at rates which are commensurate with the risks. The Wyatt Earp, which was purchased at almost a gift price by the Commonwealth Government, will make the Defence Department independent.

Wyatt Earp was transferred to the Royal Australian Navy and a lengthy debate followed about what her name should be. Initially *Wyatt Earp* was renamed RAFA *Wongala* (Royal Australian Fleet Auxiliary) and made one voyage from Sydney to Darwin loaded with a cargo of "stores". It is possible that stores included munitions.

Following the sale of *Wyatt Earp* to the Australian Government the 'Ellsworth Expedition' was disbanded. Ellsworth later announced plans for another expedition but with the outbreak of World War II these plans were cancelled. Ellsworth arrived back in Los Angeles on 20 March 1939. On 18 April 1939, Ellsworth gave a full report of his four expeditions in *Wyatt Earp* to the Department of State, dated 17 April 1939. His plane, *Polar Star*, is in the Smithsonian National Air and Space Museum, in Washington. Lincoln Ellsworth died in New York on 26 May 1951.

Hubert Wilkins' plans for another submarine trip to the North Pole were also abandoned due to World War II. Throughout 1939 he put several proposals before the Australian Government for

---

[29] Macquarie Island Research Station, managed by the Australian Antarctic Division, was in fact established in 1948.
[30] *Advocate* (Burnie, Tas.) 11 March 1939, p. 9.

the use of *Wyatt Earp*, and offered his services in various ways. Under the heading "Wyatt Earp – Fisheries Research – Suggested Extended Cruise" Wilkins said that, in a letter to the Prime Minister, he had suggested the *Wyatt Earp* "might be used for meteorological and fisheries investigations". He claimed that information from the Australian sector of the Antarctic would aid Commonwealth meteorologists in the provision of more valuable weather data.

While awaiting a response from the Government, Wilkins spent several days in Canberra. Here, on 13 March, he gave "A most informative address" to members of the Canberra Rotary Club.[31] The following day he visited Canberra Grammar School and "with the aid of elaborate colour films, he delivered an absorbing lecture ... greatly appreciated by the students".[32] Wilkins travelled to Sydney by car on 16 March. From a "Special Representative at Canberra" an article under the heading "Sir Hubert Wilkins Visit to Canberra – Map of the Antarctic" appeared and reported on Wilkins "few days" in Canberra during which he had visited the cartographic branch of the Department of the Interior and:

> inspected the work that has been done on a new map of the Antarctic. "It is expected", he said, "that the map will be completed about June next. I have never seen any finer work and the officer who has it in hand, Mr. Bayliss, is to [be] very highly complimented upon it. The National Geographical Society is at work on a new Antarctic map, but I do not think it is making any attempt to include all the valuable historical data that is being included in this large Australian map. I was happy to be able to supply Mr. Bayliss with some first-hand information, which I feel he will be able to use to advantage."[33]

By 12 April 1939, Wilkins was on board the SS *Ceramic* in Fremantle, and he was in Oslo on 5 June. In July, it was reported from New York that Sir Hubert Wilkins had sent a cable to the Australian Prime Minister (Mr. R.G. Menzies) "offering 'privately to equip and maintain' a landing party of Australian naval men and

---

[31] *Canberra Times*, 14 March 1939, p. 2.

[32] *Canberra Times*, 16 March 1939, p. 6.

[33] *Daily Mercury* (Mackay, Qld), 23 March 1939, p. 6.

scientists for the Australian sector of Antarctica to take advantage of co-operation with the Byrd expedition, provided the Australian Government would transport them in the Wyatt Earp."[34] This was a different proposal to his one made in March. The following day the *Canberra Times* reported, under the heading "ANTARCTIC Sir Hubert Wilkins's Offer – Government to Investigate", that the Minister for External Affairs (Sir Henry Gullett) advised "that the Defence Department would have to be consulted" about the use of the ship. It was noted that Cabinet would consider the proposal on 31 July.[35] The heading, on 5 August on page 2, again from the *Canberra Times*, said it all "No Expedition to Antarctic", saying that any action by the Commonwealth Government to establish a base in Australia's Antarctic Territory "had been postponed indefinitely, at least for some years".

World War II officially began in September 1939. In Ottawa on 19 December, Sir Hubert Wilkins offered his services to the Canadian Government. Small paragraphs appeared in newspapers all over Australia, in which he said "that the Australian Government told him his services were not needed immediately". Within a short time he was in the United States, with an American passport, working for that Government and probably thinking he had made his final Antarctic trip. One more was still to come.

"In 1956 the Australian Antarctic Division in Hobart purchased equipment used by Wilkins in Antarctica for 2000 pounds, from Sir Hubert Wilkins."[36] The collection includes an anemometer, a theodolite, a sextant and two deck watches. It seems likely that they were used on this 1938-1939 voyage of Wilkins on the *Wyatt Earp* and are the items referred to in Lincoln Ellsworth's letter to Prime Minister Lyons earlier in this chapter. They are all now in the National Museum of Australia and images are shown below:

---

[34] *Warwick Daily News* (Qld), 12 July 1939, p. 2.
[35] *Canberra Times*, 13 July 1939, p. 4.
[36] Information received by email from National Museum of Australia, that they received from the Australian Antarctic Division at the time these items were transferred from AAD to NMA.

Wyatt Earp arrived in Hobart on 4 February 1939.[37]

As HMAS *Wyatt Earp* she would return to Hobart on 22 December 1947, on her way to her final visit to the Antarctic, on the first Australian National Antarctic Research Expedition.

---

[37] This photo is from *The Mercury,* Hobart, Australia, according to Lincoln Ellsworth's "My Four Antarctic Expeditions: Explorations of 1933-39 Have Stricken Vast Areas from the Realm of the Unknown." *National Geographic Magazine,* July 1939. Despite research it has not been possible to confirm this.

Theodolite (top), Anemometer and case (centre), Sextant (bottom) all used by Wilkins in the Antarctic. Courtesy National Museum of Australia.

 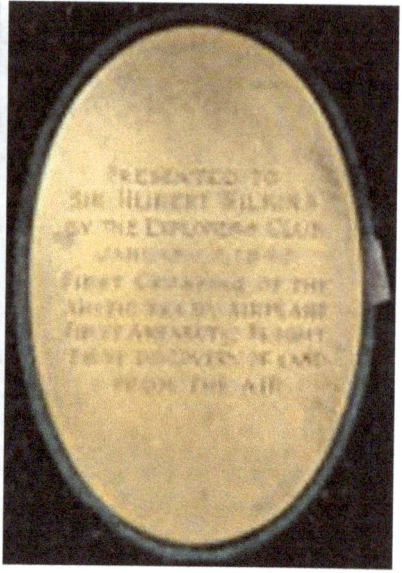

This medal inscribed
"Presented to
Sir Hubert Wilkins
by the Explorers Club
January 6, 1940
First Crossing of the
Arctic Sea by Airplane
First Antarctic Flight
First Discovery of Land
From the Air"
From the Sir George Wilkins Papers, BPCR, OSU.

10

1957-1958 OPERATION DEEP FREEZE III PREPARED THE UNITED STATES FOR THE START OF THE INTERNATIONAL GEOPHYSICAL YEAR ON 1 JULY 1957

Wilkins Final Antarctic Trip, with the US Navy. In the Antarctic again Wilkins visited every United States base and station, sending back detailed reports on conditions. He arrived by air at McMurdo Base on 12 October 1957 and departed from Wilkes Station by ship on 30 January 1958. While there he also visited Scott Base, the New Zealand Station, and Scott's and Shackleton's huts at Cape Evans and Cape Royds.

Hubert Wilkins's final voyage with Lincoln Ellsworth on the *Wyatt Earp* ended in Hobart on 4 February 1939. After some negotiations the ship was sold to the Australian Government. She made one more Antarctic voyage, as the Royal Australian Navy's HMAS *Wyatt Earp*, in 1947-1948, on the first Australian National Antarctic Research Expedition.

Wilkins' plans and ideas for his next journeys had to be put to one side with the start of World War II. He tried to enlist in the Australian Forces but, being 51 years of age, he was told he was not eligible. He was in Ottawa, Canada, when it was reported that he was offering his services to the Canadian Government. "Being Colonial", he said, "I am more anxious to serve in the Dominion forces than in those of the Netherlands or the Motherland."[1]

He must have come to some agreement with the United States Government for, as his American passport shows, he became a frequent world traveller. In June 1940 he left New York "for China and the Far East, ostensibly on a survey for the Detroit Economics

---

[1] *Courier Mail* (Brisbane), 20 December 1939, p. 1.

Society, but, by all accounts, on a spying mission for the American Government. Later in the year he goes on a similar "intelligence-gathering mission to Europe".[2] In 1945, when World War II ended, Wilkins became a permanent United States government employee. He worked for the US Army until his death in 1958. However, he never relinquished his Australian citizenship.

Under the heading "Sir Hubert Wilkins' Work in Arctic – Secret Services for USA" it was reported:

> Sir Hubert Wilkins disclosed to-day that he had flown over the North Polar zone six times in the last 12 months. He said: "My work there is still on the secret list, and all I can say is in the capacity as consultant for the United States army, navy, and Weather Bureau, I am making regular flights over the Arctic regions in United States service planes. I expect to make another flight soon".
>
> Sir Hubert Wilkins said the United States' policy of studying the Arctic conditions was "the only intelligent thing to do" and added that the United States now regarded the Arctic as its third coast, and as an even more important strategic area than its east and west coasts. Sir Hubert Wilkins said he expected to finish his work in 1949 when he will return to Australia.[3]

His extensive travels continued, as his passports show, visiting, at least, Algeria, Morocco, Tripolitania, Casablanca, Libya, Iraq, Karachi, Syria, Saudia Arabia, Lebanon, Turkey, Algiers and Panama. In a letter to J.K. Davis, dated 30 December 1952 he says: "I had visited all these desert areas to make a survey for several departments of the Department of Defence …" and he mentions being "on duty for the Army" from which it appears his work has merged into the effects of both hot and cold climates on clothing for military personnel.[4]

---

[2] Papers of Elizabeth Chipman, National Library of Australia. MS9635, MS Acc11.071. Timeline for June 1940, Winston Ross, in interview with Pulsifer, Sir George Hubert Wilkins Papers, BPCRC, OSU.

[3] Papers of Elizabeth Chipman, Wilkins – Timeline 1948, p. 3, *Cairns Post*, 29 January 1948, p. 5.

[4] Papers of Elizabeth Chipman, Wilkins – Timeline 1952, p. 2.

In 1953, in his Australian hometown[5] it was reported, under "Explorers Post", that "Sir Hubert Wilkins, the famous Australian explorer and author, has been named geographer to the research and development division of the US Army Quartermaster Corps. Sir Hubert, 64, has lived in the US for the last 28 years." He worked for this section of the Army until his death.

Wilkins work in cold climates was recognised in 1955 by the University of Alaska when they conferred on him the honorary degree of Doctor of Science. This occurred on 16 May 1955. A Doctor of Science is the highest degree awarded by any university. It is only awarded in Science and to individuals with an outstanding record of research and discovery and a recognised standing in their field.

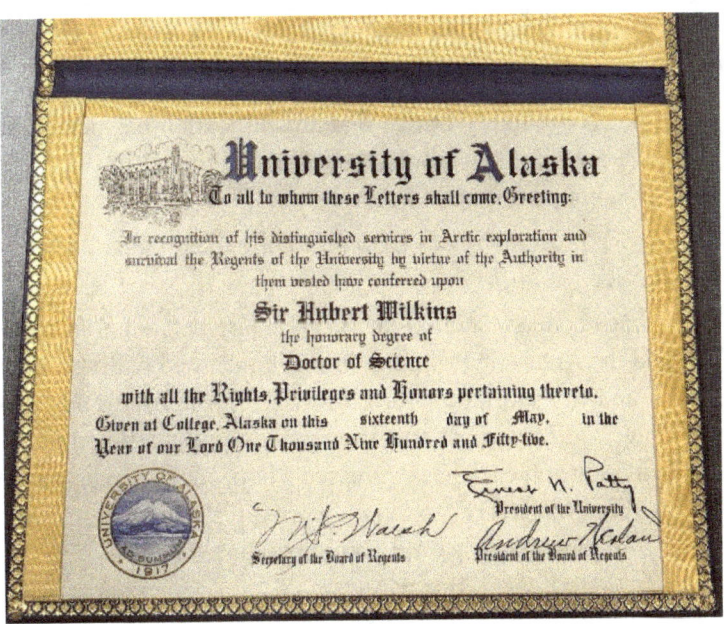

Box 125, Sir George Hubert Wilkins Papers, BPCRC, OSU.

Wilkins and Captain J.K. Davis corresponded on mutual interests over many years. From 1947 to 1962 Davis was a member of the Australian government's planning committee advising on Antarctic policy and action. On 28 August 1956 Wilkins begins his letter: "So you have returned to Australia. Am

---

[5] *Advertiser* (Adelaide), 8 June 1953, p. 4.

glad for you to have a copy of the plans for the Antarctic – they are tremendous and money to carry them out is much more liberal than the talent examplified [sic] in the carriers". He notes that he gets "an occasional scientific report from [Philip] Law and finds that the Australians are doing a fine job". He refers to his visit to the Vestfold Hills with "the Lincoln Ellsworth Expedition 1938-39" and that he had "left a record there claiming the land for the Australian Commonwealth".

In 1957 Wilkins turned 69. He was still working for the US Army Quartermaster Corps. The International Geophysical Year 1957/58 was planned and the US Navy would head south in September. Dated 17 May 1957, Wilkins submitted a "Disposition Form". The "Subject" is "Observer duty in Antarctica, 1957-59" and it is addressed to "Commanding General QM R&D[6] Command, Natick. Mass". It was signed Hubert Wilkins. It reads, in part:

1. It has come to my notice that an application has been made to have an Observer from QM R&D Command in the Antarctic this coming Antarctic summer.
2. This expresses my desire to be among those considered for that service.
3. It has been ascertained that several key personnel in the Navy and the Antarctic Program Office, concerned with the approval of and transportation for Observers to the Antarctic, have no objection in respect to experience, age or nationality, to my selection and each has expressed a hope that I will be appointed as the QM R&D Observer. Approval by the Deputy Chief of Naval Operations would, of course, be necessary.
4. It is my suggestion that if approval for a QM R&D Observer in the Antarctic is granted, a further request be made for the Observer to be provided with facilities, subject to circumstances, to visit bases at McMurdo Sound, Little America, Byrd Land, Cape Hallett, Knox Land, and other bases if and when opportunity occurs.
5. It has been ascertained that Admiral Dufek expect to fly to McMurdo Sound late in September or early October in order

---

[6] United States Army Quartermaster Research and Engineering Centre.

to start delivery of supplies by air to various bases long before ships arrive this season at Antarctic bases.

6. It is possible that an early arrival in Antarctica by the QM R&D Command Observer would insure a wider field for observation.

7. It is suggested that among other features the QM R&D Observer, en route and in the Antarctic, should investigate are:

8. a. Nature and distribution of significant factors in natural environments.

   b. Significant factor of Antarctic and other living activities as provided and experienced.

   c. Operational effectiveness of Quartermaster and other Services-equipped personnel, while wearing items provided for environmental protection.

9. It is suggested that arrangement should be made for the Observer to be provided with photographic equipment and film, and permission to carry and use same.

It was signed Hubert Wilkins. Below is a copy of the Authorisation from the Office of the Quartermaster General of the United States Department of the Army. And so it came to pass!

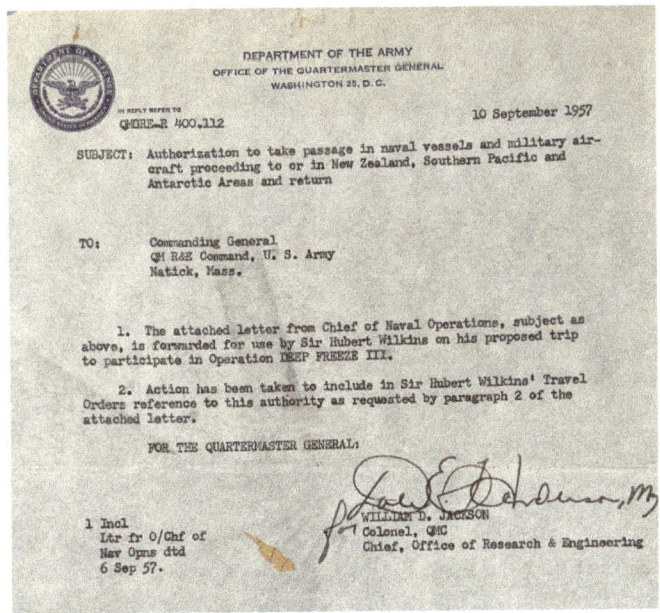

Papers of Elizabeth Chipman.

Wilkins first "official" report to the Commanding General at the QM R&E at Natick was dated Noon 15 October 1957, and titled "Report of arrival in IGY area and initial activities". He mentioned the visit to Admiral Dufek by Sir Edmund Hilary and his staff from New Zealand's nearby Scott Base. He commented the "N.Z. cold weather winter clothing quilted, down-filled parka and trousers, light and comfortable, of good appearance and protective".

Wilkins' "official" report after his return was typed, has no date and the file copy held at the Polar Records of Ohio State University is not signed. It states the purpose of his travel was "To observe the activities of Operation Deep Freeze III. Apart from ship service to and from the USA to Antarctica, Operation Deep Freeze II was concerned with the resupply and maintenance of McMurdo Naval Air Facility Base and IGY stations at Little America, Byrd, Pole, Liv, Hallett and Wilkes Station".

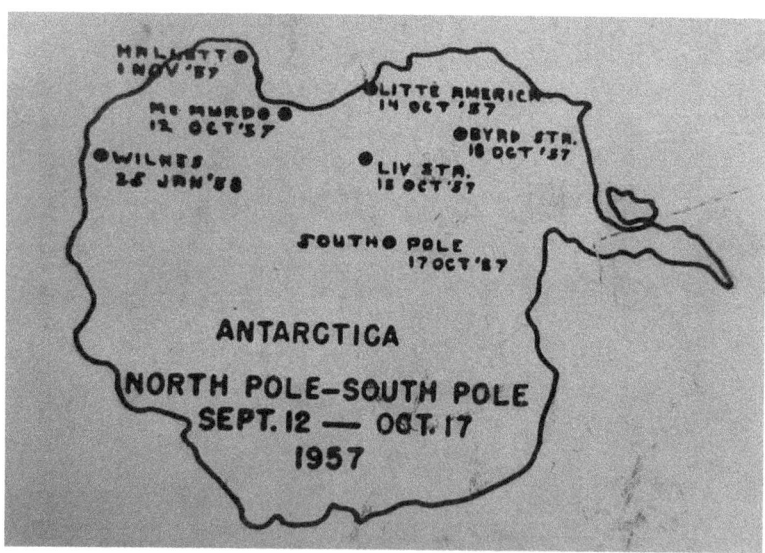

It is presumed that Wilkins made his own rubber stamp for marking envelopes. Stamp Box 42 Sir George Hubert Wilkins Papers, BPCRC, OSU.

His "official" report and his "travel claim" give conflicting details of the dates and places he visited. Both, however, agree he travelled from Natick to Donaldson Air Force Base S.C. for transportation to New Zealand. He spent nearly two weeks in Christchurch before flying to McMurdo and visiting other Antarctic bases, as follows:

12 Oct. 1957	McMurdo Naval Air Facility Base, Antarctica
14 Oct. 1957	Little America V
15 Oct. 1957	Byrd Station
16 Oct. 1957	Liv Station
17 Oct. 1957	South Pole Station
18 Nov. 1957	Little America V and IV
22 Nov. 1957	Shelf Ice Traverse Party, Travelling on Ross Ice Shelf
3 Dec. 1957	Scott Base (New Zealand Station)
6 Dec. 1957	Cape Evans Scott's old base Ross Island
10 Dec. 1957	Shackleton's old base Cape Royds Ross Island
12 Dec. 1957	Cape Bernacchi and Dry Valley (Near new landing field on mainland of Antarctica)
16 Dec. 1957	Hallett Station (80 miles south of Cape Adare)
26 Jan. 1958	Wilkes Station Wilkes Land, Australian Sector

From Wilkes Station, Wilkins travelled by USS *Arneb*,[7] to Sydney, Australia, arriving on 8 February 1958. He left Sydney two days later, by plane, for a few days in Adelaide before arriving in Manila on 18 February, and arriving back at Natick on 23 February 1958. John Grierson's biography of Wilkins covers this expedition, **very** briefly, in the following words:

> In 1957, Sir Hubert was sent on one of his testing missions, to Antarctica, in order to carry out on-the-spot research for five months with various items of equipment, emergency rations and other material. *En route* he called in at New Zealand in October and gave an interview to the *New Zealand Freelance* in which he said, 'Research must keep at least four or five years ahead of actual use, and the International Geophysical Year activities in Antarctica present a magnificent opportunity for

---

[7] *Arneb*, an attack class cargo ship, served in the US Navy throughout WWII in Naval Transport Service. In 1948 she was modified for Polar operations, in the North Atlantic, Mediterranean and West Indies before in 1955 becoming Flagship for Operation Deep Freeze I. During Operation Deep Freeze II she had several 'difficult encounters' with ice.

such observations." This was the time, it will be remembered, when Sir Vivian Fuchs was just about to set out on his historic journey from South Ice to the Ross Sea, not merely as a demonstration of human daring, but as a major contribution to the research of the International Geophysical Year. Seldom has so much public attention throughout the world been centred upon developments in the Antarctic.[8]

But there was so much more to this journey.

Following Wilkins' marriage and during all his many frequent and lengthy travels away from home including this trip to the Antarctic (over five months) he sent, mostly handwritten and mostly one page, notes to his wife, Suzanne. They all started "Hello Hello" and ended "Best love Hubert"! Wilkins also kept detailed diaries of his work-related experiences. As can be seen in the following, his two records about the same event often differ in their content.

Starting on 23 September 1957, he writes to Suzanne from Donaldson Air Force Base.[9]

Donaldson Air Force Base
Greenville S.C.
Monday 23rd Sept [1957]
Hello Hello
At last it looks as if all delays in starting for the Antarctic are over. Luggage aboard the airplane papers signed and we are due to start at 8 am tomorrow Tuesday morning. Stopping at Travis Air Force Base near San Franciso, Honolulu and Canton Island on way to Christchurch New Zealand. I should get to NZ by the 30th and will not know until I get there when I leave for the far south.
Hope you are well and that all is well at the Farm.
Thanks for coming to see me off.
Best love Hubert.

---

[8] John Grierson, *Sir Hubert Wilkins: Enigma of Exploration*, p. 206.
[9] Letters to Suzanne transcribed and edited by Trish Burgess. Diary Entries transcribed by Philip van Dueren and/or by Trish Burgess. All have come from the Sir George Hubert Wilkins Papers, BPCRC, OSU.

Please leave the two papers herewith in the envelope and envelope in the bottom drawer in the bathroom chest of drawers.

Officers Mess
Travis Air Force Base, California
Tuesday night [24 Sept] 6 pm
Hello Hello

Here we are at the first stop over for the night, about 100 miles from San Francisco. Had a very comfortable flight. 11 hours – plenty of room to walk about in the plane which is a big one.

The Air Force Officer with us turns out to be a Squadron Leader Parker from Melbourne Australia going home on leave. There is only 3 passengers and some crew men. The other man is a Mr. Becker of the New York Times. Both very nice. We leave early in the morning and stop tomorrow night at Honolulu. Expect that will also be a comfortable flight. Hope all is going well at the farm & that you are well. Best regards to Winston. Best love Hubert.

Clarendon Hotel, Christchurch
1 October 57
Hello Hello

We arrived here late Sunday afternoon. A big crowd to meet us partly because some old World War I friends are here and there was some notice in the paper that I was coming.

Had a comfortable flight out but at each stopping place we arrived after 5 pm and left before 9 am so no local post offices were open. Weather here is nice. Spring Flowers are coming out.

Don't know when I will leave for further South but expect it will be before the end of the week? the weather is bad down there but probably will soon clear up; The several friends here, the press and preparations for departure keep me busy and I will be glad to get away to the ice bases.

Hope the trip to the Farm was Enjoyable and that you had a safe trip home. Best love Hubert.

Sent some clippings in Winstons letter.

Clarendon Hotel, Christchurch

5 October 57

Hello Hello

Are still here – waiting for the Admiral Dufek (with whom I will fly South in a 'comfortable' plane,) to recover from a 'bad cold. We expect to get away in a day or so.

There are so many people waiting to fly South that you would think McMurdo Sound was a popular suburb. Am enjoying visits with old Friends of World War I but will be glad to get away. The Stamps are for Winston. Ask him to keep the typed list so that I can refer to it when I get back.

Hope all is well with you. Best love Hubert.

Diary entry: Sat 12 Oct 57 Takeoff 0500 Navy Skymaster C54, Admiral & press. General Wade Kingston left for McMurdo so arrived before us. Had Cornish pasty for breakfast & lunch. Coffee on plane. Over cloud until Cape Adare, did not see Hallett under cloud. ... McMurdo Sound clear no cloud. Everest (sic Erebus) smoking. Landed fine no transport for Admiral he disappointed. I rode on sled behind weasel. ... Sir Edmund Hillary & two others came over after dinner. Discussion on effect of oxygen.

Mount Erebus, still smoking 2008. ©Trish Burgess.

Diary entry: Sun 13. Full sunshine, comfortable night ... After lunch Commander Downey & Admiral included me take quick round trip on Neptune to LA.[10] Loaded in plane. Met Lockheed's rep who here to report on skis. Much delay arranging load. Took off with aid of jets, got off easily. Climbed well. Flew along edge of Barrier, a large section split off but not yet adrift, no icebergs near Barrier one deeply cracked but not yet split right off. Open water along front of Barrier for most of way, mile or so wide. Ice for 25 miles much broken but fresh skin of ice over open water. ... Clear for many miles but 110 miles from LA clouded over. LA reported zero zero[11] so turned back. Takeoff 2.30 landed 6.30.

Diary entry: 14 Sept [sic Oct]. Monday. Clear, wind 10mph temp 8-14 degrees F. Up 5 AM after breakfast walked to Scott's hut 2 carcasses mutton under veranda. Looks well preserved, picked up matchbox, penguins skin & feathers, lichens & 2 rocks. 2 oil barges still tied to beach. Hut well preserved, partly full snow. Visited dogs & dog house 20 dogs, 3 pups. ... Refuelling of PV4 began only at 11:30 went to plane at noon no lunch. Taxied out but just before take-off 1 hydraulic line leaked took 1½ to fix. Then took off for Little America. Long crack on Barrier had widened since yesterday. Water yesterday 1 mile out from Barrier edge is today 30 miles or more out. High wind on surface, new ice & snow streaked on water drifts at angle. ... About halfway over low cloud flying blind but Radar showed direction. ... But could see Little America clearly when we got there when approaching saw cat tractor. Later told that they searching for Weasel lost some days ago – it tumbled down crevasse 10 feet. Storm came along men rescued but now cannot find weasel.

---

[10] Little America visited here is not the same one Wilkins visited in 1936. The original base was set up by Admiral Byrd in 1928 and he used it again in 1933-35. Lincoln Ellsworth used it at the end of his flight across the Antarctic continent in 1936, when Wilkins brought *Wyatt Earp* to the Ross Sea. Byrd extended it to become Little America III in 1940. Little America IV was built for US "Operation High Jump" in 1946-47. In preparation for the IGY Little America V was set up in 1956, as parts of earlier LA sites had vanished due to calving of the ice shelf. LA V was built near Kainan Bay several miles north-east of earlier sites.

[11] "Zero zero" flying term referring to ceiling and visibility. Not good!

Little America pretty much under snow. ... Way out of Little America okay as planned on map, passageway ample, some leaking, also leaks in rooms badly. Meteorological quarters good. Photo decorations good, placards of photos of all men. IGY Navy, Air Force scenes. Had steak dinner.[12]

Diary entry: Sept (sic) Oct 14 Monday continued. Took off from LA 7.10 pm on course for Beardmore Camp about 30 miles from front of Beardmore Glacier. Wind drifts conspicuous. Course until 9 pm, then drifts confused lumpy. By that time could see dim outline of mtns. By 9.30 mountain scenery clearly seen but in shadow. Triangular peak marks entrance to Glacier. Hill tops rounded mostly. Landed at Camp on fairly smooth surface, irregular & lumpy but lumps not high, taxied easily. 2 Jamesways (type of building) close together 1 living, 1 engine room & stores. Jamesway heater, potbellied stove uses 50 galls in 6 days. 24 hrs a day. Jamesway not put up too well but just as good. Snow drifts in but ventilation thus provided. Air bad when all plane crews & passengers were inside. Cooking done on Primus and 1 3-burner there also. 3 army cots for sleeping two spare double bunks.

Boys talk of fantastic mirages, seem to like the job, say it is not much different to other camps except cook for themselves. Had two tubs of water with stove going all day. Water no problem. Huts clear of drifts. Drift forms about 6 feet away. 1 hole out house, ice on seats. We had to take on 400 gals of fuel to get back. ... Landed at 1.40 am on 15th. Had supper, to bed, found birthday card from office & letter from Winston. PanAM expected 5 pm.

Diary entry: 15 October. Wrote report to Commanding General. Went up Hill overlooking but did not visit New Zealand base. ... Visited mechanics. Repairing plane in open. Using Herman Walter heater for warmth. Great waste of heat – could have used tent. Has available a special nose hanger of type used for Radar screen but this is too fragile as designed, had to strengthen it. Now it serves well in high wind but it was being used on another plane. In the evening Pan American Charter plane arrived with US Ambassador

---

[12] Wilkins' comments about state of living quarters, decoration and photos of men are a measure he used at all stations he visited to assess them.

to NZ Mr. Russell & Mr. McAlpine NZ Minister for Railways. Had party in mess. Spoke over tape recorder for NBC & Monitor correspondents.

McMurdo Sound
15 October 1957
Hello Hello
Arrived here on comfortable flight, living quarters with Admiral Dufek fine.
Have been fortunate to be able to visit two other stations. Little America on Beardmore Base and expect to fly to South pole on 19th or 20th.
Very busy times here – everybody coming or going. Pan America passenger plane comes in tonight with two hostesses on board much preparation to honor them, and presenting them with penguin feathers. Here is one for you.
Glad to hear that the painting is going so well.
Will write more when things are going a little quieter out. Expect to be busy for several weeks.
Best love Hubert.

> Jim Mathews, from the Old Antarctic Explorers group, comments:
>
> The first two women ever at McMurdo Station, Antarctic: Ruth Kelly and Patricia Hepinstall, both stewardesses on a Pan Am flight the Navy chartered to bring people to McMurdo in October 1957. Admiral Dufek was adamant that no woman would visit Antarctica while he was in command, but he didn't figure on commercial air carrier union rules. They flew with a full crew at all times and stewardesses would be on the flight, whether or not the Navy objected. So, they arrived, took dog sled rides and visited the station where, among other people, they met Sir Hubert Wilkins, there for the IGY. When Wilkins learned ladies would be arriving, he promptly put on a tie – a different world. This event was forgotten for years, but the stewardesses have received some recognition lately.[13]

---

[13] Downloaded from Old Antarctic Explorers Website: https://oldantarcticexplorers.com on 9 September 2024.

Sir Hubert Wilkins (centre in black) with Kiwi (New Zealand) field party about to be flown to joint US/NZ Hallett Station on Moubray, North Victoria Land, November 1957. The aircraft behind them, Que Sera Sera RD4-5 Skytrain, was the first plane to land at the Geographical South Pole on 31 October 1956. Photo: Arnold Heine. Courtesy: www.colinmonteath.nz.Polar.Archive.

United States Navy photograph, with the caption: 'Sir Hubert Wilkins, the noted Australian-born explorer and naturalist, photographed with the two Pan American Airways stewardesses, Miss Patricia Hepinstall (left) and Miss Ruth Kelly, during the visit to McMurdo Sound of the Clipper America.

In her Timeline Elizabeth Chipman noted that Wilkins sent a press clipping[14] to Captain Davis. She said that in it, the two women are seated (probably at a table in the mess; coffee mugs etc. on table) looking up at Sir Hubert who is standing. His eyes are rolled heavenward as if saying: Things were never like this in my day. Across the top of the page, he wrote: "October 21, 1957: Last week, from McMurdo Base I visited the Pole, Litte America and Beardmore Auxiliary station. If Law, or Casey would arrange to duplicate the scene below I might consider visiting 'Mawson'. Best Regards. Wilkins".[15] His use of the words "visited the Pole" may be misleading as he did not land there but was on the plane on 17 October (see entry below) when "Drop pole successful" took place.

Diary entry: 16 Oct. 57 Morning walked to hill over Scott Base. Saw plane take off to visit Hillary who on the way, 4 tractors & weasel. NZ Ferguson tractors work well. Afternoon 3 pm. Took off in Admiral's plane for mapping flight to Cape Bernacchi where a land-based landing field is contemplated. Field now covered with great hills of ice streaked every which way with water courses. Some streams in summer will pour over a glacier, mud stains show conspicuously. After mapping flew up Dry Valley beside which is Ferrar Glacier which is far too crevassed for dog team passage. Many bull-nosed glaciers pour down into Blind Valley. Scenery spectacular, like a little Bryce Canyon area. Many dykes and great variety of color. After Dry Valley flew over mntns tried to locate Hillary, could not until returned to McMurdo Sound to pick up trail which we followed until locating party. ... Returned to Base after 11-hour flight 2 am.

Diary entry: 17 Oct. 08.13 takeoff to drop supplies from C-124 ... Followed Scott's route to Beardmore, NZ Rep wanted to see spot where Oates walked out. Grand flight up the Beardmore. Very much crevassed, split with steep sided snow free hills, really mountains. Must have taken great hearts, much courage to face such conditions. A puzzle to find a suitable route. Plateau occasionally covered with scattered clouds necessitating climb to 13000 ft to top them. In

---

[14] *Press* (Christchurch), 19 October 1957.
[15] State Library of Victoria: JKDAVIS Papers Box 3271/7.

between we descended to 7-8000 ft. Some passengers did not stand altitude well. I did not mind it. Was clear at Pole. Saw base from some distance. A wide circle of drums was seen at McMurdo side of Pole Station. Didn't seen any people on first passing but was very busy speaking for taped record for Richard J. Jennings N.B.C. made a speech ... Drop pole successful. Great white expanse impressive, described difference between Nth & Sth Pole. ...Turned back low over plateau ... Glided down Beardmore. Great topographical sight. After over Ross Shelf lunch was served. In-flight individual food packet, solidly frozen. Nobody had thought to warm the packages ... Some commented unfavourably on frozen state of food. (Some correspondents released this in press release) I explained to as many as possible that the food was designed for crew with heat available & plenty of water for coffee. Plane reasonably warm. ... Back 6 pm, almost 12-hour flight.

U.S. Naval Air Facility McMurdo Sound Antarctica.
17 October 1957
Hello Hello

The Pole flight took place today. Earlier than expected – weather was good so we took off. A wonderful flight & much learned. At the Pole talked for Monitor. NBC. A Mr. Richard J. Jennings was the man with the recorder. He is starting back for New York tomorrow and kindly said he would telephone you to tell you when the talk might go on. He seems a very nice fellow. I also gave him Winston's name and address. Please tell Winston he might like to meet him.

Things are running very well for me. Admiral Dufek and all others are very kind and helpful. I am going over to Byrd Land Base tomorrow. That will cover all the bases down here from the air. But I will go back to each and stay at each for two or three days – but don't know the dates yet.

We get up each day at 5 am for breakfast and have lunch on board the planes and dinner when we get back sometimes 11-12 o'clock at night. Busy times and expect that will continue.

Hope all is going well in New York and that you are not working too hard at the paintings. Best regards to Winston. Hope the play leads to something for him.

Best love Hubert.

Diary entry: 18 Oct. A 12-hour roundtrip to Byrd station provided opportunity to observe variations in wind snow drifts while crossing Ross Ice Shelf, and when over Marie Byrd Land. Our route was direct ... made successful drop ... no trouble. But the accompanying plane had one engine failure – oil leak and trouble ditching load ... As is customary the plane without trouble – as soon as heard of the damage – turned back (we were about an hour ahead) to escort the damaged plane. Had some trouble finding it. Radio communication trouble and while we were above the cloud 5000 feet and the damaged plane unable with 3 engines to climb above cloud and was flying at 4000 – in cloud. Finally in a spot between clouds it was located and the two planes returned safely together to McMurdo. A long trying day, our pilots tired, was interested in noticing that all our crew – when conscious of trouble in the other plane became quite tense and started chewing gum rapidly – which seemed to calm them slightly.

Diary entry: 19 Oct. There was considerable wind and some snow today. This condition affects the living quarters noticeably. Had to put on full Arctic outfit while in room writing report ... During afternoon made inspection of mechanical sections. As we were about to start a Bulldozer cut the main power cable. There is no emergency light for the Admirals HQ. There are emergency power plants which of course are no help when the cable is cut. Communications building had emergency lighting. Admiral Dufek agreed that emergency lighting should be available, also windows, in buildings. Only one window, one end of 6-room two Jamesway Huts which is Admiral's quarters. All buildings would be better with double windows. Also camp discipline – clearing snow from doors is neglected & slippery steep entrances has caused some nasty falls.

Wilkins spent the next few days around McMurdo talking with people about emergency rations, clothing, footwear and accommodation:

> The same conditions as in Alaska are noticed here, very few if any of officers or men make any effort to use some of the best basic principles built into environmental protection.

Many workers said they found Navy underparts of uniform unsuitable, too warm if buttoned up while working, too cold if unzipped. Many said the nylon zipper for hood failed. All those dressed in Army outfits tonight on landing strip – unloading freight that had just come in from NZ, were well satisfied with Army outfits except white coats which 3 said were too warm, did not know how to manage them. Even one who had worn them while wintering over had not learned. (Diary 20 October 1957.)

Wilkins "Mentioned to Rennie, AP reporter, my disappointment at how the camp was looked after and coincidentally this evening Captain Dickey called in all officers and gave them a dressing down" for a lengthy list of problems which confirmed Wilkins observations. It included things like lack of safety precautions against fire or road traffic. A fire had broken out in the powerhouse, to which plenty of people responded, but there was no means of putting the fire out! The fire hoses were frozen stiff, the hose cart would not wheel, there were no fire axes and no one knew how to put it out. Wilkins questioned the distribution of fire extinguishers, noting there were two in the lavatory but none in VIP HQ. And, he noted, there is no one in charge of "Safety"!

He questioned the drainage around the base, pointing out that water from the hospital and the barracks runs down to a dump "but water freezes & gradually builds up a small glacier of varied colored ice. Coffee grounds, urine stains & melt ice holes in same from emptied basins all around quarters." His list included the dress and manners of men in the mess, their morale, busting of cartons of fresh fruits and milk on the landing strip, uneconomical multi handling of supplies and a "good deal of yapping about going home among crews, some angrily." Each officer was asked to put forward recommendations for better running of the camp by the following evening.

Sir Hubert Wilkins [printed]

McMurdo Sound. [with not very good Operation Deep Freeze stamp]
24th October
Hello Hello
Do not know when I will get to the pole with this letter or whether it may have to be sent plane for posting. The weather here today is too bad for us to leave and the landing field at the Pole is not fit to land on – so that's the way it goes.

There are so many flights turned back from various places that we are running short of fuel for planes – plenty of fuel for the houses but our rooms are just? too warm. My bed, for instance is 53 degrees Fah. and I use 2 blankets and a sleeping bag.

Outside it is always windy 18 to 20 miles an hour and the wind makes it cold & uncomfortable. Otherwise all is going OK but I do not get far away from the camp.

Last night 2 men got stuck in a jeep about a mile from camp. They waited in the jeep but one man who went out to rescue them froze his face so that he could not close his eyes. They just will not be careful about dressing properly.

Hope all is going well with you. Best love Hubert.
Keep the envelope if it has the Pole station mark on it. I might need it.

Wilkins' Diary of 24 October comments a little further on the "frozen face". "Last night Commander Flynn (2 years experience) started for airstrip. His jeep broke down, another commander went out to rescue him but not properly dressed and froze his face so that he could not close his eyes. Was not long exposure and frostbite only 1st degree." Wilkins spent part of the day measuring the temperature inside buildings and listed "Things least liked by men" starting with "No liberty here. Work every day, no day of their own. The sailors used to Leave only in port. Would regular day a week (like a Saturday or Sunday) be best or surprise leave every so often. No one much interested in these matters. Great interest in "Home for Xmas".

C/o Commander Task Force 43
McMurdo Base Navy Post Office #20
Fleet Post Office San Franciso
29 October 57
Hello Hello

Hope things are going well in New York and that the painting is doing nicely. There is an artist with us down here doing landscapes but it is too uncomfortable outside to sit for long – temperature about zero every day with a wind at about 20 mph & blowing constantly night & day. There has been only one partly comfortable day although the sun is now shining almost every day and does not set even at midnight.

There is some delay in flights to the Pole. One plane is down there because of engine trouble & a new engine is being flown in today. It will be dropped by parachute and we hope it will land safely. If not we will have to get a new plane from the U.S. and leave the one at the pole for a monument(?) – But I suppose you might search the news from here in the paper since there are 8 correspondents including The Times, Associate Press, United Press here. Some of them have sent out some long stories about me – Especially New Zealand and San Francisco papers – also newsman from Portland Oregon – 2 stories.

The cold makes all things brittle and ear aid cords break. Will you please get from any hearing aid shop (you will find the addresses of those selling Zenith in the Red Book). Two cords of the kind sold in package herewith and mail them in your next letter to me. Address above. Best love Hubert.

(Sideways along edge) Give the news and best regards to Winston. Hope his job is going okay. Christmas cards via the Pole and one on the way via the Pole you. Do not know when they will get there by.

Wilkins spent his days at McMurdo finding out all he could about how the utilities, power lines, drainage, storage, bathhouse, clothes washing and drying and just about everything else worked and writing up notes about what could and should be done better. He pointed out the clothes drier is in the bathhouse but the bathhouse is also an engine house. Fluff from drying gets into the oily areas of the engine. He suggested hanging clothes or using new types of dryers, it could become a fire hazard. He took time to photograph two seals on the ice on a sunny day, as he also recorded the conditions of the access road and the pumping system for fuel from storage tanks to drums that provided supply to the stoves.

On 1 November, after tidying up his quarters, he walked down to the Navy plane parking area:

> Some people were getting into a plane. They had everything loaded and the door closed. The engines were warming up, then the door opened, a Lieutenant Ackman came running up to me and said would you like to go. I of course said yes and climbed in. He said we are going to Hallett. ... While out with the seals I missed the press conference during which the flight may have been mentioned, and might have had a chance to be taken – or maybe not, I don't know. ... My Guardian Angel again.
>
> Flew out about 30 miles to the edge of the fast ice, then onward for about 100 miles over broken pack, large open patches. Then we went over cloud to get clear weather about 50 miles from Hallett. By that time we were near the coast, a magnificent almost vertical coastline (2-3000) thousands of feet high with hardly any icefoot in fact in some place water reached the cliff bottom. We had arrived over pack of Lady Newnes Iceshelf, between Coulman Island and the mainland and closely followed the coast to Cape Hallett.

The base at Hallett was surrounded by penguins, some Emperors and many Adelies. Once again Wilkins made a thorough and quick collection of the details he required to put together his report on the Station – weather, living arrangements, clothing, kitchen, storage. He noted that the cooking was excellent. They had lunch and returned to the plane. "As it was warming up they heard from McMurdo that it was blowing and snowing, visibility almost zero zero. ... All but three members of the crew and myself returned to base. We slept in plane."

Hallett base sent out hot apple pie for their breakfast, with coffee made on the plane. On return to McMurdo they found the man from Portland Zoo was just leaving for Cape Crozier, 50 miles away, to collect some Emperor penguins. In two return trips he brought in 22

Emperors. Wilkins, because of his unexpected and sudden departure to Hallett the previous day, had not advised of his absence from the base at the administration office. Luckily when an alarm was set off that he was missing, and a search was about to start, one of the men reported they had seen him get in the plane. "I am usually roaming about the camp and my black uniform is conspicuous. Everybody knows who I am."

Wilkins' Diary on 3 November, noted that a plane was expected from Little America with a German who had fallen 60 ft down a crevasse and had severe injuries including a ruptured spleen. Two days later he noted the man had still not arrived … "Bad weather one end or the other". A plane carrying "sick men" finally left for Christchurch on 10 November. If these included the German, Wilkins does not say.

C/o Commander Navy Task Force 43,
U.S. Navy Post Office 20,
Fleet Post Office San Francisco Cal.
Monday 4 November 1958
Hello Hello

Thanks for your birthday letter received today. Received a card also from my office with about 50 signatures.

Glad you got the King & Queen portraits on exhibition. The artist here is busy when the weather is fine – doing landscapes but it is not too comfortable trying to paint outdoors in a temperature of zero. However, the temperature is going up a little and I can now, sometimes, sit in my rooms without all my winter clothes on – it is usually about freezing on the floor and not much warmer higher up until yesterday when the snow on the roof melted and dripped into the room.

Had an interesting trip two days ago. Went to another station about 350 miles from here (Hallett Station). We landed in a high wind and as the weather got worse we had to stay overnight – sleeping in the plane. Had a pleasant visit with the men at the station and got back here next day.

I have only two more long flights to make and the rest of the trip, probably, will be made in an icebreaker ship – to New Zealand anyway.

I will send Mr. Devers a letter on McMurdo Base stationery which he might receive in a few days.

I was lucky not to go on a flight to the Pole the other day. After the plane had landed it could not start. New a new engine is needed and it has not been flown in yet – waiting for good weather at the Pole.

The men may be there yet for several days – probably uncomfortable because the Pole which is small must be very crowded. Some seals come up occasionally on the ice near here but no Penguins except those brought in by plane. A man from the Portland Oregon Zoo now has 31 Emperor Penguins and two Adelie penguins which he hopes to deliver by plane to the Portland Zoo within a week.

Not much excitement here but plenty of work to do. Hope everything is going well over there.

Expect Winston's play will do well. Had a letter from him the other day. Give him my regards when you see him.

Best love Hubert.

Was amused at the paragraph. It is funny that no Eskimo would act in the Arctic and no penguins near here except those flown in. I miss the penguins and hope that before long I will be able to find a rookery and stay for some time.

PS If you put airmail stamps and the address above Task Force 43 Navy Post Office #20 Fleet Post Office San Francisco postage as for as San Francisco is all that is needed. No extra for air mail to NZ.

Wilkins spent the days between 2 and 12 November checking into everything he possibly could at McMurdo. He also noted that he had finished reading *The Magic Power of Your Mind* by Walter M Germain. He lists the titles of the chapters in this book and about twenty other books it recommended. The Base is told that "six senators expected to arrive Christchurch on 19th to spend two weeks visiting all sections with Admiral Dufek. They will fly first over the North Pole before coming to McMurdo. Hope to do it within 30 days, must watch to see if they beat me. Doubt it if the planes here are not replaced." Wilkins requested to relocate to Little America Base before the arrival of the Senators and landed there at 1 am on 12 November. He learned that two ships, the icebreaker *Glacier* and USS *Arneb* will both visit Wilkes Station. He thinks he might meet the latter at Hallett as she will go to Melbourne, Cape Town and Rio on her way home.

Little America Base Antarctica

14 November 1957

Hello Hello

You might notice that I have changed Bases. Came over here from McMurdo Sound two days ago to stay at the Base until the first ice breaker arrives in about 3 weeks time.

Have more comfortable quarters here than at McMurdo Sound. No dripping from the roof in my room but a great deal of dripping in the passage ways and big icicles hand down from the roof and stand up from the floor. It is very difficult to walk in the passages but outside the weather here is not bad – cloud but not as windy as at McMurdo.

I was lucky – the plane I came with to Little America broke down on its way back but landed safely on the ice. The only trouble had by the crew was sleeping out for a night on the ice. Things are going on alright down here – lots of work to do.

Hope everything is well with you and that the painting is going well.

Give my best to Winston. I will write him soon.

My mailing address will still be the same but mail reaches here very seldom. Best love Hubert.

The clipping is from a New Zealand weekly.

Wilkins' Diary noted on 13 November that he went to the edge of The Barrier[16] and saw Major Dawson blasting:

> Awful job, why not tunnel up to level. The Barrier edge slopes for 500 yards. Kainan Bay very small, cliffs 60 ft high, open water several miles out, couple of miles of pack ice at edge of bay ice. Bay ice 10 ft think. Great number of crevasses under 4 feet of snow. Builders would never know that crevasses there. Snowcat fan belt broke on way back, walked home.

Also on 13 November, the party of Senators and VIPs arrived

---

[16] The Ross Barrier is a huge ice shelf in the Ross Sea. Currently (2024) it is about 970 miles long and 500 miles wide. The ice above sea level varies in height from 15 meters to over 50 meters. It was discovered in 1841 by Captain James Clarke Ross. Wilkins had been in the Ross Sea previously (Chapter 8).

at Little America but Wilkins "did not stay up to meet them", and made no further mention of them. Three days later, on Saturday 16 November, Wilkins "Flew out to Crary,[17]" returning to Little America on the afternoon of Monday 18 November. Almost certainly Crary was at the first Byrd Station that was commissioned in January 1957, to support the Traverse of the Ross Ice Shelf and lasted about four years before collapsing under snow. A new Byrd base was built in 1960.

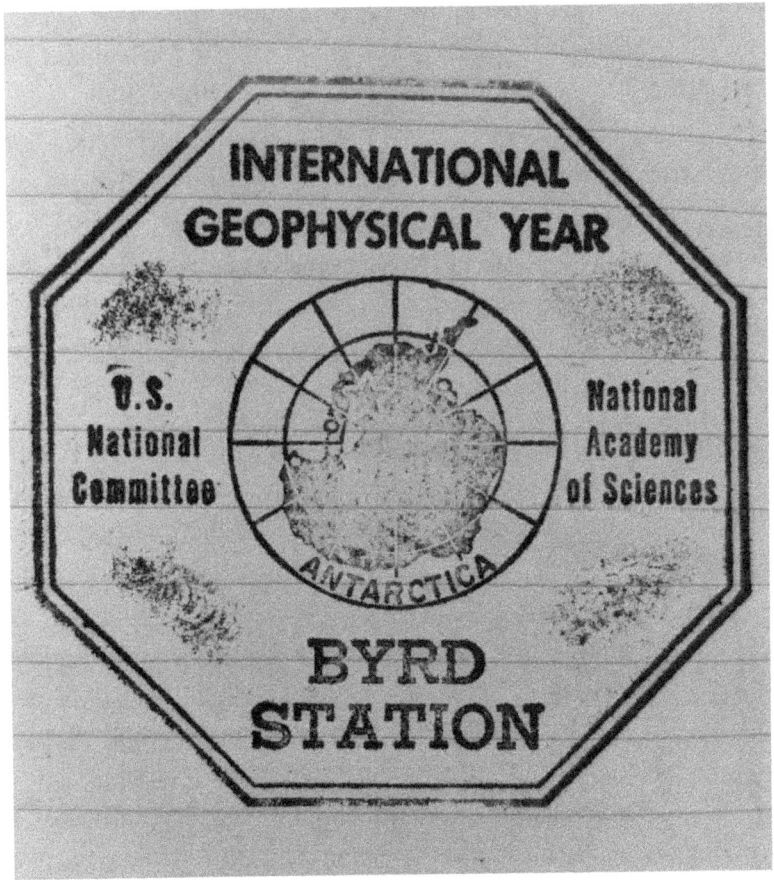

Stamp for IGY Little America Base.[18]

---

[17] Crary, a person not a place. Albert P. Crary who was Deputy Leader of United States Science during IGY 1957 and Leader of the US Seismic Traverse of Ross Ice Shelf 1957-1958.

[18] Sir George Hubert Wilkins Papers, BPCRC, OSU.

November 17th (1957)

Hello Hello

Thanks for the letter and earphone cord together with the snow shovelling pictures and Buffalo in Meshoppen. Hope the Associated Press did not bother you too much. Their correspondent down here has sent two or three stories. The T.V. you mention was not the one done at the pole. That will be on "Monitor". But one done in a general assembly when the Pan American plane was here. The whole show that night was silly and I had only a very little to say and do not know what part of it was used. The girls at the beard contest said that if I had entered they would have given me first prize but I did not enter the contest.

Am very busy going here and there and expect to stay about Little America until about 1 December then go to live and travel on a big ship (ice breaker).

The other letter you spoke of with the first hearing aid line has not arrived but no doubt it will arrive. Anyway 'saxet' ones will do.

Give Winston regards. Have had no time to write. Reports and lectures take up a lot of time. Best love Hubert.

From Wilkins' Diary it appears he returned to Byrd Station on 20 November on "VX6 Navy flight" and spent several days checking how well the base performed. His list included that:

> Lock doors and doors need to be cleared after each storm, supplies have kept well, wireless in roof not satisfactory, latrines are warmed by heat drawn by fan from garage, exhaust from engines sufficient to melt snow, supplies mostly undercover ... are gettable but neither well segregated or accessible, deep 36 ft snow pit at one end of wings – easily accessible and comfortable in which to work, pit about 6 ft square, no illness psycho or physical, morale high during visit, quarters clean & tidy ... men are satisfied with clothing but variety of boots worn.

On 21 November he returned to Little America at 4 am, breakfast at 6 and he spent the day digging with Paul Dalrymple "to uncover wires 3 to 5 feet deep about 200 yards long. ... I did not mind the work. Took pictures of balloon ascent."

Wilkins digging snow at Little America V, when retrieving Paul Dalrymple's buried cable. Photo by Paul Dalrymple, courtesy of Wilkins Family Collection.

Wilkins read and wrote and noted problems the following day – "shower water basin too small hole for drainage" and "food acceptable but nearly always cold". On 23 November he went to The Barrier again and down to the sea ice "which is about 10-11 feet thick in Kainan Bay". It seems the digging and bulldozing is to make a ramp from The Barrier to the sea ice for the forthcoming traverse on the Ross Sea Ice Shelf, but he notes "I do not believe it would be safe to leave much cargo on the ice". And further comments "the ramp is steep, with a sharp turn at the top, too sharp for more than one sled behind the cat".

In a personal email to a Wilkins family member, Paul Dalrymple said:

> When Sir Hubert came to Little America in November 1957, he was a young 70 [sic 69]. At the time I was an aging 37, so he was 33 years younger. I was digging up my cables from the station to my mast 500 feet from camp, as I felt that I might need them at the Pole. Sir Hubert was a digging dynamo. By that time, they (the cables) had become buried in two feet of snow. So we were digging side by side, but in spite of his age,

he could outdig me by at least two to one, probably three to one. The snow was flying off his shovel like it was motorized! I would toss aside a couple of shovels, then stop to scratch my ear or nose. Not Sir Hubert, he kept right on shovelling. He was a marvel at shovelling snow. He must have been a giant in the field when he was in his prime!"[19]

Accompanied by the Army transport officer from Fort Eustis, it appears his visit to The Barrier was by dog sled "Dogs sleds good but snow gathers in the scoop shaped wide sleds. The over bearers of the track ice up. Even in cold weather, ice removed by hammering. Tried alcohol but would not last long. Cat(erpillar) drivers are satisfied with clothing."

24 November was a Sunday and he read and had a "Hamtalk" (amateur radio) with Suzanne, and on 25 November the party of congressmen were expected to arrive at 2 pm and leave again the following day. "Shortly after lunch word came to get ready to go back to McMurdo. By 8 pm we were there."

On 26 November, two twin engine Cessnas arrived with 10,000 lbs of frozen foods and fresh milk for various stations. The following day Wilkins comments: "Frozen foods not so good, eggs only fair. Milk much less rich than powdered milk". News came too – "US to build station at Sth Pole. Russia will build at geomagnetic pole named Vostok, 14,000 ft altitude, 5000 higher than Pole station. Maybe colder than Pole." Wilkins also gathered some interesting facts about "Teeth pulling at Little America – 112 teeth. 52 pulled during Byrd's expedition, 109 men."

Two planes went to the Pole on 28 November. It was a clear windy day. "Feels cold". The Congressmen are going home and there was to be a Thanksgiving get-together party at 10 pm. And the following day Wilkins had long talk with two men from the Pole:

They had a pleasant winter – Temp low but not too much wind, No difficulty with exposure of 20 minutes except hand & feet. ... Scientific lecture three times a week. Not much contact with outside

---

[19] Personal correspondence, Paul Dalrymple to Wilkins Family Member, 15 January 2014. During the IGY he served two consecutive years, 1957-1959, at Little America V and at Amundsen-Scott South Pole Station.

or peripheral stations. Every two weeks ham schedule. Could not get much help from weather central for analysis of weather. Seems to be a blanket of cold air up to about 3000 feet. ... Anemometer cups blow clear of snow at 15 to 20 mph. Grand Aurora displays not often 2-3 but considerable other types. Mostly darting white, sometimes all over sky. Dog looking fat.

On 30 November he noted "Sunshiny day, quite warm" and when, yet again, he was talking with everyone and collecting comments for his reports. On 1 December the news is that the plane with Admiral and staff had crashed at Little America. "All shaken but none seriously injured. Admiral flew with helicopter to Glacier [icebreaker]." This was followed with "Later heard the helicopter with Commander Flynn on board crashed on deck of ship attempting to take off. The Heli was still tied to the deck when the start was made, both Flynn and pilot badly hurt and burned – face and hands."

McMurdo Sound Base

2 December 1957

Hello Hello

It was good to hear your voice the other ... But sorry to have wakened you at that hour.

I came to McMurdo a couple of days ago with the intention of going to the Pole station for two or three weeks. But now plans have changed and I expect to wait here until the ships come in – about 15 December and then join a ship and go westward to visit a couple more stations. If that happens I may not get back until late March. However one never knows what may happen here. The Harbor is still frozen solid and the ships may be delayed.

It is still cold down here – about zero and as we are about out of light bulbs the buildings are dark and gloomy.

The new men have arrived and most of the men who wintered here have flown back to New Zealand. All of them glad to leave.

The plane that carries this, we believe, is the last to leave before sometime in January so I am writing to wish you a happy Christmas, New Year & Birthday. There may not be a chance to send another letter for some time.

We occasionally see The New York Times, sent here to The Times correspondents. I saw the Review of Winston's play. Hope it still going well. Give him my regards.

There is always something going on down here and I have a lot to write to the office.

Everybody here gets cold after cold – some of them have to go to hospital for several days. So far I have not had to go to hospital but the colds are bad. I take 9 vitamin pills a day. Hope are you well and not working too hard.

Best love Hubert.

[sideways along page] Am sending some envelopes to the pole to be posted. Addressed to me at 37W53rd. If they arrive please keep all of them, 23 all told until I return. HW.

Wilkins' Diary of the same date as his letter to Suzanne, and in contrast to it, tells that the plane that came in from Little America had one shattered engine. "New one must arrive and be installed before the plane can fly. This means another plane from NZ ... The Air Force is indifferent to scientists and their equipment. What they doing & why? Air Force under agreement which Navy determined to complete, fuel, food supply, let the scientific gear go. All the scientists have now been relieved and returned to NZ. The place is no longer crowded. Not comfortable, still dark cold & gloomy, but we now have a free table to write. The card playing boys have now gone."

Over the next ten days Wilkins continued his observations and conversations and information gathering around McMurdo. He "saw job of installing new engine in Neptune, quite a job using a snow ramp to raise the tractor with a crane which will lift the engine". On 6 December he flew to Cape Evans, which was only 15 miles away:

> Landed near Scott's 1910 Expedition Hut. Three tents were up but I found an old tarpaulin so set that up over a plank resting on an oil barrel and had a good but rather penguin smelly shelter. Had a sleeping bag but slept in clothes on top of bag, was cool but not cold. A blessing to be in the open where one could see daylight.

Scott's hut is still in good order but almost jammed full of snow so did not go inside. A great amount of stores were scattered about round the hut and on the hill nearby – jars, marmalade, biscuits all seem to be in good order & fit to eat. We used a couple of tins of jam blackcurrant and green gauge both very good, but nothing else. Had with us several cans of trail rations 56 although package stated "use within one year of packing". The meat bar was of course too thick to bit off easily in the cold, almost & 20 but made into hoosh by Washburn it was good.

I took along five loaves of bread, 3lb butter & strawberry jam, all of which was appreciated by the group. It is interesting to note how the men cling to accustomed habits of food & eating.

Scott's Hut at Cape Evans. Courtesy: © Colin Monteath Polar & Mountain Archive.

Wilkins continued:

An interesting relic at Scott's hut is the old motor vehicle from which the engine has been removed but all other parts are there. It was a friction drive on a plate type transmission and a gear variable throughout the range of its drive plate. Thrust on the snow was by water wheel type about three ft diameter with controls at the front & Ski's wider than the drive wheel.

Transmission by chain with double revolution, all made heavy & strong, if the engine had been reliable it would have worked well. Several traces for harness were lying about. A leopard seal skull very dried out was near, I saved this to show to the dentist at Framingham or send to Dr Nelson at Caulk shop.

Magnet building & met stands are about 100 yards away on side of hillock. Another met box & anemometer staff on the top of the hill. Many seals were lying about the Cape.

Wilkins spent 7 December wandering over the volcanic rock surface, picking up specimens "for self & the office". He noted that there were about 100 skua gulls about, each with two eggs hatching. The birds, he said, were quite tame but often both of a pair would leave their nest and charge intruders, swooping up as they came too close. The following day he "roamed the hills" watching gulls and seals. "Mt Erebus a pleasing sight in sunlight which changes direction and lighting each minute. Was very active today, main column atomic explosion shaped, must have been 1000 or more feet high. Saw two star like flashes in the column about halfway up."

On 8 December Wilkins had washed his clothes and his Diary records:

As they were drying, the Admiral, all correspondents & others came in a helicopter. The party included Harold Harper correspondent of London Daily Mail. They were going to Cape Royds. Admiral asked me to go along. The Royds hut is smaller than hut part of Cape Evans. A party of New Zealanders had been there this year, shovelled snow from the door & used the inside but left it very dirty. The hut was one big room with bunks around the side at floor level, table in centre, shelves above.

On one of the boards was marked Joyce's skiing material, Ernest Joyce who made one of the first manhauled journeys to depot supplies at foot of Beardmore for Shackleton in 1914. Many supplies scattered outside including about 20 hams some of which have been eaten by skuas, other hams hung inside, the ones inside seemed in good order but did not open up. A medium sized penguin rookery covered the point, a few seals lay on the ice at the northern landing. Near the landing was a sled in very good order. There is a landing on both sides of the cape, neither very good – rocky interference. The hut is set back in a hollow between hummocks of lava – well sheltered but liable to heavy snow drift.

Shackleton's Hut at Cape Royds. Courtesy: © Colin Monteath Polar & Mountain Archive.

After they had wandered around for about an hour the helicopter returned and took most of the group back to McMurdo. It returned and took the remainder to Cape Evans, where they packed up and then returned to McMurdo. Wilkins moved "from Building G which is crowded with VX6 aircraft pilots & crew to Jamesway J3. Where Washburn's group had their base. This much more comfortable but draughty due to bad setup".

On 11 December the Admiral and his staff left for New Zealand taking visiting VIPs with him including the US Ambassador to Australia, the Deputy Chief of US Mission to NZ Embassy, both having had a talk with Wilkins, who also spoke with several other visitors.

McMurdo Base

12 December 57

Hello Hello

A plane just leaving for the Pole so I am asking the correspondent from the London Daily Mail to post this. You might or might not get it before Christmas but anyway Season's greetings. Expect to join the icebreaker Glacier tomorrow or day after & go to Hallett Station 600 miles from here. All is well here. Hope things are well with you. Best love Hubert.

Still at McMurdo on 12 December, Wilkins continued his information gathering – checking on how the "clear up" of the base was progressing. Special orders had been posted about comfort, cleanliness and recreation. Not, he noted, entirely due to his earlier report but, in part, to the arrival of new crews, new broom!

Diary entry: Friday 13 December was a day of action around the base. A plane arrived from Christchurch with Christmas trees and ice cream and mail. The *Glacier* had stopped beside the edge of solid ice to overhaul two engines and there was a flight to the Pole. Wilkins could have gone but chose not to and then found there was a flight to Hallett, with four New Zealanders, but he decided to wait for *Glacier*. A flight went to Camp Bernacchi and another left for Christchurch taking many of the Little America staff. On 14 December the plane at the pole is held there by bad weather. The *Glacier* would not be going into Hallett so air operations decided to send one or two planes with an eight member New Zealand geological party, and their equipment. Finally on Sunday 15 December, Wilkins is advised that a plane for Hallett, with space for him, was scheduled to leave at 9.00 am:

Got my gear to the flying at 8.30. We were in the plane – Engines running but a routine test of all parts revealed that the ITG Danke System was not in order. Men worked all day & repairs still not effective. The NZealanders food amounted to 4000 lbs instead of the 2000 assumed. That meant two plane trips or two planes to Hallett. The other plane took off at 1.00

pm the weather came up bad during the afternoon. The plane did not return from Hallett until early morning.

Monday 16th. The plane we were supposed to use had not been repaired so the load was transferred to the plane that made the trip yesterday. An example of a fission efficiency was that two of my fore bags clearly marked for Hallett left behind but as usual I made a search before starting out, found bags & put them on the right plane. The weather was bad at McMurdo but at Hallett weather was good so we took off & soon in clear weather landed at Hallett. ... I was given a comfortable twin bunk in the hospital with Dr Shear. All very nice & clean. A sitting room in the building, which few of the staff used – they usually assemble in the recreation room or mess hall which also includes the communications & meteorological instruments.

Wilkins spent the time photographing Hallett Base – the scenery and he took some film of penguins. The small library there included several polar books and he listed those he read, sometimes two per day, in his Diary: Debenham "In the Antarctic", Evans "South with Scott" – "This good". And Evans again "The Antarctic Challenge". Roald Amundsen's autobiography "My Life as an Explorer", of which Wilkins noted Amundsen's "... trouble started at the beginning of arrangements at Rome" statement about Umberto Nobile, an Italian pioneer in Arctic aviation, who with Amundsen and Lincoln Ellsworth flew over the North Pole in the dirigible *Norge* in May 1926. Wilkins noted that, for the first time on the trip, he had a typewriter available and started writing his final report for typing.

Hallett Station
23 December 57.
Hello Hello
This I suppose will be a surprise – a typed letter that that you will be able to read – but it is a new typewriter and it seems strange. Arrived here from McMurdo just a week ago and am enjoying the stay. We are surrounded on three sides by beautiful mountains – one of them 13,000 feet high. The snow is gone in patches and the scenery is grand. There is rough ice on the beach and on the beach and for about half a mile

square are about 10,000 penguins just hatching out their young. They make an awful noise – which I can switch off – and the smell is a bit high but they are most amusing to watch. I will have some film pictures of them but not much because I am just about out of movie and still film – must save some for the next station at Wilkes Land. Nobody knows when the ship for Wilkes Land will arrive – have probably had my last flight down here, it will be shipboard hereafter perhaps until I get back to the U.S.A., can not tell yet because we do not know where the ships will go after leaving here – some one way, some another.

The weather is fine – sunshine all day – 24 hours and the temperature only about 2 degrees below freezing. The 14 boys here are fine, half New Zealanders, half of them from the U.S. all clean, respectable and busy at their jobs, I am left much to myself and have both a comfortable bed and plenty of room and a table to use for my work – conveniences I did not have at any other place. We have just received word that a plane will be here about 5 pm today with Christmas mail but I do not expect any since it was not expected that we should get any mail after I arrived here and I had left word at McMurdo to send all mail back to the senders. I may not get more mail until I return. Hope everything is going well with you. Hope you have had a nice Christmas and New Year. Ours will be quiet but we do have a tree. Best love Hubert.

(Hand written) My best to Winston.

On Christmas Eve Wilkins noted that the ice was breaking up and there was much clear water in sight from the beach. However, it snowed from 8 am until lunch time. There was a Service on Christmas Day. On 26 December the ship *Atka* was only 26 miles away but it turned back because of heavy ice. The following day the New Zealanders left on a geological mapping survey and there was a Ross or Crabeater seal on the ice. By Monday 30 December there was a Ross seal on the beach and on New Year's Eve there was threat of a "blow" and the ice was drifting. Wilkins was writing his Report and there was a party! He continued working on his Report through the first week of January. On 2 January he noted "Sunshine" and the "white penguin caught & preserved". More sunshine on 3 January and he took pictures but a fog came up about 6 pm. Noted by Wilkins, Sir Edmund Hillary reached the South Pole on 4 January 1958. Over the next few days the ice was clearing, the weather was fine and Hillary left the Pole. *Atka* came in on 8 January, unloaded and departed the following day. NZ items were moved by helicopter and they dropped a boat from about 200 ft. It landed right side up, slightly damaged but floated. And news was that *Arneb* left [where?] yesterday and may be in on Monday. Wilkins found a large sea flea on the beach! The weather continued fine and he continued writing his Report, finishing the last of the draft on Sunday 12 January. By 14 January *Arneb* had arrived at Hallett and unloading continued well into the following day. Wilkins went aboard the ship about 2 pm on 15 January, and had coffee with the Captain. The following day there was close pack ice about the ship. *Atka* "disappeared during the night". The remaining landing craft were loaded on the morning of 16 January. "Good bye to Hallett".

Hallett Station
Jan 15th 1958
Hello Hello
Just a note as we are leaving by ship for Wilkes Station about 500 miles west of here. Expect to stay on this ship until we reach some port from where I can fly back. Do not know which Port yet. May be New Zealand, Africa or South America.
Expect to get back about the end of March. Hope everything is going well with you.
Regards to Winston. Best love Hubert.

The sea was calm on Friday 17 January, "no ice, just about Cape Adare at 6 am. Penguins, Ross gulls, about 11 Prions … Still see land on portside. Asked to give a talk on Sunday evening." On Saturday Wilkins continued recording his observations: "Few Bergy Bits, few lumps of ice. Antarctic petrel, penguins, Wilsons petrel, 2 whales. Mostly cloudy." The ship went in and out of ice. On Monday 20 they had life boat drill on stand to. "Nobody had informed us of No of boat".[20] The next few days were stormy, in

---

[20] In an emergency on board ship passengers and crew muster at allocated lifeboats, identified by a number.

the pack ice, went further north to avoid ice and by the afternoon of 24 January there was more ice ahead. Turned north again, then westward then north again.

On 25 January Wilkins noted:

> Came to ice about 6 am. Working ice all day. Many examples of inexperience. In company Atka took up lead, Burton Island followed then Arneb. About 11.30 Atka broke 2 blades of propellor. The Burton Island took lead. Ice pack fairly thick. Many icebergs. About half tabular. Many Cape pigeons & Crabeater seals. About 8 am said to be about 98 miles from Wilkes. Expect to arrive early tomorrow morning.

They arrived at Wilkes at noon on 26 January ... and on 27 January, Wilkins recorded that he stayed ashore, made a trip to the ice cap recording the temperatures at 1 ft, minus 25°F, and at 16 ft, minus 70°F.

On 28 January he took pictures, posted rocks to the office and stayed on board the ship all day. There was a "Beer party ashore for men". Again, he remained on board on 29 January and his note for Thursday 30 January says "Expect to sail".

Wilkins continued on USS *Arneb* from Wilkes Base to Sydney, Australia, arriving on 8 February. The *Canberra Times* of 10 February (p. 3) reported that "Sir Hubert returned from his ninth voyage to the Antarctic yesterday on the U.S.S. Arneb. The attack cargo ship sailed from Antarctica to give the American crew a fortnight's leave in Sydney. Sir Hubert is now a geographer with the U.S. Army Research and Engineering Command, and has not visited Australia since 1941."

Wilkins' official travel documents show that he left Sydney on 10 February for Manila in the Philippines, where he arrived on 18 February. And that he paid cash for his air fares home. However, it seems he travelled via Adelaide for a quick catch up with his family. He arrived back in Framingham on 23 February 1958.

(George) Hubert Wilkins, with his sister Annie and brother Tom, Adelaide, on or about 17 February 1958. From Wilkins Family Collection.

A short article appeared in a newspaper, probably the *Advertiser* (Adelaide),[21] with the above photo on or about 17 February 1958. Part of an original newspaper cutting of the article is in Elizabeth Chipman's papers in the National Library of Australia. It may be the last interview given by Sir Hubert in Australia. Part of the article says:

> Noted SA-born explorer Sir Hubert Wilkins, 69, who is in Adelaide visiting relatives, is still working on an idea he had when he was a young man on his father's farm at Mt. Bryan East.
>
> This is the possibility of making climatic forecasts for hundreds of years ahead.
>
> Sir Hubert Wilkins, also well known as meteorologist, aviator, naturalist, author and war correspondent, is now a geographer in the Research and Development Command of the US Defence Department.

---

[21] The back of the photograph states "Advertiser Newspapers ... Photo Sales Service" but despite lengthy research the original publication has not been found.

He has been away from Australia for 17 years – "but I am still an SA citizen."

He said yesterday that as a young man he had seen the way animals on his father's farm had suffered in dry seasons,

This had roused his interest in long-range forecasting.

"Forty years ago I suggested that it might be another 450 years before we got even a foundation for the study of long range climate forecasting," he said.

I did not get much support at first, but received it later in America.

"It depends a great deal on sunspots."

Sir Hubert Wilkins, who cruised under the ice in a submarine to within 300 miles of the North Pole in 1931, has spent the …

Wilkins worked very hard on this final Antarctic trip. He was no longer young, although still apparently very fit and all his life he had spent time in inhospitable climates. This was no different, despite being fully supported by the US Navy and the resources of the IGY and Operation Deep Freeze III. He was very keen to visit all the bases and it must have been a disappointment to him to only overfly the South Pole. However, he was never one to complain about what life handed him and he made the most of every day of his final visit to his "white heaven" for as the quote at the start of this books says "Antarctica beckons to the mystic" – and Wilkins was certainly that:

> Alone and apart, defiant and inexorable, Antarctica beckons to the mystic. For the man who cannot dream, for the explorer with no soul, it is a white hell. But for the visionary it is a white heaven, and it is no fortuitous accident that makes the same men return time and again to its pitiless wastes, some of them to master a few of its secrets, many of them to die.

Opposite are pictures of some of the memorabilia that Wilkins collected while in the Antarctic for the IGY 1957-58. All are held in the Sir George Hubert Wilkins Papers, SPEC.PA.56.0006, Byrd Polar and Climate Research Centre Archival Program, Ohio State University.

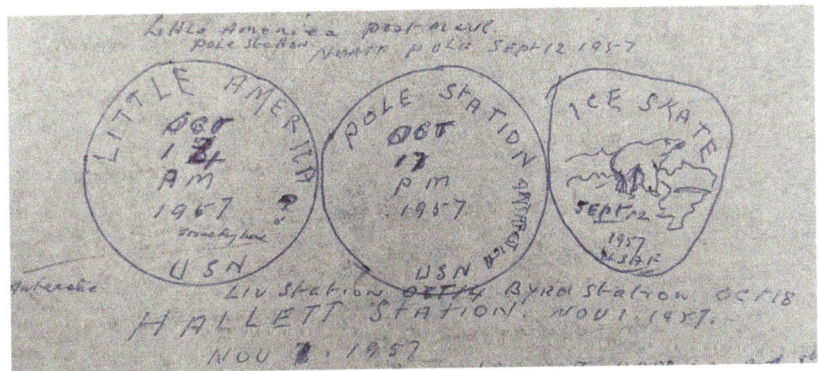

COMMANDER SUBMARINE FORCE, U S ATLANTIC FLEET
23 March 1959

My dear Lady Wilkins,

    I am grateful that USS SKATE has been able to carry out Sir Hubert's wish concerning his remains. In a fitting and solemn ceremony in keeping with the high regard the people of the world, and particularly the explorers, hold for Sir Hubert, Commander James F. Calvert, Commanding SKATE, committed the ashes to the elements at the North Pole on March 17.

    If you so desire, upon the return of SKATE from her present Arctic operations, I will be happy to have Commander Calvert call on you at your home.

    You may recall that Commander Calvert had the pleasure of meeting Sir Hubert before his passing. On Saturday, October 18, 1958, Sir Hubert was the distinguished guest of Commander Calvert in SKATE, which was then moored at Electric Boat's Shipyard in Groton, Connecticut.

    Since there has been no public announcement about SKATE's present Arctic operations, you are requested to keep the contents of this letter confidential. Once information about the SKATE cruise has been released by the Department of Defense, there will be no further need for the secrecy concerning the disposition of Sir Hubert's remains. I anticipate that a public announcement will be made within the next few days.

    I will be in touch with you again as soon as Commander Calvert returns to New London.

Very sincerely,

F. B. WARDER
Rear Admiral, U. S. Navy

Lady Hubert Wilkins
37 West 53rd Street
New York 19, N.Y.

From Sir George Hubert Wilkins Papers, BPCR, OSU.

Epilogue

What did George Hubert Wilkins achieve during his Antarctic expeditions and what is his legacy?

Although George Hubert Wilkins only lived long enough to see the start to his life-long ambition of establishing weather forecasting stations across the north and south polar lands this has been well and truly achieved by countries across the world. This life-long goal continues to benefit people across the globe.

Throughout his life, whenever the opportunity arose, when being interviewed by newspaper reporters or giving an important lecture or just a lunchtime talk, whatever the audience, Wilkins returned to expounding his plan for weather stations to help farmers, in particular, have a better idea of the weather they could expect to come their way.

One of the common threads throughout Wilkins' expeditions, to both the Arctic and the Antarctic, was the establishment of weather stations. As early as 1919 he had submitted a plan to the Royal Meteorological Society for the establishment of 32 points of observation in the Arctic and 12 in the Antarctic. He hoped that the knowledge gained would enable long-range weather forecasting. He suggested that by establishing observation bases at St Paul Island in the Arctic and others in the Antarctic or sub-Antarctic – Amsterdam, Kerguelen and Heard Islands and at MacRobertson Land as well as on Graham Land and in the Ross Sea area – these stations would not only communicate with each other, through wireless communication, but right across the world. "This far-reaching scheme for a greater efficiency in long-range weather forecasts on the success of which to such a great extent depends the commercial prosperity of the world".[1] Speaking at the Commonwealth Club luncheon in Adelaide on 20 September 1938, Wilkins said that although he made no claim to being a scientist or meteorologist, he had been committed to the

---

[1] "Polar Forecasts: World Chain of Stations", *Sydney Morning Herald*, 7 August 1934, p. 9.

establishment of meteorological stations in the Arctic and Antarctic regions,[2] certainly before his first Antarctic trip in 1920.

George Hubert Wilkins died on 30 November 1958, aged 70. He was found dead in his room at the Grand Central Hotel in Framingham, Massachusetts, not far from where he was still employed by the United States Army Quartermaster Research and Engineering Centre at Natick. "This simple, dedicated man died the way he had lived – working."[3] Wilkins spent the previous afternoon working on and cleaning his much-loved 1939 Chevrolet car. His funeral was held in Framingham at St, Andrew's Episcopal Church on 4 December 1958.[4] While one newspaper report stated that his ashes would be placed in Westminster Abbey in London,[5] after cremation in the United States they were taken aboard the submarine USS *Skate* and scattered, during a Navy memorial service at the North Pole, on 17 March 1959, as he had wished.

Wilkins would likely be delighted and astounded at the proliferation and automation of weather stations throughout the world. And of the information available online to anyone who cares to look. The Australian Government Bureau of Meteorology shows the "Latest Weather Observations for Antarctica", issued every 10 minutes, from eleven stations. They include Australia's three main stations, Casey, Davis and Mawson, along with the French base Dumont D'urville, the American McMurdo, Japan's Syowa and two Russian stations, Mirny and Novolazarevskaya. The two Australian airfields, Casey Skyway and Wilkins Runway are also included with the small remote Bunger Hills and the sub-Antarctica's Macquarie Island.

Perhaps Wilkins most enduring and recognisable legacy, though, lies in the countless places and objects that bear his name, serving as a testament to his contributions to scientific discovery and exploration. Many of the things that he discovered are named

---

[2] "Sir Hubert Wilkins", *The Argus* (Melbourne), 21 September 1938, p. 22.
[3] "Australian Explorer of the Poles", *The Biz* (Sydney), September 1959, p. 17.
[4] *The Washington Post and Times Herald*, 5 December 1958, p. C2.
[5] "Wilkins' Ashes for Abbey", *Canberra Times*, 6 December 1958, p. 3.

after the sponsors of the expeditions on which he travelled. On the Shackleton-Rowett Expedition, for example, a new finch that he identified on Gough Island in the Tristan da Cunha group he named *Rowettia Goughensis*, the Gough Finch, after the backer of this expedition. But Wilkins identified two more new species of finch on nearby Nightingale Island and these were named *Nesospiza questi* and *Nesospiza wilkinsi* after their ship, *Quest* and Wilkins himself.

There are, however, many things that have come after his death that are named in honour of George Hubert Wilkins. Although not from his Antarctic travel there is the Australian skink, *Lerista wilkinsi* named in 1926, and the Australian Wilkins rock wallaby, *Petrogale wilkinsi*, only identified and named in 2014. In Australia, and a testament to his pioneering flights, there is Sir Hubert Wilkins Road at Adelaide airport and the Sir Hubert Wilkins Aerodrome in Jamestown, South Australia. Nearby is the Wilkins Visitor Centre, which has outdoor story boards sharing insights into Wilkins' life and displays inside telling his story in greater detail. Sir Hubert Wilkins Memorial Park is on the Barrier Highway in Mount Bryan, South Australia. There is a Wilkins Street in the suburb of Mawson in the ACT where there are also streets named after other Antarctic notables: Bernacchi, Colbeck, Debenham, Heard, Hurley, Mawson, Rymill and Shackleton. And there are a number of Wilkins Streets, Roads, Crescents and even suburbs across Australia and, no doubt, in other countries.

Named after Sir Hubert in the Antarctic are the sites of Wilkins Island, Wilkins Sound, Wilkins Coast, the Wilkins Ice Shelf, Cape Wilkins, Wilkins Mountains, Wilkins Nunatak and Wilkins Aerodrome, near the Australian Casey Station.[6]

In the United States, at the Army Quartermaster Research and Engineering Center is the Wilkins Arctic Test-Chamber with a portrait of Wilkins in the entrance foyer. From the Commanding

---

[6] From the Australian Antarctic Gazetteer at the Australian Antarctic Data Centre and the SCAR (Scientific Committee on Antarctic Research) Antarctic Place Names.

General of the Headquarters of that Center came the following announcement immediately following Wilkins death:

> Sir Hubert, the Quartermaster Corps' most colorful, best known, and most beloved employee, has been associated with the QMC since 1942 and with the Center since 1953. His 31 Arctic and Antarctic trips have assured him of immortality. His achievements will constitute a living monument to his memory. The love of his co-workers will live forever.

There are many expressions similar to this one, reaching out not only to express sadness but also to honour Wilkins' memory and his lifetime of achievements. Another that stands out came from Dr Larry Gould,[7] President of Carleton College, Minnesota, who when talking about "prima donna" explorers, said:

> The one brilliant wonderfully generous exception was Wilkins. I do not think I have ever known anyone who was more kind toward the people with whom he worked or more generous. And while we remember Wilkins for the magnitude of his achievements as an explorer, I think I shall always remember him more because of his generosity and kindness as a human being.

---

[7] Gould was a geologist, professor and polar explorer. He was chief scientist on Byrd's first Antarctic expedition. He was President of the American Association for the Advancement of Science in 1964.

www.ingramcontent.com/pod-product-compliance
Lightning Source LLC
Chambersburg PA
CBHW052058300426
44117CB00013B/2193